The Fight to Enlight

Initiation Through the Heart is the
Only Way to Win

How a modern hemp pioneer discovered profound healing, resiliency and self-liberation after facing terrifying but enlightening near-death experiences, severe childhood bullying, extreme drug addiction, incarceration (for a non-violent marijuana crime), financial collapse, debilitating chronic illness, almost irreconcilable heartbreak - and how you can overcome any challenge you're facing with compassion for yourself and the world.

(Copyright held by Seth Leaf Pruzansky)

I dedicate this book to my Mother and Father, and the rare family, friends and loved ones who have stood by me through everything... you know who you are.

And of course I have to most especially dedicate this book to the indescribable source of energy that is causing my heart to beat and gifting me the opportunity to be alive, for without that, I surely wouldn't have survived through the countless trials, tribulations, near-death experiences and initiations.

With infinite gratitude,

Seth Leaf Pruzansky

Contents

Chapter One: "Conception" 1

Chapter Two: The Dysfunctional Ego 10

Chapter Three: Bullied 17

Chapter Four: The Seeker Is An Addict 22

Chapter Five: Damian 34

Chapter Six: Hemp Shoes 42

Chapter Seven: Into The Wild 50

Chapter Eight: Thawing Out The Deep Inner Freeze 65

Chapter Nine: A Labor Of Love 82

Chapter Ten: Cosmic Court 88

Chapter Eleven: The Ascended Master? 110

Chapter Twelve: Going Public 124

Chapter Thirteen: "Who Am I To Judge You?" 134

Chapter Fourteen: You Can Run, But You Can't Hide 151

Chapter Fifteen: I'd Rather Rise In Love, Than Fall In Love .. 164

Chapter Sixteen: Glacial Blue Skin 173

Chapter Seventeen: Frozen Turkeys...177

Chapter Eighteen: Jamaica's Got Soul 190

Chapter Nineteen: To Resurrect..211

Chapter Twenty: A Grand Mystery..223

Chapter Twenty-One: John Of God...229

Chapter Twenty-Two: Change..238

Chapter Twenty-Three: Candida..244

Chapter Twenty-Four: Stars..250

Chapter Twenty-Five: In The Prison Of Mind, Body, And Soul......269

Chapter Twenty-Six: There Are No Victims, Just Volunteers...........277

Chapter Twenty-Seven: Sweat Lodge..283

Chapter Twenty-Eight: Reverse The World 293

Chapter Twenty-Nine: Free While Chained 299

Chapter Thirty: How Does My Story Help You?.............................313

In Conclusion (What I'm Doing Now And Where To Find Me)......327

CHAPTER ONE

"Conception"

Just before I was conceived, my father was struck by lightning.

It happened on the property of my parent's beautiful home in the mountains of northern Maine. They were both from New York City and chose to move away from the madness of urban life deep into the north woods, as part of the back-to-the-land movement of the late '60s and early '70s. They no longer could bear an industrialized society. They'd hoped, like many of their generation, to discover the much spoken of "utopian hippie paradise." It was rumored to exist if one found the right commune with other city-to-country refugees.

My longhaired father (his appearance was a cross between Michael Douglas and John Lennon) was showering naked in the heavy late afternoon rain. He was sweaty and covered with dirt and wood chips. When out-of-staters ask what life in Maine is like, most locals will respond with: "It's winter for six months, and then we spend six months getting ready for winter!" And that's exactly what my father was doing. He'd been splitting wood all day in preparation for the long, cold winter that was still four months away.

Years later, he told me that during that time, he was ignorant of how powerful nature could be. He heard thunder in the distance, but it seemed far away, and he was so grimy after a hard day's work that a cool soak in Mother Nature's tears seemed perfectly natural and inviting.

As he showered, he noticed how beautiful the ancient granite outcropping under his feet was. It was embedded with fine quartz crystals, groupings of mica, and cubical pink feldspar formations. And then, before his mind could process it, lightning struck the ledge a few feet in front of him. In the same moment, it traveled into his right leg and up through the side of his body, temporarily paralyzing him. He felt time stop.

In those moments of paralysis, his normal state of awareness shut down - but something was still aware. Whatever that was, it was a part of him, but it was also beyond him. Flashes of insight related to otherworldly awareness opened up. Suddenly all that existed was energy. It was an endless sea of oceanic electromagnetism spanning throughout many realms and into the abyss of forever. And then, just as quickly as it came, this shimmering blue sea of frequency receded into the farthest reaches of the infinite, and my father found himself back on the familiar shores of his waking mind.

When the momentary bliss of realization wore off, he remembered it was a life-threatening event that caused it. He'd heard my mother scream before he fell to the ground; she didn't know he'd been struck by lightning, but at the same time he was struck, she was seeing flashing orange lights that appeared through the wall behind her. They danced across the room and then disappeared out the picture window.

Once my father regained his mobility, he feebly limped into the house to see if she was all right. After finding her somewhat jolted, but unscathed, they discussed what had happened. They concluded that she had seen the same bolt of lightning that had hit him. After traveling through his body, it must have transformed into the crazy flashing phenomenon that she observed.

As a result of this experience, they were both deeply humbled - not to mention literally and figuratively shocked. My father, in particular, had learned first-hand that the forces of nature are powerful beyond comprehension. Had the lightning gone into his left leg rather than his right, it may have led to his heart and possibly his physical demise.

Albert Einstein said something to the effect of, "There are only two ways to live your life. One is as though nothing is a miracle. The other is though everything is a miracle". My father is an optimist. Even though he still hasn't deciphered what the deeper meaning of getting struck by lightning was, he is confident that there is one - and one far more meaningful than being in the wrong place at the wrong time.

My mother was in labor for thirty-six hours before I was born. Growing up, I always felt she had a hard time forgiving me for that. Sometimes I think that she still does!

She's often claimed that I didn't want to enter the world. On some levels this wasn't to far from the truth. Though love pulsed through my soul, I always seemed to be aware of a past life knowing that human incarnation was wrought with challenges. Growing up, the one thing people always said about me was that I was hypersensitive. They had no idea how true this really was.

My most vivid and frequent memories of being a small child are sitting in the front yard of my parent's serene mountain home in Canaan, Maine. I knew nothing of formal meditation or any ideas or concepts related to it, yet I would sit naturally in that state, listening to the sound of the brook bubbling beside me, the different birds singing their distinctive songs and the leaves rustling in the wind. I would also listen to something much deeper. It was a sound in the core of my being, sometimes faint and other times more pronounced, depending on how closely I listened. At first, it was similar to the sound you'd hear if you put your ear to a conch shell. But the closer I listened to it, the more I realized that somehow, that sound was communicating through me.

I would listen more and more intently until I began consciously experiencing the sound that I was hearing. Suddenly I wasn't just a little boy in the woods anymore – I was an energy field, a frequency that was animating my human form.

Acknowledging this interplay of extrasensory transmissions that fluxed between the dense feelings of this material world, before ascending into the lightness of the non-material dimensions – and then back again, allowed my body to be filled with euphoric feelings. Metaphorically they were like waves from an ocean of energy that was endless in its size and depth.

Also present was something similar to music, but it was nothing audible like the music that humans make. I can only describe what I heard as a celestial harmonics, or music of the spheres, and even that does nothing to describe the majesty of its sound. As a child, I clearly understood that somehow my soul – the miraculous animating principle of my consciousness itself, was related to this music, if not entirely birthed from it.

As I listened, I simultaneously stared at where the tree line met the sky. Slowly everything in my field of vision would become brighter and brighter until all that I saw was transformed into the white light of pure, unadulterated consciousness, interspersed only by the electrical sensation of my heartbeat.

Once everything faded into light, making the material world invisible, another dimension emerged. The soothing feel of the euphoric ocean, the sound of celestial harmony, and the sight of incandescent white light all fused together. I became aware that their source was birthed from a place within me. At this point in my life, my undeveloped ego identified my true sense of self as this miraculous animating energy that caused my heart to beat and thoughts to arise in my mind. It was a substance much finer than the bioelectric and bio-magnetism that pulsed through my human form. Later in life I learned that these states could be easily attained by anyone who knows how to practice heart-brain coherence.

But, as a young child, I knew that my consciousness came from this energetic 'stuff,' and I also knew that who I was as a person was an expression of this miraculous, living geometric field. This expression conveyed itself through a type of love, but it wasn't love, as most believe it to be. It was a supra-rational, unexplainable love, and in the arms of this force, I so deeply loved nature and all the little creatures living in her that it would cause me to jump for joy when interacting with them. The stars, the trees, and the bubbling brook: they were all expressions of this celestial and terrestrial love I was enveloped by.

I'd often tell my father that I loved being alive. I would literally jump and down with joy because the feeling was so strong in me! This always caused him to laugh, because he could feel in his bones how serious I was.

If this meditation process was the key that unlocked my soul's freedom, then the lock that blocked it was not engaging in it. As I grew older, this naturally occurring meditation process occurred less and less due to the constricting circumstances of my life, brought on mostly by social and societal conditioning.

As a young child, I never made plans to do this meditation, and I never questioned its occurrence. There were also no words I could use to try and articulate it. It was a natural expression of my normal consciousness.

Every time I entered into this state, my perception of the material world deepened and expanded, and at the same time, I could see, hear and feel this incredibly refined substance that emanated from everything around me, animate and inanimate alike. I was simultaneously aware of how everything was connected through this same electrical-like substance. This perception led to the awareness that my entire sensual experience of life was being projected (and recorded) from a vibratory center at the core of my being, but it was non-localized, meaning even though it mostly seemed to reside in the core of my being it wasn't stuck there, it could be anywhere it wanted. With this awareness came the ability to transcend everything of the physical world, including my little body.

Engaging in this process regularly totally transformed my conscious awareness; I fully understood who and what I was...and it was no big deal aside from being the BIGGEST deal. It was just reality, being what it is – miraculous.

Like I said earlier, as a young child, I didn't possess the intellectual capacity to clearly articulate these transcendental experiences to inquiring adults, but I still tried. I used to say things to my parents and their friends like, "People, birds, and trees are all the same" and, "Everything comes from the same place." When they asked how I knew that, or who told me that, my only way of explaining was to point at the tree line and tell them that I knew this from looking up there. Instead of embracing my suggested love of life, this caused them concern, because they had no idea what I was talking about.

Although the majority of my childhood was sublime, there were rare moments laced with a sharp element of fear. Occasionally I suffered from fevers that produced the opposite reaction of my meditations. Instead of my awareness harmoniously transcending the confines of my physical reality, it would sometimes become tortuously incarcerated by it. It produced terribly frightening sensations that cut into my normal serenity like a salted wound. And during these moments I would feel hellish disharmony. The sensations shifted from porous, soft and velvety to dense, hard and razor-sharp. I was certain that I could sense the presence of something nebulous, almost monstrous, observing me.

Whatever it was, I felt certain it wanted me to suffer. Scared to death, I'd scream and cry out for my mom to rescue me, and she always did.

The anticipation of these fevers and the dreadful sensations that accompanied them instilled a slight anxiety complex in me. These fever experiences lasted into my pre-teen years, then finally stopped. Little did I know that later in my teen years, they would be dramatically relived through the greatest awakening of my life.

When my parents first moved to Maine, they built their home on a low-lying mountain in Canaan. Before long they'd made friends with most of the homesteaders in the surrounding area, including the members of a hippie commune on the other side of the hill. Our property was gorgeous. We were about two-thirds of the way up the mountain.

The top of it was covered with granite outcroppings surrounded by expansive beds of lush green moss and stunted pine trees.

The western part of the mountain was characterized by picturesque meadows lit up by seas of colorful wildflowers that rolled like waves on the ocean when the breeze would blow. From this vantage point, one could view the western mountains of Maine. The entire place looked like a Monet painting. It was in one of these meadows that my parents told me I was conceived.

The northeastern side of this mountain was composed of steep knolls littered with giant granite boulders left by the last Canadian glacier ten thousand years earlier. My younger brother Davy and I spent countless hours playing there.

Next to our house, a stream wound its way through our land and far behind the property. It was here that I often found ancient fossils and chunks of clear quartz, spurring a lifelong obsession with rockhounding. The land was so vibrant and primordial that it looked like something out of the Jurassic period. It was easy to imagine dinosaurs roaming around every corner.

Being the hippies that they were, my parents often held or attended parties with their neighborhood friends. These parties were always very exciting, filled with an eclectic mix of unique and colorful people. There were musicians, intellectuals, volleyball players, and drunks sprinkled amongst bikers and local rednecks. Everyone was always having a great time.

One of the things that always stood out at every party was marijuana smoke. The smell of it, the way it dispersed itself across a shaft of sunlight. It always mystified me. Growing up, my brother and I were always taught that hemp and marijuana were beneficial to people and the planet in so many important ways. It just seemed like common knowledge.

For me, childhood was sublime. I was born completely in tune with my authentic nature. Little did I know that a change was going to come…

CHAPTER TWO

The Dysfunctional Ego

The first time I had ever become afraid of humans was during my first day of kindergarten. It was so traumatizing that the negative memories of that school day, and many others after it, would unconsciously become the basis for many of my destructive decisions and habits in the years to come.

Trapped inside of a strange concrete building with other beautiful children who also possessed innocence, awe and wonder in their eyes, were now also conflicted because they too were being told what to do and were being given agendas by strangers that were new, and in my mind, unnatural.

It felt like my parents had dropped me off at a prison that was brainwashing children. I felt that this wasn't supposed to happen. There wasn't a trace of familial and community love in here. I spent the day quietly sobbing, wondering why my folks would leave me somewhere like this.

The very summer before I started school, I was raving to my father about how much I loved life. There was a day when I was literally jumping up and down with joy exclaiming, "Dad, I love being alive! I love life so much, Dad!" Now, after only one day in school, my loving childhood felt seriously contaminated. It was no longer peace, love, and confidence; it was control, fear, and confusion.

The meditative state that was the cornerstone of my life experience began to crumble, and I was clueless as to how disconnected to this part of myself I was becoming. The structured school environment, by its very nature, attempted to condition my outlook with its own values and institutional concepts. The attitude was, "All you need to know about the world is what we tell you." It was totally contrary to my naturally occurring meditative states, the lens through which I'd always viewed the world.

As a young child, I had no idea how this type of conditioning was so deeply impacting me at all levels of my being, and so over time I unconsciously surrendered to it and became brainwashed by agenda-driven thoughts, ideals, and philosophies.

The day before I began kindergarten, I was a luminous being, with a balanced sense of self - in alignment with my innate intuitive wisdom. The day that I finished sixth grade, I was an unbalanced, self-centered maniac that used my egoic knowledge to imprison my innate wisdom, and I had no idea what had even happened.

With my spiritual wisdom jailed, my criminal ego was free to commit any crimes that justified its existence. But sadly, I was too young to understand this type of self-inflicted psycho-spiritual repression. My guiding light had been severely diminished, and I never even saw it coming.

After graduating from elementary school, my parents decided that we should move out of the woods and into a more suburban environment. They tried explaining to my brother and me that the way we were raised no longer applied to the way the world had become. Instead of living off the land and communing with nature, we were to continue with institutionalized education, with the goal of eventually becoming doctors, lawyers, engineers, or any other of the myriad job positions offered by society.

News of this move came at a pivotal and vulnerable time in my life. I was twelve years old, and my brother was only nine. I was too young to have developed a frame of reference for what society expected of me. But naturally, I trusted my parents, so I followed their lead. Their choices were made out of love for my brother and I, but they didn't realize that my sensitivities to nature would not adapt well in a suburban environment.

We moved to Waterville, Maine, a suburban college town of about 30,000 people. Gone were the days of finding fossils in the brook. Gone were the days of running around mostly naked with other hippie kids. No longer could I ride my bicycle for miles down endless dirt roads and through otherworldly rock pits. But the most tragic loss of all was that by the time we moved into suburbia, I had completely forgotten meditating and the enlightening information transferred from my spirit to my developing awareness.

Now we lived somewhere that was far removed from nature. It was a place where kids had distinctly different interests than my own, and they weren't at all interested in relating to me.

According to my parents, my only concern was to work hard, get good grades, and think about what career path I wanted to choose.

The only good thing about living in town was the art lessons. My parents found an incredibly gifted teacher who thoroughly inspired me with constant encouragement and instruction. Because of her, my general creativity flourished. She claimed to see something exceptional in me. Even though her focus was on drawing and painting, she declared that I would excel at whatever form of the arts I was attracted to. I adored her for the positive attention and, as a result, my artistic abilities continued to flourish.

Only one week after moving to suburbia, I broke out in a rash caused by poison ivy. Before moving to town, my friends and I used to recklessly roll around in it just to show off, and not once did we get even a small outbreak. I continued to get it repeatedly over the next few years, and my allergic reaction to it was severe. For me, living in this environment was like a fish living out of water. It was like living in the sanitized environment of a hospital ward.

As I began junior high, I soon realized I didn't have any friends, and I didn't fit into any of the cliques or groups that normally congregate in schools. I was completely ignorant of the existing social cliques. I tried devising ways that a smaller-than-average country boy like myself could get noticed and start making friends. As I came up with ideas to introduce myself, I didn't consider how my peers would perceive me.

One day during a social studies class, the teacher was discussing different religions of the world and how those religions often determined not only the social identities of their specific regions but also nearly every other single function of those societies, economic or otherwise. Upon hearing this, I decided it was an opportune time for me to introduce myself to the class by telling them about my family's traditional heritage. I thought if the other kids knew more about me, then they would like and accept me more. However, I was completely oblivious to the cascade of harsh peer abuse and rabid bullying that I would be subjected to over the next few years for making that decision.

I raised my hand, and the teacher called on me. I told the class about my Russian Jewish heritage, including that we did not celebrate Christmas.

After talking for a little while, I noticed that some of my classmates were giggling and making odd facial expressions. One of the students mumbled, "stupid Jew," and the entire class erupted into gales of laughter. Even the teacher chuckled before telling the class to quiet down.

I thought that by sharing this intimate aspect of my life with my classmates, I would interest them and earn some friends. I could not have been more wrong. From that day forward, I became the subject of severe anti-Semitic bullying.

It lasted until I quit school for the first time in the ninth grade.

After a few months of hateful remarks, having swastikas drawn on my study books and being told that I "should be gassed to death" by kids I didn't know, the abuse became physical. I was spit on almost daily. There were a few kids who would cough up phlegmy wads into their hands, sneak up behind me, and splatter it over my face. I dry heaved every time it happened; occasionally I vomited. Being sucker-punched and shoved into lockers was a regular occurrence. I once had my head shoved into a flushing toilet. But it became really scary off of school grounds. I was often chased, pelted with rocks, and twice took a heavy beating when I got too close to my oppressors.

Every time that I confronted my parents, guidance counselors, or school faculty about it, nothing was done. My parents told me to get tough because they had endured much worse, growing up in New York City. But they still didn't understand how sensitive I was - not to mention how bad the bullying actually was. I thought about fighting back, but these were seasoned bullies, and their threats to kill me left me afraid they might. I wrote an article about it that was published as a letter to the editor in the school newspaper. My father still has that article today. The entire school, students, staff and all read it, but nothing was done, and the bullying continued.

My father finally realized how serious the issue really was when he witnessed a group of kids openly hitting me and stomping on the spokes of my bike during a soccer game at a public park. Seeing this, he came running at the group of kids, waving his arms and yelling. The kids all fled. He felt terrible for not doing more than he had. Later that night, the same group of kids pelted our house with rocks and eggs. My father called the police and the school, but nothing was done about it.

Around this time, I began tentative study at the local Synagogue to prepare for my Bar Mitzvah. I was hesitant about going because I knew what would happen to me if my schoolmates found out where I was and what I was doing. I felt deeply conflicted because our family traditions were definitely a part of my upbringing (although not a big part) and I was proud of that (at least I thought I was), but I was horrified by how I was incessantly treated by my peers for the same reasons. I started to feel ashamed of my heritage and myself. My self-esteem had been all but decimated.

My grandfather was a Russian immigrant who came to America in his early teens. He knew about struggle. He was very proud when he heard that I was studying Hebrew in preparation for my Bar Mitzvah. He was sometimes an angry and troubled man, but he adored my brother and me, and he head a heart of gold.

Around the time of the Bar Mitzvah, he sat me down for an important talk. He told me that being Jewish would always bring adversity into my life, but that it was no different than what our people had endured for millennia. He told me of the significance of our holidays, and of the unspeakable actions of the Nazis'. Then he told me about my great-cousin Marty, who escaped from one of the concentration camps. During his escape, an SS officer attacked him. It wasn't clear whether Marty killed the officer, but he managed to get his knife before fleeing to safety. My grandfather then handed me that very knife to keep as a reminder to endure whatever hardship was in my path. He told me to remember what my great-uncle Marty had endured - that it would give me the strength to get through my struggles. But just holding that knife, I felt that pain that resided within it - it was as dark as anything I've ever felt, brimming with evil. I told him I didn't want to keep it, but that I would always remember the message of the story. It was a defining moment in my life. I now had a broader perspective of tribulation. I empathized with the suffering that was endured, not only by my relatives but also by people all over the world.

My grandfather's story instilled a warrior-like strength in me. I can only describe it as a feeling of sorrow intermingled with unwavering confidence in the process of life, like in astrology – Chiron "The Wounded Healer"

After my Bar Mitzvah, I faced the world at age thirteen with a greater feeling of maturity; I felt a little more ready for what life had in store for me. Little did I know of the trauma that was coming next…

CHAPTER THREE

Bullied

Being the recipient of such constant and intense bullying severely injured my self-esteem. I began to think that if I wasn't Jewish none of this would have ever happened.

As a result of such thinking, I began to develop a degree of religious intolerance. It wasn't intolerance for religions other than my own, though - it was intolerance for all religions, *including* my own. How could a loving God allow what I was experiencing to happen, especially in the name of religion?

Interestingly, I developed two different perspectives that were very opposite of each other: because I felt so singled out by constant assaults, I began to think like a victim - but I also began to feel a lot of compassion for those who victimized me at the same time. I knew that most of their actions towards me stemmed from the abuse they received from others. Some part of me realized that most of it was learned behavior that they unconsciously adopted. It was not their true nature; their true nature had been crushed so long ago that they didn't even know what it was, if they ever did.

I tended to flip-flop between these two viewpoints. My conflict created a lot of anticipatory anxiety. I also began harboring a lot of guilt.

I thought there was something wrong with me. I figured that at some point in my life, I must have done something terrible to be treated like this, but I couldn't figure out what it was. Sometimes I wondered if God wanted to punish me for a reason I wasn't aware of. No matter how I looked at it, it hurt. Even after my Bar Mitzvah and supposedly becoming a man, I still felt alone and powerless to change my situation.

I looked for ways to escape the torment of this terrible situation and discovered that marijuana was well suited for the purpose. I started smoking it at age thirteen, and by fifteen, I was using it daily.

The first time I tried it, it did nothing for me. The second time, it blew me away. I saw aspects of myself that prior to using it were unimaginable. There were feelings of deep peace, but at times it was shrouded in turbulence. I caught brief glimpses of many parts of my early childhood that I had forgotten about, as well as glimpses into my future. I'd experience an intense fear of death; then that fear would turn into peace.

Smoking cannabis daily helped me to mentally escape from the constant threat of physical abuse. Even though I was still unsure of how to handle the constant bullying, being high allowed me to see their behavior for what it really was: complete ignorance on all levels. It became clear to me they had very little, if any, family or community guidance. These kids were damaged goods, and sadly most were destined to remain that way.

While living in suburbia, I was still able to spend time with the kids that I had grown up with. On random weekends our parents took turns shuttling us out to see one another. Three of the boys I grew up with (two Bens and a Nick), I considered my best friends. When I was in their company, I could be myself without concern for the constant threats of violence in suburbia. I rarely discussed these issues with them; I was too overjoyed to be in their presence and reconnected to the childhood that I loved.

At this point in our early teens, we were all infatuated with smoking marijuana, listening to incredible music, and learning about the hippie counterculture that we were raised in. All the cannabis smoking took place at my friends' parents' homes; their parents knew we smoked, and they left us alone without a word about it. I think they realized we were good kids exploring a lifestyle they themselves had lived. And they were right - it was harmless, and we all bonded even deeper as friends during that time period. However, combined with the other circumstances in my life that I had no way of handling, my dysfunctional personality was developing rapidly.

The first out-of-body experience that I had since I used to meditate as a child occurred in a car accident when I was fourteen years old. I was with Ben's dad and my good friends, Joe and Lily. We were headed back to Ben's house. Ben's dad was driving, and I was in the front passenger's seat when Joe actually claimed to see a UFO hovering above us in broad daylight!

Ben's father became interested after hearing his excitement. We were moving around 35-40 mph, and he craned his head over the steering wheel to catch a glimpse of it, and I watched the Saab 900 we were in drift over to the next lane and into oncoming traffic. A giant Chevy Suburban headed directly towards our little car.

Time slowed down a few seconds before impact, and then I lost all awareness of myself in a body. All I could perceive was my skeletal structure and the energy that animated it. In the span of a few short moments, the only knowing left in me was that of a skeleton receiving and transmitting electrical impulses from its bone marrow. On impact, the electrical impulses in and around my skeleton started to dissipate from my bones like smoke dispersing into the air.

After that, my awareness hovered above the scene of the accident and observed it. It seemed to be in another dimension that was looking into the world where the car accident had just occurred, a space that was nothing at all like the world I had been living in as a fourteen-year-old boy. There was a flood of geometric patterns along with a stream of predominantly imperceptible information that seemed to be related to the car accident itself. I had no physical body in this dimension, but my awareness was still there.

I was not alive, and I was not dead, I was someplace in-between. It was another existence, real and, from what I could gather, very important. Simply put, this experience completely rocked my world. In a single instant, I became completely transformed on all planes of my existence: physically, mentally, emotionally, and spiritually.

It felt like my soul was hovering above the accident site; taking in the smoke billowing from the two crushed vehicles…then suddenly I was opening my eyes in my human body again. The airbag's inflation had covered the interior of the car with powder, its scent was intertwined with various other noxious fumes emitting from the wreck. The engine compartment of the car was almost sitting in the cockpit, and I heard my friends in the back seat sobbing. But none of this was as shocking to me as what I'd experienced outside of my body. It was more than I was able to deal with on a psychological level. It took months for me to process the mind-numbing intensity of this experience.

I had a sense that something profound had just happened, but I wasn't sure what it was. Nevertheless, coming back to the reality of the car crash itself was a shock to my whole physical system as well. I had never been in such a terrifying situation. There were no serious injuries, just cuts, bruises, and some mild fractures. The people in the Chevy Suburban had no serious injuries either. I emerged with hardly a scratch.

We were brought to the hospital to be examined for injuries, but since there was nothing serious, we were all released. That night at Ben's house, I was still in a state of shock. I wasn't sure how to make sense of what had happened during these multidimensional moments of the collision. Deep inside, I had figured something out—that a part of me existed outside of my body. However, I was clueless as to what that part of me was or where it actually existed.

That night, as we passed around a joint and talked about the accident, I wasn't able to take more than two tokes. As the effects of the marijuana kicked in, I felt the energy of my body wanting to leave its physical structure, and I didn't like it. I remember thinking that once was enough for the day. I wanted to feel grounded in my young body after the trauma of the accident. Getting high was not helping at that point. I didn't want to slip away. I wanted to be me, in my body. However, I was about to get hooked into some addictive patterns of perception…

CHAPTER FOUR

The Seeker Is An Addict

After the accident, the bullying no longer fazed me. It still happened with frequency, but now I mostly just laughed it off. Normal life was not nearly as real as what had occurred in the moments of the collision. My day-to-day experience in this world, no matter how challenging, simply seemed insignificant by comparison.

But I still wanted to know what that entire experience meant to my day-to-day life. The problem was, I wasn't sure how to replicate the same out-of-body experience and without being able to do that, how could I investigate it further? Neither was I able to effectively communicate what had happened, which made it difficult to discuss with other people. It was before the prominence of the Internet, and I couldn't find any books on the subject. What occurred during those moments when I was aware, but not in my body, seemed to be beyond this planet - yet connected in some important way to it.

Years later, I learned that indigenous people across the globe had trained their whole lives to make sense of out-of-body experiences like the one I underwent. Without that foundation of knowledge and training, I did my best to figure it out on my own. Since I'd felt a similar experience beginning to occur after smoking cannabis on the night of the accident, I reasoned that perhaps smoking a lot of it might trigger a similar experience. So that's exactly what I did. But no matter how much I smoked or ate, nothing brought me anywhere near the intensity of that first experience.

However, I began to develop a substantial psychological addiction to it, which further fueled my dysfunction. And, I eventually concluded that I wasn't going to have an out-of-body experience from constant use - but by this point, my priorities shifted. Instead of seeking to replicate a profound otherworldly experience, I was looking to stay high. I began selling small amounts of pot to maintain a steady supply, but I also realized that I was really good at selling it. This is when my entrepreneurial mind really began to take root in my awareness as I devised better strategies to get better weed in order to sell it for greater costs.

However, my reasons for using it the way I did, was definitely not for medicinal use. I was abusing it. Obviously, none of this made for a healthy scenario; it was my way of coping. But it didn't incur any serious repercussions until the winter of my freshman year of high school. I'd decided to smoke a joint in my room after a particularly brutal day of being bullied at school. I knew my parents would be home before long, but I wasn't concerned; they'd warned me about the dangers of drug use in the past, but having been raised in a pot-friendly environment, I didn't think that cannabis was drugs. But when they arrived home to the smell of marijuana smoke, they completely flipped out - and somewhere amidst their screaming, my father called the police. I was in a complete state of shock, and so were they. They loved me so much and felt I was going off the rails, and I was, so they dealt with it in the only way they knew how to at that point.

Once the gravity of the situation really hit home, I didn't take time to think. I plowed through them and ran out of the house as quickly as possible. It was the end of winter in Maine, and I was headed down a hill towards North Street Park wearing sneakers and no winter clothes. Suddenly, I saw the light - only it was blue and flashing. The officer in the car began yelling through a megaphone, ordering me to stop. I ran across busy North Street and into a snowfield without looking to see if cars were coming. The snow was deep, and every step I took slowed me down. I knew there was nowhere to go as I approached the freezing river, but I was terrified.

Out of nowhere, I felt a giant hand grab my shirt at the scruff of the neck. The shirt started ripping as I attempted to squirm out of it, but the cop grabbed my arm and threw me face down into the snow. The next thing I knew, I was cuffed and dragged into his car. He began yelling at me, and I began hyperventilating in the backseat. None of it seemed like it was really happening. It was surreal.

Instead of bringing me to jail, he took me to a rehabilitation center. My parents were already there and, along with a chorus of others I'd never met, they began a militant intervention. They took turns lecturing me about how I was ruining my life and the lives of my family members. Then I was brought into a room where an enormous man demanded that I pee in a cup. At this point in the proceedings, I was so stricken with fear that I couldn't pee. He threatened to administer a catheter if I didn't produce a urine sample immediately. I still couldn't do it. He responded by going into graphic detail, explaining that if I didn't urinate into the cup within five minutes, he would take a tube, shove it up my penis and collect the urine sample that way. I was mortified. The trauma from this experience was so severe that for over a decade, I couldn't urinate in public bathrooms if people were nearby. But the real damage occurred to my relationship with my parents. They were the only people left that I felt I could truly trust and I felt that they'd betrayed me. This event destroyed our relationship for a long time.

Suddenly the world had become a very dark place. In the past, no matter how bad the bullying was, I never let it get the best of me. I knew I had the love and support of my parents. But after this event, I completely alienated myself from them. This caused them to try harder to connect with me. But in my mind, I wanted no part of their support. Every word they uttered sounded empty and duplicitous.

After many years had passed, I truly realized that they feared for my wellbeing because I was so reckless. Eventually, I was able to understand and even empathize with their intervention. They loved me deeply, and they thought they had my best interests at heart. But at the time, I wasn't mature enough to understand how much they loved me and how worried they were. But after that, I no longer trusted them, which meant I no longer trusted anyone. I certainly wasn't mature enough to trust myself, either. With the exception of my art teacher, I lost all respect for authority and adults in general.

My only goal now was to numb my emotions however I could. Of course, I was oblivious to the fact that this would make things much worse in the long run. I was unable to understand how immature I was and how powerful these substances were. I didn't use them recreationally. The emotional turmoil I felt caused me to abuse them. I became relentless in my quest to get high.

Hallucinogens were my first priority. I began using high dosages of them, hoping I would invoke some kind of forced enlightenment. I needed to know what the purpose of my life was because at that point, I felt there was none. The people I got drugs from did them to "party" and have fun. My intentions were very different. I was letting God know I was coming to visit - even if I had to die.

The small amounts of cannabis I sold to sustain my habit were no longer enough to feed my level of consumption. Since I was unable to sell more due to a lack of supply, I began stealing marijuana and other substances from my parent's hippie friends. These were the parents of all my cherished childhood friends. Deep down, I was jealous that these parents allowed their kids to smoke, and mine did not and of course I was setting myself up to become completely disowned from my friends and their parents, and rightly so – I was stealing from them.

I'd borrow someone's car or get someone to drive me in exchange for a shared portion of whatever was plundered. Altogether, I would visit three different houses over the course of a few months. I knew that what I was doing was terrible, but my desperation, lack of guidance, and emotional disarray drove me to act without conscience.

Of all the places I stole from, one, in particular, was on especially sacred grounds. The family living there had fully dedicated their lives to living off the land. They hand-produced almost every element of their existence themselves through gardening, animal husbandry, and wild harvesting. They were people who lived, breathed, and loved Mother Nature so passionately that they devoted their lives to harmonious cohabitation with her. Living off the grid to this degree was no easy feat in the seasonal state of Maine. These people were the real deal and they worked hard; a labor of love. They represented the life that I felt had been stolen from me in our move to suburbia.

Incidentally, the small amount of marijuana that they produced for their personal supply was the highest quality grade I had ever tried. It was like no other weed I had smoked.

The first time I looted their house, I noticed a giant ceramic container filled with a peyote cactus. I recognized it from my elementary research on psychedelic plants. I also intuitively believed that there were powerful spirits associated with these cacti and that for me to uproot them would be a sacrilege. I was so frightened by the presence of this sacred medicine that it gave me chills just to look at it. Stealing these plants was not an option. However, I nicknamed their stolen pot, "peyote weed." This pot was so strong that it produced hallucinogenic effects in the few who smoked it with me.

Word spread about the peyote weed, and soon I was approached by an acquaintance named Asher, who became my temporary partner-in-crime. I didn't really trust him, but he had a license and easier access to cars than I did.

On our first attempt at stealing peyote weed together, I immediately realized that I had opened Pandora's box. We parked the car, ran inside, and began a mad search for the pot. I quickly found it, and we headed for the door. On the way out, Asher noticed the ceramic pot filled with peyote cactus.

"That's the peyote, isn't it?"

"Yeah, but don't touch it! Let's get the hell out of here before they catch us."

As we rode back to town, I began lecturing him about the peyote - how messing with it in any way would cause horrible things to transpire in our lives. My life was out of control, but there were some lines

I thought I knew better than to cross, ironically. Asher listened, but he didn't say a word.

I was harboring tremendous guilt about all of this because I knew how wrong it was to steal from those beautiful people. It was becoming all too clear that this wasn't going to end well.

Not more than a couple of weeks after I went to the peyote house with Asher, I was informed that he had a peyote cactus in his possession, and was asking random people if they knew how to 'get high' off of them. I was livid. I found Asher at his house and began screaming at him. It seemed to amuse him; he couldn't understand why I was so infuriated. He claimed there was no such thing as spirits, and that I needed to grow up and stop believing in fairy tales.

I tried to make my case, but I was armed with so little knowledge about the spiritual consequences of desecrating sacred substances that I started sounding foolish. I began staring into space, seeking the presence of mind to say something of value. Then, looking to his left, I saw the uprooted peyote cactus next to him on a plate, its long, carrot-shaped root dangling over the side. I began shaking with fright. I wanted to hit him, but instead, I turned around and ran out of his house.

The image of the murdered peyote cactus was imprinted on my mind. I felt like I'd just seen a dead human body. *What have I done?* I thought. This was serious.

Not long after the peyote incident word, got out amongst my parents' friends that I was the one responsible for the string of thefts. Apparently, I'd been seen leaving one of the houses. On top of that, I hadn't considered that my co-conspirators might decide to make trips to those houses on their own. I had no idea how many times these places had been hit.

Then the inevitable happened: I came home to find the peyote people waiting for me, along with my parents. Everyone went ballistic when I walked in. The family I'd stolen from told me I would have been shot had they caught me in the act. But even more terrifying, they told me of the spiritual implications of my actions: "Because you fucked with Mescalito, Mescalito is going to fuck with you!" I was so afraid that I dipped my head in shame and began crying. There was nothing I could say - I knew I had brought this upon myself. I got up and ran for the door. Before I stepped out, I told them I was sorry - but of course, that wasn't going to make any difference. And it didn't matter that I wasn't the one who actually killed the peyote cactus because I knew I was still responsible for its death.

It took a few more days for me to fully realize the implications of what had happened. Once the word got out, none of my dear childhood friends or their parents wanted me around anymore, and I couldn't blame them. What I'd done was a betrayal on every level. I was now engulfed by a feeling of complete loneliness, mixed with a fear of being attacked by evil spirits. Being cast out by my peers in suburbia was beyond my control; being ostracized by all of my childhood friends and family was entirely my own doing, and it was crushing. And without intending to, I'd alienated my parents from their friends as a consequence.

I had one relationship left in my life, and it was as emotionally unhealthy and dysfunctional as I was. Interestingly it was with the prettiest and most popular girl in my suburban high school. Her name was Lucinda, and she was a blond-haired, blue-eyed girl of Native American and Irish descent, two grades above me. I often tricked myself into believing that she was in love with me. In reality, while she might have thought I was cute, the real attraction was that I was good at having an ample supply of pot on hand. Still, I was in awe that this gorgeous girl would hang out with me. She could be with anyone she wanted to. And she was.

Through the grapevine, I'd often hear of her numerous sexual exploits. Every time I heard about a new guy she'd slept with, my heart would ache. For her own reasons, she abused sex in the same way I abused drugs. We were never lovers, and while she only attempted to seduce me a handful of times, I always refused. I suppose I wanted her to know I was different than anyone else she'd been with. I really wanted her to love me as I loved her, but she had too many of her own issues, and the fact was, I did too. We'd have only hurt each other - and that's what we ended up doing anyway.

Lucinda knew I was stealing the pot I shared with her, and while she didn't condone it, she didn't try to stop me, either. I even convinced her to drive me a couple of times for these burglaries. But everything changed when she discovered what had happened with the peyote theft. Her mother, Anais, was almost full-blooded Native American and a very spiritual person. She liked me a lot. She'd given Lucinda a book by Carlos Castaneda, and when Lucinda found out about the peyote plant, she waved it in my face as she lectured me on the consequences I would be facing from the spirit world - that by messing around with sacred medicine, I was sure to be attacked by dark spirits. That was my greatest fear at the time. She told me she no longer wanted to be my friend, threw the book at my feet, and said, "This book is about spirituality and being one with the universe. Something you know nothing about!" Then she walked away.

It hurt tremendously - because to a degree I knew she was right. I really didn't know anything about being one with the universe...not anymore. My profound childhood experiences were a distant memory that I'd lost touch with almost completely.

I was lost in a victim mentality that said I was all alone and completely separated from any goodness or unifying force that might exist in the universe. Yet somehow, buried deep in my unconscious, the wisdom of my childhood meditations were trying to emerge - wisdom that I would need to re-experience to remember.

I was certain that I had cursed myself with all of my recent actions. Of course, at that point in my life, I wasn't able to see how all the trials and tribulations I was experiencing were lessons that one-day would teach me to uncover my latent potential. All I felt was loneliness, betrayal, and the confusion of an out-of-body experience that didn't seem to have anything to do with my life on Earth. I really began thinking that perhaps I wasn't meant to live in this world. The moments of bliss I'd felt during the car accident made more sense to me than anything else.

All I had left now was seeking enlightenment through getting high. I became seriously introverted as drugs further fueled my desire for internal exploration. The peyote theft and Lucinda's response ignited my motivation for some kind of forced enlightenment. I would wake up early at my parent's house and come home late at night. My days were spent riding my bike along railroad tracks and through abandoned industrial zones. I used to frequent an area where retail outlets that lacked funding had been abandoned. I sat and looked at the destruction done in the name of industry. Broken bulldozers and dumped scrap metal looked like the skeletal remains of dinosaurs that had struggled to survive in inhospitable lands. The sounds of tractor-trailers on the highway filtered through the woods sounding like demons clawing their way up to the surface from hell. Death was in the air; I couldn't shake the premonition of species-wide planetary extinction from the periphery of my awareness. My will to live felt obsolete.

But at the same time, I was able to recognize that my suffering was not to be compared to that of many inhabitants on the planet. I didn't physically suffer the way countless others did; but still, there was something that was suffering deep inside me. I just couldn't put my finger on it. On the surface, it was emotional, but where it truly was, was somewhere deeper. Either there was peyote curse, or I was unconsciously cursing myself with inexplicable suffering from the guilt I harbored.

About a week after the confrontation with Lucinda, I returned to school. Between classes, a senior who was jealous because of the time I'd spent with Lucinda, marched belligerently toward me. He was the captain of the hockey team, and he was huge. He grabbed my shirt, threw me against a locker, and proceeded to scream. Spit flew out of his mouth into my face. "I hate you fucking Jews! I wish you all were dead!" Usually, when something like that happened, I'd run off and hide somewhere to smoke some weed to calm down. This time though, I was on fire. It felt like some other force was coming through me. I looked him dead in the eye and started to laugh. I told him that spirits had cursed me, and because of what he just did, he too would be cursed. It felt like demons of righteousness were speaking through my body. He and his friends gathered around and began laughing. One of his pals shouted out, "Yeah, the kike is cursed alright! He's cursed by us!"

The next week, the hockey captain's father died. He and his friends never bothered me again. They actually went out of their way to avoid me. Though they never said anything, I knew that my declaration was forefront in their minds. I saw the same fear in them that I felt in myself. It was the fear of that which they didn't understand, the fear of the unknown, the fear of death. It permeated their facial expressions. They were unable to hide it. And I was getting ready to fully face it…

CHAPTER FIVE

Damian

My existence had become a contradicting mixture of the incessant need to know the meaning of life, with the emotional turmoil of loneliness and a nagging feeling of separation. I had tried to reach my own Nirvana by getting high enough to numb my internal conflict, but it wasn't working. At that time, I thought that maybe I could find something to get me so high that I would transcend all of it and project my consciousness beyond space and time! I had to at least try.

Word had spread that an upperclassman was having a massive party at his parent's place while they were away. I knew I could get drugs there. My plan was to go, get high, and leave, because I was sure no one there wanted to socialize with me and I was pretty sure I didn't want to socialize with anyone there, either.

Upon arriving, I was able to score a hit of acid with five dollars in quarters I'd taken from my father's change drawer. Mission complete. I headed for the door. I wanted to trip somewhere in the woods, where the nurturing goodness of nature would comfort me.

Just before I stepped outside, I looked to my right. The guy standing there didn't look like he belonged at a party; he looked like a Native

American medicine man. He had really long brown hair, and his tall figure was adorned with silver and turquoise jewelry. His dark, hypnotic eyes seemed to hold and cradle the awe of galaxies. He was wild like a savage, yet sophisticated in an unexplainable way, and he held an audience captive, intrigued by his yelling, singing and erratic movements.

His name was Damian. I recognized him from early in my youth. His parents were acquaintances of my parents, although Damian and I never hung out. I definitely remembered who he was, but back then he didn't have the mystique that he did now.

Lucinda was there and was watching him intently; she was practically drooling. His actions were like those of a chief leading a ceremonial dance. *He is unlike any human that I have ever seen*, I thought. He seemed to be more like a spirit than a human. I had just taken the hit of acid, so I knew it wasn't affecting me yet, but the aura around him was so bright, I wondered if it was real or imagined. Was I losing my mind? Not yet. This was no normal human being. He was fierce, yet joyous, glowing with multi-dimensional vibrancy. He seemed almost alien.

I waited until he calmed down and then I decided to introduce myself. As I walked up, I listened to the conversation he was having. He posed a question to the people gathered: "Why do you all think you feel so attached to everything in this world?" And then he turned, looked directly at me and said, "Don't be fooled by the normality of what you think is reality."

"But why does it hurt so much if it is not real?"

"You think it hurts because you have tricked yourself into believing this to be real, when in fact, what is real is beyond any belief that you could ever believe in."

"What do you believe?"

He smiled. "Why would I allow something as limiting as beliefs to interfere with the innate intelligence that's pulsing inside me? Your thoughts and beliefs about life will often stunt your ability to be aware of this inner intelligence. But once you are aware of it, the thoughts and beliefs that you produce from it will make you more aware of it! I keep my heart open, and my mind pure so that life flows through me. When life flows through me, then I know I'm living in reality. I perceive the world this way because I have removed the inner obstructions that once inhibited life's natural flow."

As profound as his words were, I realized that something even more profound had taken place. I didn't just understand his words with my mind; I could literally feel the message that they conveyed on a much deeper level. It seemed like *something* in him, some sort of energy that was projected through his words had momentarily unblocked the dysfunction that I carried around. Suddenly, a wave of deep-seated peace came over me, so powerful I had to sit down. I felt like a monk centered in a perpetual place of bliss, rather than the prison of pain I'd become accustomed to over the past few years. *Is this really happening?* I asked myself as I sat there reveling in those indescribable moments.

But after a few minutes of this heightened awareness, doubt started creeping in. Did that really just happen? Was it a just placebo effect of the LSD? If my pain wasn't real, then why do I feel it again?

After a little while, the LSD actually started to kick in, and I could sense a dark presence enveloping me. There was something ominous about this party house. The words of energetic wisdom that this medicine man had spoken were now blanketed by it. I could feel a bad trip coming on. I fled into the woods where Nature was sure to comfort me, and she did.

It was around this time I moved out of my parent's house and began couch surfing at random suburban locations. I mostly stayed with Lucinda's older brother, Manny. He was a bona fide hellion whose interest in heavy metal music trumped that of anyone I'd met, and he personified it: long brown mullet, ever-present jean jacket with various band logos sewn on it, beady snake eyes, and skeletal frame. He was a master manipulator; he'd often lead people on with cryptically entertaining stories, only to trap them with guilt. By the end of it, they'd usually feel obligated to give him money, drugs or food. I remember watching him ride his sister's old ten-speed bicycle around town. With his riding style - standing up, swaying back and forth - it wasn't hard to picture Luciferian wings sprouting from his back. Hell on wheels!

Coincidentally, Damian lived near Manny's apartment. One day, I saw him walking down the street, so I approached him. He recognized me from the party. I told him I was staying with Manny and that he was welcome there anytime he wanted. He knew Manny and warned me to be careful - the guy was trouble. I told him that I'd figured that out, but I had nowhere else to go.

The day after I spoke with Damian on the street, he began showing up at Manny's place almost every morning at the crack of dawn. He would usually bring food that he shared with us. Manny appreciated this, but he got frustrated because he was unable to play the mind games with Damian that he could play with everyone else. Damian had a thick psychic wall that Manny's predatory hooks were unable to penetrate.

About a week after Damian began visiting, Manny had a meltdown in his apartment while he was trying to impress two overweight girls that he'd lured into his lair. He had a thing for big girls - as he enjoyed saying, "I love fatties, bro! I eat fatties (fattening food), I smoke fatties, and I fuck fatties." The guy was a real class act (sarcastically).

Manny was smashed. He started screaming at the top of his lungs, then heaved his electric guitar through the sheetrock wall. One of the girls started screaming, which prompted him to grab her by the hair and yank her head to the ground. He covered her mouth with his hand and began threatening her. Meanwhile, the downstairs tenants had wasted no time calling the police. They arrived, kicked in the door, cuffed Manny, and took him to jail.

When Damian found out that Manny was in jail, he invited his friend Leon over. Leon was all right, but like most of the guys I'd met in town, he wasn't shy about picking on me. It wasn't anti-Semitic; more like a pecking order type of thing. I'd learned to pay that behavior no mind at this point, and he eventually treated me as well as he was capable of. Leon was relatively immature, but the three of us did share a common vision: escape from suburbia. We wanted to get lost in the woods, where we could camp out, grow weed, and not be bothered for living the way we chose.

I suggested we go to the land where I had grown up, in Canaan. Behind the sanctuary of my old home were woods and fields that seemed to go on forever, and fresh spring water that one could drink right from the ground. It was now early spring, and I figured we could hide out there like bandits, grow weed, and make enough money to afford a warm place for the winter.

I was able to convince Lucinda to drive us up there; she was long over me, but I told her that if she brought us up there, she wouldn't have to deal with me anymore, and she agreed. She dropped us off with the little bit of camping gear that we were able to salvage from Leon's parent's garage.

The plan was to find a clearing way back behind my old house, far out of earshot of any residential neighbors. After some scouting around, we found the perfect spot. One hour into setting up our new camp a wild-eyed man with unkempt hair and a bushy pirate's beard found us. He had a shotgun.

"What in the hell are you guys doing here?" he barked.

Leon, the most gregarious of us, spoke up in a half-joking tone. "We needed to leave our old lives in town so we could smoke pot and eat acid without getting into trouble." Damian and I were flabbergasted; neither of us could believe he'd said that to a complete stranger. But the man's hardened face suddenly cracked into a wide smile.

"Have you got anything to smoke?"

"Yup, we certainly do," said Leon.

"Well, come meet the old lady," he offered merrily. "My name is Allen."

We all introduced ourselves. I explained that I'd grown up on the property next to this one and that we really were escaping from suburbia. I told him that I was searching for the meaning of my life. He chuckled and said nothing about it.

He and his wife, Marianne, had always owned the property next to my parent's place, but I had not visited it since before I was born. They pulled a little camper behind their car all the way from Oregon. Just before we made it to his camper, he turned to me and said, "We knew you guys were coming." Perplexed, I asked how. He just smiled and said nothing.

The three of us became close friends with Allen and Marianne. They took us under their wing and allowed us to stay with them, do chores, and grow some pot. We all seemed to share similar values, but they had much more practical life experience than we did. They coached us with ideas, instructions, and techniques for survival in the world. They were concerned that we thought we could just show up a random people's property and try to live off it. In many places around the country, it could have gotten us shot. For the most part, it seemed like Allen and Marianne assumed that the three of us were wet behind the ears. Leon and I may have been, but Damian was not.

Marianne was the wise leader of this wife and husband duo. At times she would get very anxious when trying to explain things to us. Other times she would zone out mid-sentence as though she had entered a deep hypnotic trance. She did this so often that eventually I asked if she was all right. Out of the blue, she explained it to me.

"My spirit guides are communicating with me. Someday you will understand how to do this, but it will be hard for you to get to that point." I had no idea what she meant, but she continued,

"When you do, you'll have a strong connection. Keep fighting temptations that will hurt you, and develop the inner peace that you sometimes feel. You'd be wise to make this your focus. You'll have to constantly do it. Your life will be consumed by tremendous hardship for years to come, but eventually, you'll be aligned with unparalleled beauty. Don't give up. Keep going. You'll make it."

Chills shimmered throughout my body. I was shocked. I noticed that although she was the one speaking this prediction, it had come through her from somewhere else, not from her thoughts. I was unable to comprehend the magnitude of her message or what it really meant - what resonated with me most was its intensity.

Based on the way she communicated with me, I began to suspect that Marianne was able to predict or have intuition regarding the future. When I pressed her about a subject, her eyes would usually get very shifty, and she would look away. Once she told me that it didn't matter what she saw because the future could always change as long as I was willing to change. Sometimes she would say things in a cryptic and hard to understand way. I feared that she saw something dramatic in my future and didn't want to share it with me. But I took what she said seriously, and she knew it. She became careful about what information she revealed to me.

Summer turned into autumn, and the chill of winter wasn't far away. Allen and Marianne packed up their camper and headed for warmer climates. Nearly destitute, Leon, Damian and I headed back to suburbia to sell the small amount of marijuana we'd grown. It had been a great summer, and we'd learned a lot, but now we were back in town, clueless about what to do next. I was sixteen and scheduled to be a sophomore in high school. The thought of it was nauseating and I knew that I wasn't going to make it.

CHAPTER SIX

Hemp Shoes

My parents were overjoyed to have me back home, even though it was clear that although my body was home, my mind, heart, and soul were not. I didn't know who they were anymore, nor did I understand the life they were living. From my perspective, it was a cookie-cutter version of reality, representative of everything I was against.

However, they did plant the seeds to further encourage my entrepreneurial ways when we visited Mardens Discount Furniture shop in Waterville Maine one day. As we walked into the shoe section of the store, I was astonished to find hundreds and hundreds of pairs of hemp sneakers that were made in China.

Mardens bought big lots of discount items from all over the world that had been damaged or discounted in some way, and for whatever reason, they now had an abundance of hemp shoes, and they were selling them at a discount price!

"Dad," if you buy all of these for me, I will sell every single one and make a great profit from them"! He looked at me oddly, but then smiled and actually made a deal with the storeowners to buy every single pair. I observed the way he used his New York City skills to negotiate, or 'dicker' with the guy as they say in NY! It impressed me.

Except for the few shoes that didn't have matching sizes, I made good on the deal and sold every matching pair. Between a few local outdoor hippie concerts and the rare few people I felt good enough about approaching, it soon became evident that the entire town of Waterville was wearing those hemp shoes! I made about $1000, big money for me in those days, plus I had refined my sales abilities. This was around the year 1991. The modern, booming Hemp/Cannabis industry was not even a blip on the map at that point, aside from the black market.

However, for me, the scarring around the interactions that took place at my parents' house, that town, and most of the bullies who lived there, still felt like an open scar with salt being poured on it all day long.

Although my parents convinced me to enroll in an alternative school rather than the high school I'd gone to the previous year, it really wasn't much different. It was still school. I only made it through the first quarter of my sophomore year before I decided I'd had enough. Between dealing with my parents and the politics of high school, I realized I had to either leave, or I would self-destruct. Quitting school terrified them, but they were even more terrified of Damian, who had become my only friend. In their eyes, he represented everything they had come to stand against. So, they made two offers that were difficult to refuse: 1) they would fully finance a move to South Florida so I could work at an incredible health food store/restaurant owned by my father's longtime friend, and 2) if I successfully earned my GED, they would buy me a new guitar.

Playing guitar was one of the few things I truly loved - so, between the new guitar, the fast-approaching winter, and my contempt for living with my parents in a suburban town, I took them up on both offers.

At the time, I didn't realize how desperate my folks were to get me away from Damian. They believed that my association with him would be the end of me. I didn't know it at the time, but this belief turned out to be profoundly accurate from an ego death perspective.

With my GED in one hand and my brand new Taylor guitar in the other, I moved to Ft. Lauderdale where the warm air, the glowing blue ocean, and the lush palm trees felt welcoming.

The experience of working at a big bustling health food store amidst all sorts of colorful people was exciting. The store had a health food restaurant that was always packed - and the pretty, charismatic head waitress would constantly flirt with me (despite the fact that she was at least fifteen years older than I was). The conversations that she would engage me in often left me feeling aroused, and she knew it. I started confusing my arousal with love and began to have a serious crush on her.

One day she told me to go to the staff bathroom and look behind the toilet. When I did, I was surprised to find a lighter and a pipe that contained a big white crack rock in its bowl. I had never tried snorting cocaine, let alone smoke crack. I had no idea what this stuff would do to me. My adrenaline began to surge just thinking about it. Here I was, working at a fancy health food store owned by one of my father's closest friends, and I'm in the staff bathroom thinking about smoking crack for the first time. I stopped thinking about it and decided to just do it.

I put the lighter to the pipe, lit it, and inhaled. I watched the rock melt and tasted a mixture of lemon and burnt plastic as the smoke filled my lungs. I began to feel a little light-headed and then...WHAM! It was like a cathedral bell had been set off in my head. An infusion of dopamine-fueled euphoria began to gush out of my brain like a waterfall, cascading into every part of my body. My knees became too weak to stand, and I hit the floor. The euphoria was intense. It was like having a whole-body orgasm. My eyes were shut as my brain bathed in this new sensation. Swirling streaming images of recent events leading into that very moment began flooding through my mind's eye. I was now living in a new state, around new people, while currently experiencing a new state of mind. I was thinking about how this first hit of crack felt, and the pretty flirtatious waitress who gave it to me and how turned on she made me feel, and what it would be like to have sex with her and…then came a loud knock on the bathroom door. The simple sound felt like a hammer pounding relentlessly in my head. I opened my eyes to find my face was buried at the juncture of the toilet and the floor.

With the smell of urine and disinfectant burning my nasal passages and the feeling of my body pressed against a damp concrete floor, I realized I was at work and was expected to do a job. The euphoria was gone. All that remained was a hollow void in my head; it was the polar opposite of the initial rush brought on by my first hit of crack. I felt emptiness, not peaceful, but turbulent, the kind that feels like something is missing, something deep and primal that can only be remedied by another hit.

What the hell did I just do? I thought to myself as the knocking on the door continued. "I'll be right out," I yelled, completely disgusted with myself for doing this in the bathroom of my father's friend's store. He would fire the waitress and me in a second if he discovered what I'd just done.

I opened the bathroom door, and shamefully emerged back into the aisles of the store and proceeded to stock shelves with health food products. Pretty soon, the waitress approached me.

"Did you like it?" she asked with a huge grin on her face.

"Well, it's all right. It's the first time I ever smoked crack, though!"

"It's not crack, honey. It's freebase! Freebase is much cleaner and classier!"

Hmm, I sarcastically thought to myself, *Of course it is!*

"Listen," she said, "I'm going to come by your hotel room tonight so that I can show you what I'm really about. Is that cool?"

I was confused; her drug habit wasn't attractive at all, but I still had a big crush on her, plus she was also the only person there that I knew. I agreed to her coming over that evening.

As soon as her shift was over, she was at my hotel. She came in, gave me a big hug and started affectionately rubbing my knee with her hand as she gazed into my eyes. I was on fire. She reached into her purse and pulled out a pipe, a lighter and two bags of white powder - one was cocaine, the other was baking soda. She dumped a little powder from each bag onto a jumbo spoon, added some water, and then used a lighter to cook the mixture up. She took little freebase rocks from the spoon, put it into the pipe, and handed it to me. I took a hit, lost my mind, handed the pipe back to her, and she took hers. We went back and forth like this for some time. After a while, I looked at her and noticed she was no longer smiling. Suddenly she seemed intolerant of my presence. She glared at me. It was reminiscent of an angry cat twitching its tail, "You're going to help me pay for this, right?"

Strung out and surprised, I told her I wouldn't have any money until I got my paycheck. She began laying down an aggressive guilt trip. "I share this with you at work, and then you have me come over here to give you more, and you have no money? You think I don't have better things to do than waste my time here with you?"

Now the entire scenario had completely dawned on me. How could I have been so naïve? This woman's only interest in me was getting my money to feed her addiction. The room was filled with tension, and I was pretty strung out from the hits of freebase that I smoked.

For a few moments, I was shaken up, but I soon realized I needed to lay down the law. "Get the fuck out of here! I didn't ask for this!" As soon as she saw I wasn't going to passively be manipulated by her, she did a 180-degree turn and completely changed her tune. "Baby, I'm sorry. I thought we were in this together. It will all be okay. Oh, honey, don't you want me to make you feel good? I'll do anything you want, just tell me!"

This was too much. I was just sixteen years old and still a minor. I went over and put my hand on the handle of the door. "I don't even know you. Get the fuck out of here."

At that moment, someone began to knock at the door. I opened it. Standing there was a thuggish looking Hispanic guy. The waitress went flying into his arms.

Holy shit! This is insane, I thought to myself.

Apparently he had been listening to us argue from outside the door because the first thing he said was, "Don't worry, my friend. We are all in this together!"

With a huge grin on his face, he put a 9mm and a giant bag of cocaine on the table, and then looked at us both. "It's all good, right? Let's enjoy ourselves!"

Now I was trapped in my own room with a crack addict and her gun-toting dealer. "We will make this easy, my friend," he said. "I will smoke with you all night. All you have to do is give me your paycheck then we will be even. It's a great deal! Sound good to you?"

By now, I was feeling really stressed out and cornered.

"I'll do it this time, but then I'm done because I don't make much and I won't be able to afford to live down here."

"Okay, my friend, okay! No problem!"

The next day at work, I felt like I had been lobotomized. The pretty waitress - who was now looking pretty ugly to me - didn't skip a beat. With bright eyes and a bushy tail, she acted like nothing out of the ordinary had happened the night before.

"What are you doing tonight, honey?"

"I'm busy!"

"OK, I'll check back with you later!"

I started feeling like I was stuck in the twilight zone. *Is this normal behavior in South Florida?*

After work, as I was about to enter my hotel room, the dealer popped out of nowhere. He asked me if I wanted more cocaine, and if I had the paycheck, I agreed to give him the night before. I told him that I didn't want any more coke and that I would pay him at the end of the week.

By now, I realized that this was going to be a never-ending issue. I paid the dealer and, because I still hadn't found an apartment, I moved to a different hotel. The new hotel was even sketchier than the first.

Between the pretty waitress and the seemingly endless supply of coke and freebase dealers who lurked around the area hotels, I decided that living in South Florida was not going to work.

I didn't tell my father's friend, the owner of the store, that any of this was happening. He would have been far too upset. I just told him

I was out of my element and just wanted to live a simple life. He was disappointed with me, but he would have been far more disappointed had he known the type of scene I had gotten myself into.

With only a duffle bag of personal items and clothes, I got on a Greyhound bus and headed back to Maine. *Wow,* I thought as I sat on the bus, *the bad spirits were out to get me down here.* Being subjected to the hellish Florida crack scene made me realize how sick and twisted this world could be. When I first came down here, I thought that working at a health food store would have exposed me to a healthy life, a *simple* life. The whole experience only served to fuel my feelings of inadequacy, victimization, and hopelessness.

After that experience, I was certain that the whole world was falling apart. It didn't seem real, but it also didn't seem like a dream. Was there any good left on earth? My pure heart was aching.

I didn't tell my parents why I was coming home. I only told them it wouldn't work out for me down there because I was so displaced, like a fish out of water. I told them that I missed the woods where I felt comfortable.

My mother had taken it upon herself to find a commercial organic farm up in the woods where I could work. It was still winter, but the owner of the farm had plenty of firewood that needed to be split. He said he would provide room and board in addition to a small paycheck. It sounded way better to me than South Florida!

CHAPTER SEVEN

Into the Wild

Ian Robertson owned a two hundred acre farm in Athens, which is known as one of Maine's biggest hippie towns. Although it still had a thriving scene for all things "hippie" - it was nowhere near its heyday of the '70s and '80s. But the inspiration for the lifestyle was still alive. There was even a section called "Creep City" where parties would happen.

Ian's property was beautiful - big open fields, dense woods, and a stream with whitewater that bordered the far end of his property.

Ian gave me a gracious welcome when I arrived. My first impression was that everything about the place felt right. I spent the winter days chopping and stacking wood by hand. At night, Ian prepared hearty meals with ingredients produced on his farm. After conversation and dinner, I'd retreat to my room and play an antique Martin guitar that was passed down through Ian's family. The abalone shell inlay was exquisite, and the sound was enough to bring me to tears.

But the most impactful moments of my experience on Ian's farm occurred when I was alone in the woods. Every day at dawn, I'd hop on his tractor. He'd bring me out to the far end of his property with nothing but a bagged lunch and an ax, and I'd spend hours working in quiet contemplation before he picked me up at dusk. The sounds and smells of the frozen forest were divine. There were times I'd stand perfectly still without making a sound, and just listen. The silence was all-encompassing, and blissful. When the gentle breeze wasn't blowing, I could hear an internal oceanic sound that began to trigger deep memories of my childhood meditations. I was on the verge of remembering the profundity of these experiences, the transcendence of them, the deep peace. But then it would abruptly stop. It felt like something was blocking me from being content and at peace with myself. This, in turn, caused me to feel agitated. *Why is it so hard to be at peace with myself?* I knew there was an inner obstruction, but I was clueless about what it was or how to deal with it.

I had stayed in touch with Damian since I moved to Florida and then back to Maine. He asked if Ian needed an extra farmhand, and as it turned out, he did. Damian moved up and brought his dog, Princess, with him. Even his dog was an enigma. She always looked like she was engaged in deep thought. It was almost comical how alike they were.

As winter turned to spring Ian, Damian and I began sprouting massive amounts of organic squash, tomatoes, cucumbers, pumpkins, and other assorted vegetables to be planted after the frost was gone. We tapped hundreds of maple trees, running lines tree to tree to collect their sap or (*tree juice*, as I called it). The maple syrup we made from it may have been the most delicious thing I've ever tasted.

I really loved this lifestyle. I envisioned owning a farm and living off the land, but something else was stirring inside of me. I was brimming with emotional uncertainty that was surfacing from being in such a pristine environment, and I needed resolution. But even stronger than my need to resolve this inner conflict was that desire to uncover the purpose and meaning of life.

After the peaceful moments experienced alone while splitting wood in the back of Ian's property, I had decided that complete solitude was a key piece of the self-discovery puzzle. Damian agreed with this.

As spring turned into summer, Damian and I decided to make a move. Life at Ian's farm was great and so was he, despite the fact that he couldn't figure Damian and me out at all. But the one thing in us he *could* relate to was our intense desire for the stillness and solitude only found through immersion deep into the far reaches of the wilderness.

He told us about a cabin roughly 45 minutes north of his place on a tract of forest called Brighton Plantation. It was two-and-a-half miles off the main road and roughly twelve miles from the closest convenience store. It had no electricity, but it did have spring water and an outhouse. He said we could stay there until it got too cold outside.

After we had finished planting the plots on Ian's farmland, we decided to make the move. I bought a barely-functional Volkswagen Rabbit for a couple of hundred dollars, we loaded up what little we owned, and we drove north. The entire inventory of our possessions at that point was our clothes, sleeping bags, two bicycles, a little bit of weed, food stamps and a giant box of twenty-year-old MREs (meals ready to eat) someone had given us.

When we arrived in Brighton, we knew we were somewhere special. Just the ride from Athens to Brighton alone was enough to evoke the wonder of nature's sublime beauty.

Driving out of the village of Athens, the houses became fewer and fewer. The telephone poles and electric lines ended; beyond that, all signs of human disruptions vanished except for the empty road. Like a gigantic serpent slithering through pristine wilderness, it wound around mountains, up and over hills and through marshes and bogs filled with the creatures of the wild.

For me, the parts that made the biggest impact were the knolls. They were similar to the ones on our land in Canaan but even more beautiful. Magnificent rocky granite outcroppings covered with stunted conifers and other trees, like majestic *bonsai* sculpted by Japanese masters in days of wonder. Expansive blankets of green moss and tiny particolored wildflowers surrounded the knolls. The flora and fauna that were so rare in the rest of the modern world were common in this place. Some of the areas were so pure and primordial in appearance that it was obvious human hands had never touched them.

Eventually, the winding tar road gave way to a brutal upward dirt road that became impassable for our little Volkswagen Rabbit. Only a third of the way in, we had to park and walk - but once we got there, we knew we had *arrived*. After miles and miles of hardly a man-made structure to be seen, we came to a small log cabin on the side of a hill. It was literally in the middle of nowhere. A sense of peace completely overwhelmed me. I knew this would be our monastic training center for the next five months.

After we placed our possessions into the cabin, we began exploring the area. There was a small field on the top of the hill where the cabin was located. From the top of the hill, it was nothing but mountains, lakes, trees, and sky as far as the eye could see. During my first night there, the stillness permeated the core of my being. The brightest stars I had ever seen blanketed the forest bed around me like fireflies hovering just overhead. I had to remind myself that I was seeing the light from stars that had long since ceased to exist. The sacredness of it all sent shivers through me.

Aside from the breezes and occasional roving packs of coyotes, it was so silent that I could almost hear celestial sounds that would normally be inaudible: the ultra-low bass rumbling of the Earth as she swooshed around the sun; the expansive open-air sound of the universe continuing to expand forward from the Big Bang. Peace indescribable.

The next morning we got to work planting a garden with seeds that farmer Ian gave to us. We also sprouted around twenty cannabis seeds that would hopefully provide our income for the year. There was fresh asparagus growing in a garden bed planted over ten years earlier, as it was a perennial that grew back every year. We savored every sweet bite of it as though it was a gift from the gods.

That day was a silent as the night, especially considering that Damian was a man of few words. He'd usually only say what needed to be said. His priority was focused on the awareness of his awareness. Since I'd known him, I noticed how almost every person he came in contact with was intimidated by his presence. Nobody could read him. But his stoic demeanor was occasionally interrupted by party nights when he was in rare form, like the night I met him. However, there weren't any party nights this far out into the woods. Our first full day into our retreat, he probably said no more than a few sentences.

After we were all set up and settled in, we explored the forested domain even further. Whenever we discovered a scenic vista or a spot with some sort of profound beauty, we sat in silence, absorbing it. Sometimes I noticed that even surrounded by silence my mind often wasn't silent at all. The serenity of nature just amplified the thoughts that were already occurring in my head.

After about a month in Brighton, my car died on the gnarled dirt road leading up to the cabin. A gasket in the engine had blown, and we lacked the tools and income to fix it. Twice a week we used the car to drive into a small one-horse town, acquiring the few groceries we could afford with our food stamps. Now, all we had were our bicycles. Every few days we'd make the twenty-four-mile ride to buy pancake batter, V-8 juice and discounted stale donuts at five boxes for a dollar. Between the groceries, the ancient army food, wild foraging, and minimalist fishing, we thought we were doing pretty good for ourselves! We loved the bike ride until we ran out of money. Being this far out in no-man's land with no money, little supplies and no outside support was an issue.

However, the timing couldn't have been better; we ran out of money just as the potatoes and onions in our garden were ready to harvest. We figured we'd make do with the new crop, the packaged army food, and what little we were able fish and forage. As time wore on, both of us began to get really skinny. The one thing that seemed to carry us through it all and make the lack of food more tolerable was the crisp, cold mountain spring water. The cabin had it piped in, and it also bubbled directly out of the ground behind it. This water felt alive, as though it carried the spirit of the area with it. It was "adaptogenic:" if you were tired, it woke you up; if you were wired, it would sedate you. I'd never experienced effects like that from drinking only water. It was a true healing spring. If it weren't for its remarkable properties, hunger would likely have driven us out - maybe out of our minds. Personally, I was coming closer to that reality every day. Teetering on the brink of starvation was stirring up some deep emotional stuff inside of me.

Our living conditions were making this incredibly peaceful environment anything but. The hunger for food that I felt brought to the surface a much more ravenous hunger that had been temporarily suppressed by the beauty of nature. It was the intense desire to know who I was and what the purpose of my life was supposed to be. Being at peace was not working for me anymore. There was a fire burning in my heart and a battlefield forming in my conscience. It felt like my mind had incited a riot between my body and soul, leaving each vying for dominion over the entirety of my existence. I was stuck in the middle of this conflict, in the middle of nowhere, and unsure of how to resolve it.

Damian knew all too well what I was going through. He had been through it countless times himself. One day, out of nowhere, he confronted me in a very direct and almost agitated manner while I was sitting on the front porch of the cabin.

"Why are you thinking like this? You are stuck in an endless cascade of cyclical thought patterns that are incarcerating the essence of your soul, and you have unknowingly been doing this for years and years of your life. You are so trapped in your head that it's almost like you've forgotten you have a body!"

I was astonished and ashamed. Astonished because even though his words acknowledged the more obvious aspects of my inner dilemma, he understood it so precisely that it was spooky. And I was ashamed because although I wasn't sure how I knew he could see right through me. At that point, he probably knew way more about me than I knew about myself.

I didn't know how to respond to this in any rational way.

"I just feel so trapped, like I'm stuck in life with my wheels spinning. All I want to know is who I am and why I'm alive. What's the point of being human? What is the point of this conversation? I don't see any good reason for any of it!"

"Who do you think *you* are to not see any good point or reason for being human? You think you don't know who you are - that's your problem - but your real problem is you're trapped in a world of thought where you're either imagining the future or remembering the past from a place of fear! You have hardwired a version of reality into your perception based on the trauma of your past, and you anticipate it continuing into your future and it's running like a computer program on autopilot. Your entire perspective of reality is based on your mind primarily identifying with this very narrow version of anticipated reality. But that version of reality is filtered through the microscopic lens of belief systems that you yourself don't even know that you believe. You have tricked yourself into believing that the existence you are accustomed to perceiving with your worldly conditioned senses is all there is".

Then, in a very hypnotic tone, he began speaking: "If you were to suddenly become fully aware of who and what you really are, it would shock you so severely that irreparable damage would occur to the tissues of your brain. It would be such an influx of information that your mind would essentially short-circuit. That's why I'm helping you realize all of this incrementally, so you can rewire all the neural circuitry of your brain and body to raise your frequency, thereby holding and emitting a greater "divine" charge…because inside of you is the source of reality that you are actually seeking, and when you find it, you will realize that it was always there and that you were never separated from it, you only tricked yourself into believing you were.

The world you see through your eyes is being projected from the energetic nature of your consciousness itself, but the narrow lens of your habitual minds egoic filter shuts out anything that threatens your egos low-frequency existence. It's a defense mechanism your personality has created in order to protect itself. This can be beneficial to the human part of your existence, but if you really want to know who, or more precisely, *what* you are, you will have to open up the filter on your lens."

As before, I conceptually understood everything he was saying... but it was the *WAY* he said it that forced me to be aware of it to a degree I didn't think I ever had been. The pressure of considering this caused obstructions in my perception to break down, opening new levels awareness that I was previously unaware of. I didn't just understand his words - I was experiencing the energy of their meaning. I was flooded with a feeling of bliss. "How do I open the filter on my lens?"

"Look, you can learn to perceive reality through a mind that is infinitely more vast than the limited one in your head. You can reach a place where this infinite mind starts *perceiving this world through you.* But to get there, you'll have to constantly work at rewiring your conditioned mind - by redirecting your awareness towards the miracle of life that is animating your being. It takes a lot of practice, but you'll create new pathways in the neural circuitry of your body that will reinforce your ability to remember what you are. Eventually it will become second nature, because the reality is, that it's your primary nature."

There was nothing that sounded or felt strange about it. What I was able to grasp made perfect sense; what I wasn't able to - still felt right. I could somehow feel the vast, seemingly hidden mind that he spoke of.

"Okay," I said, a huge smile still on my face. "I am ready to get to work. How do I redirect my thoughts?"

He shut his eyes and started breathing slowly yet rhythmically. After about five minutes and without saying a word, he got up and walked off the front porch of the cabin with his dog in tow. He started walking up the small hill behind the cabin, so I followed. Once we reached the top, he sat down, shut his eyes, and began that slow, rhythmic breathing again.

I thought I was going to be instructed how to implement this practice, but I wasn't sure what he was doing, and so I felt a little agitated. I sat down close-by and waited for him to speak. He said nothing. Then my mind really started to race. Thoughts emerged in a rapid-fire sequence, all of them totally random, and all of them totally negative. Shameful memories of the past, fear of what my future held, and most prominently, wondering why Damian would tease me with a little bit of the self-liberation I was looking for, only to sit in a field at the top of a hill and say nothing at all. Finally, I decided to speak.

"What is the…"

As soon as I started speaking, he interrupted me, extending his arm and pointing his finger straight up. He didn't even open his eyes. Agitated, I kept my mouth shut, laid back on the mossy forest floor, and began to let go of the anxiety I was feeling. I started to realize that even though he wasn't speaking, he was still instructing me how to redirect my thoughts because I became hyperaware of a powerful feeling in my heart. It completely overrode my thought processes.

In this relaxed state, I listened to the sound of the wind rustling through the leaves. I noticed the sun warming my body through my clothes, and the cooling breeze blowing on my face. I gazed up into the cloudless blue sky and felt the earth supporting my body. For a moment, I knew what it was like to be an eagle, living in two worlds simultaneously.

But what really caused me to focus my redirected thoughts was the realization that my breath was bringing the outside world into my body. Automatically and rhythmically, the outer world began assimilating itself into me and as a result my inner world became "activated" and "alive". It had always been doing this. I just hadn't paid it any attention to it since my childhood days. Calmly, I began to consider how amazing it was that breathing was an automatic function of my body and that even if I were unconscious, my body would still breathe on its own. It was miraculous, really. I wondered how many other automatic functions my body performed without input from my brain. It was obvious that it was more than I was consciously aware of, I knew that much.

Then, I was hit by a sudden realization: if I were able to intentionally redirect the incessant train of thoughts in my head- thoughts that are mostly influenced by how I've been conditioned to perceive the world, then what would I be aware of without any intervention from the worldly conditioning that had been causing me to suffer?

Just considering this possibility created a gap in my normal train of thought. It was in those fleeting moments that I was first grasped by what Damian was speaking of when he said, *"You'll eventually reach a place where this infinitely vast mind starts to perceive reality through you."*

I faintly remembered this long lost feeling from the meditations I did as a child, but back then, I never thought about it; it just happened on its own - a natural function of my consciousness.

How did I fall so far? How did something so natural become so foreign to me? My mind began to race again, as the victim mentality I had hardwired into my nerve tissue and brain (from years of thinking the same stressful thoughts over and over again) began to emerge and rear its ugly head. I became very concerned. "*If my autonomic physiology functions automatically, regardless of my conscious input, then why do I exist in it feeling so clueless about its overall agenda?*" I felt a moment of intense depression; after the epiphany I'd just had, it felt like a regression, like the epiphany itself was a trap. I felt more confused than I had before the realization I'd just had only moments before!

"Why is it so hard to stay awake, loving life, remembering, and knowing that we truly are pure awareness, yet so easy to forget and wallow in fearful thought?"

He said nothing. His body language and facial expressions said even less. I desperately began asking even more questions. "What am I? Who am I? Why are we having this experience right now?"

He actually surprised me by answering. "It can only be explained to a certain point. But, you basically have to choose to let go of everything that you think you know, and allow what is – to be exactly what it is; it is essentially a process of unknowing, and in unknowing - everything becomes known."

The immensity of it hit me, and I was speechless. I didn't even know how to respond to any of this: I thought it was insanity. I got up, walked down to the cabin, and got on my mountain bike. I began hauling ass down a dirt road going further into nowhere than I already was. Recklessly I flew down a big muddy hill with massive boulders strewn across it, nearly wiping out. Two-thirds of the way down the hill the trees disappeared, revealing a big marsh of cranberry bushes and water lilies. I skidded my bike to a halt, threw it down and hopped off to where the edge of the road met the cranberry bog. Something fierce came through me. I started screaming at the top of my lungs. I screamed until I lost my voice. "What the fuck is going on? Why the fuck is this happening to me? Please tell me who I am or take me out of this world! Tell me why or let me die!" I repeated this feeling-rich affirmation over and over again.

At the time, I meant every word I said. I needed to know who and what I was because I didn't want to live with this feeling of separation anymore. I was seventeen, and I'd had enough. I was no one, I had nothing, and I was in the middle of nowhere. I needed concrete answers; tangible proof that what Damian said was indeed true.

After losing my voice, I tearfully whispered to the universe. I begged it to please give me proof. I wanted it from the source. I trusted Damian, and I believed what he said was true, but he was only a human being. I needed divine intervention. I wanted God, the Universe, that indescribable nameless power to purge me of all doubt. I needed it to awaken me and provide in me the faith to believe that no matter what, I was loved unconditionally by something greater than myself and that I had a purpose. But nothing profound happened during those moments at the bog. However, with my emotionally driven affirmation I planted some potent seeds of possibility that were taking root in the gardens of my awareness.

As time continued on, we ate all the potatoes and onions that we had grown. All that was left was the twenty-year-old army food. We didn't have the heart to try hunting or fishing anymore. Every being had a right to live just as much as any other. Who were we to take their lives for food? The living spring water became our primary source of nutrition. We both became scary skinny. Even though I was becoming emaciated, I went down to the cranberry bog and pleaded with the universe every day, in essence, watering the seeds of possibility that I planted in my mind. I asked to know the meaning of life, and then I waited, but nothing noticeable happened. I was just a restless mind in the stillness of nature existing for no purpose. I was completely clueless on all levels about what to do with my life. Damian, on the other hand, didn't dwell on such matters. He didn't seem bothered by anything, really.

There was one day in early autumn that stood out as magical during my time in Brighton. In the loft of the cabin was an old banjo. It was a beautiful instrument - mother-of-pearl inlay all over the fretboard and abalone shell designing the body.

Somehow, the strings were all intact, and it sounded great. I didn't know how to play the banjo, but I had enough of a background in guitar to find my way around on it. I'd always had an affinity for expressing my feelings with an instrument, and Damian loved it; it was one of the few things that made him smile.

Later that day we went hiking through the woods in a direction we hadn't explored yet. On the side of a hill was a dilapidated cabin. The entire structure had caved in and was rotting into the ground. Aside from the cabin and the old road it was on, there were no signs of human interference. The only part of the rotting structure that hadn't completely fallen over was the front door and its frame, though they were threatening to. Damian grabbed the door handle and pulled the door right out of its frame, revealing a rotting layered mess of old cabin contents. In this botched heap, he lifted a giant piece of plastic and sitting there, perfectly preserved, was a black and purple vest trimmed with gold flowers and a beautiful gold tree on the back of it. It was an exact replica of something I've seen Jimi Hendrix wearing in pictures.

Damian noticed it, too. He took it out of its tomb and told me I should keep it because my banjo playing reminded him of Jimi's guitar playing.

It was an inspiring moment. I took it as a clear sign to further develop my musical abilities - even if I was no one, with nothing, in the middle of nowhere.

CHAPTER EIGHT

Thawing Out The Deep Inner Freeze

As the chill of autumn began to creep in, we knew we'd have to find another place to go. Someone in town told us about an abandoned cabin in Concord, about twenty miles from where we lived in Brighton.

With only the bare living essentials, an ounce of weed we'd grown, and Damian's dog, we made our move. Concord was not as remote as Brighton, but it was close. The little town of Bingham - where we used our food stamps to buy pancake batter, V-8 juice, and stale donuts - was only seven miles away. The cabin was a quarter-mile hike down a trail off of a desolate dirt road. At the entrance was a small utility building that remarkably enough, had electricity that we could use without paying. The cabin, however, did not. It didn't have running water either, but thankfully, there was a stove for wood heat.

The electricity from the utility shed turned out to be a huge blessing. We were able to trade our ounce of weed for another Volkswagen Rabbit, and it ran on diesel. In frigid Maine winter weather, diesel would have turned into a gel. The older diesel vehicles have a female plug next to the engine block that allows you to run an extension cord to heat the gas tank. This allowed us to drive it in the winter. We surely would have died of starvation that winter if we couldn't drive.

The cabin in Concord was really more like a shed than a cabin. It was shaped like a train boxcar, and the way the windows were installed made it look like one too. On top of having no running water or electricity, it also had very little insulation. There were open holes and gaps all through the 2x4 siding that allowed the winter winds free access to everything inside, including us. There was a corner kitchen and a loft. We collected our water from a small well that was on the property.

We were as prepared as we were able to be, which wasn't saying much. Almost every day, we were pushed to our limits just to survive. It was bare-bones living - absolutely brutal.

Once the snow set in, it was like death knocking at our door. Every day was a battle not to freeze. Our primary occupation every day was to just keep moving, periodically interspersed with standing next to the fireplace. The trick was to warm one side of our bodies while the other got cold, then alternate. I slept in the loft with my sleeping bag underneath a heaping pile of old blankets. There were many nights so cold that despite the fact the woodstove was glowing hot, the dog's water dish directly underneath it would be frozen solid.

During the days we were out in the woods collecting firewood from dead trees. The small amount of money we had was used for riding to town to buy scraps of food for Damian's dog, or to collect food stamps from the welfare office. Using the car to travel anywhere was intense; the heater was broken, so we dreaded having to use it. It was like driving in a chest freezer on wheels. Virtually every aspect of our experience felt like a test of will. I was so focused on survival that it created little time for me to contemplate the meaning of life. Or so I thought...

On one of the coldest nights of late December, we were sitting next to the woodstove desperately attempting to warm our chilly extremities. It was so cold that the glowing hot woodstove looked like a bellows expanding and contracting in response to the unforgiving cold. It looked alive, like it was breathing. Whenever we added a piece of wood, its near-molten chamber caused it to ignite almost instantaneously. As the stove would "breathe," its expansion looked like it might cause the whole thing to melt on its legs - and just as quickly, it would contract with a blast of arctic air. The cold was so penetrating and dehydrating that it seemed to freeze-dry all the moisture put off by my breath and skin. Chilled to the bone, I could practically hear the crystalline structure of my bones compress with every step that I took - any more of this and I thought I might turn into Jack Frost himself!

It had been almost two months since I had bathed or changed my clothes. I had been wearing the same thermal underwear and snowsuit the whole time. I couldn't take any more of it, so I snapped.

"What kind of life is this? Every day we suffer and struggle just to keep from freezing. What are we accomplishing? What is this supposed to prove?" I cried out.

"Those who ask the most questions suffer the most," Damian replied.

"What the fuck does that mean? We suffer constantly, regardless if I'm asking questions or not. In fact, our entire life out here is all about suffering and struggling to survive. For some reason, I thought we were leaving the world behind to find the meaning of why such an insane world existed in the first place - not leave the world behind to starve, freeze and go insane just trying to stay alive!"

He looked at me kind of sideways and asked, "I thought you were willing to die to know the meaning of life?" After he said this I metaphorically and, due to the cold, quite literally froze in my tracks. For a moment, I wondered if he had somehow heard my prayers at the cranberry bog. "What makes you think I'm willing to die to know the meaning of life?"

"Well, aside from the fact that it's all you think and talk about, look at you! Look at how you've lived your life since we moved out of town. Look at how you've lived your life since I saw you at that party a couple of years ago. You act like you gave up on life a long time ago, like you've been hurt so badly by someone or something that unless life gives you some explanation for its appearance, you won't participate. Do you really think life owes you that? Hasn't it already given you everything there is?"

"Can you be more specific?" I pleaded.

"Specific? Life has given you life! You have a body, brain, and a spirit animating it, along with the free will to cultivate its greater potential within you!"

"I see what you mean."

"On top of that, you have a day-to-day, moment-to-moment experience that allows you to choose not only where you want to go but how you think and feel about where you want to go and what you want to do. Are you not able to find limitless meaning and potential in that alone?"

"Yeah, I could."

"Half the time you mope around like you are the biggest victim on Earth! Seriously? For just a moment, I want you to consider a few things, alright?"

'Sure."

"I'm sure that when you were a child, your parents told you to always eat all the food on your plate because children in other parts of the world are starving, right?"

"Yeah, but I'm sure many people's parents have told their kids something like that."

"Right! But did you eat all your food after that?"

"Yeah, most of the time."

"Okay. But did you ever consider what it might be like to actually *be* a starving child in some remote section of the world, to see the world through their eyes? To feel the hunger in their stomachs?"

"Yeah, for a fleeting moment or two."

"Okay. Have you ever considered that there are *countless* children around the planet who are starving? Or that there are countless children starving with severe birth defects because their environments are so toxic? How about that there are countless children starving all over the planet with severe birth defects, many who are living in war-torn countries so violent that their innocent families spend every waking moment knowing that any day they could be hit by a stray bullet or have a rocket dropped on their entire village? Did you ever think about that?"

"Somewhat, but not in such depth or detail."

"Here is what I really want you to consider. What if countless people who are living in situations such as I have described could still accept their circumstances for what they are - and in spite of all that still choose how they feel about life? And what if, in spite of it all, knowing how dire their situations are, they were still able to be *grateful* for the small amounts of goodness in their lives, no matter how fleeting those feelings may be? Countless people in such situations have been and are able to do just that. If they can do it, you can too, right?"

"Yeah, I could."

"Good, because it really is just a choice - a choice you can make. You can make it right here, right now, despite all of your trials and tribulations, despite all of your suffering, to be grateful for the fact that life itself, your higher and inner power, the teacher of all teachers is instructing you through all of your hardship and success to learn what you really want to learn."

Everything that he said to me felt very true, but it was only scratching the surface of what I really wanted to know. So I asked,

"What do you mean when you say that 'life itself, through all of my hardship and success is teaching me what I want and need to know?' Life isn't a person teaching a lesson like a teacher teaches a student. I don't understand how life, my life is teaching me what I want and need to know. That doesn't make any sense to my brain!"

"Life *can* be an actual teacher teaching lessons to students in a classroom setting, but it doesn't have to be. Life is everything. It's life, all of it. Underneath the world you consider to be normal, there is a field of energy that unifies every single thing in our known and unknown universe. In this regard, life can choose one of a multitude of forms from which to teach you with, but you need to be open to it."

"That makes sense."

"Here's a question. When you hit a breaking point and snap, do you cry out to a higher power to help ease your pain?"

"Yes, but I'm not convinced anyone or anything is hearing me. I do it mostly out of desperation. I'm desperate because I'm suffering and I don't know what else to do."

"All right, for a moment, let's pretend that a higher power doesn't hear you. From an internal energetic perspective, you are still within yourself, invoking a deep desire for change, a desire to be eased from your current state of suffering. Think about it like this: there is the appearance of two major yet conflicting forces at work. There is you, the personality you believe yourself to be - and there's an energetic animating principle referred to as the *soul* that gives life to your body. You suspect it's there, but you feel separated from how your personality relates to it because you don't see it with your normal senses. This causes discordance in pretty much every area of your life. What if this conflict was the root of all your issues? What if all of your suffering occurred because you believe these two parts of yourself are in opposition – when in reality, they only appear that way and they are actually not?"

He continued. "What are your earliest childhood memories? Reflect deeply on it and tomorrow you can tell me what you remember."

I was left in a labyrinth of thought, feeling and contemplation. By the time we'd finished talking, it was late. I climbed the ladder to the loft where I slept, got into my army-issued sleeping bag, just as I had every night for the past couple of months. As I thought about our conversation, I listened to the wind howl outside. As it often did, a gust blew right through the shed, reminding me that there was very little keeping me from being fully exposed to the bitter cold elements all around. This reminded me that perhaps there was also very little keeping me from being exposed to the truth of who and what I really was as well. I pondered this even deeper. My thoughts went from my head to a very soft and loving feeling emanating from my heart. In those moments I felt there really was not anything between who I thought I was and the truth of what I *really* was. I felt my awareness at the edge of self and then, amidst all of the cold - I felt glowing warmth throughout my entire being, inside and out.

I could choose to be happy and content from the inside out if I wanted to be with no need from anything "outside" of me to invoke it. No matter how hard it was to survive in this temporary tundra, I felt grateful for what I did have: LIFE!

Even though it was unspeakably cold, I was warm and cozy in my snowsuit and sleeping bag, despite not having washed or showered for months. The sound of the whipping winter winds caused the chimney above me to make a melodic whistle, in rhythm with the chimes singing together outside of the window. The woodstove cracked and groaned. The combination became a winter symphony. I looked out of a window edged by geometric ice crystals to see the stars…so bright…so clear…so far away, but I knew that somehow I was connected to them. I saw how beautiful it all was - and how incredibly blessed I was to even be able to perceive all of this.

I imagined my ancestors were aware of such simple but indescribable beauty… I imagined this awareness going back through incalculable generations into antiquity, and even further back…to its origins from an energy source that was as similar to a dream as it was to reality…

I began to reflect on my own life. In my mind's eye, I rewound back through my troubling recent years, my sublime adolescent years, and into my early childhood. Then I fell asleep.

When I awoke the next morning it was still bitter cold outside, but it was sunny, and the skies were crystal clear. My awareness and memory were also just as clear. As I lay there in my sleeping bag, I vividly remembered my early childhood. I remembered sitting in the front yard of my parent's home. I saw myself staring at the point where the trees met the sky, and I remembered what happened after a few moments of observing that. Everything in my field of vision got brighter and brighter, eventually turning white. When that happened, I was in my body, but not bound to it. My connection to everything great and small was experienced by unobstructed awareness. I was aware of the deeper, subtler aspects of that one awareness, along with everyone and everything that lives or ever had: seemingly infinite oneness expressed through the dynamic individualism of my human personality and awareness. This is what felt real. This is what felt like reality, the primal reality that gives birth to all other realities.

When I reached that point, I became fully aware that I was a spiritual being experiencing this world through human senses and a human point of view. This was who and what I really was, and there was nothing left in me at that moment to question it. I also remembered that as a child, there was nothing to question. Awareness occurred naturally. It was self-evident. This was what I identified with first and foremost, and there were no problems or blockages in this awareness. The awareness of my own awareness was all that I was aware of.

So then what happened? How could I have been so hyper self-aware, only to eventually blunt that awareness? How could I have forgotten such a transcendent yet grounded and embodied state of awareness?

I got out of bed and climbed down from the loft. Damian was melting snow in a pot on the woodstove, attempting to bring some moisture into the air. He looked over at me. "You remember, huh?"

I told him everything. The first thing he said was, "All those people, masked by identity, have fallen prey to themselves."

Not only did I understand what he meant as soon as he said it - I also knew that one day I'd use that line in a song. It cuts right to the heart of suffering in the human condition and releases it if someone allows it to. He asked me to give my interpretation of that statement.

"To me, it means that a human's true form, their eternal self…their soul…is covered up by the person they believe themselves to be. This *mask* of a temporary identity cuts them off from the unification between their spiritual form and their human form, causing them to suffer. This results from the perpetuation of a vicious cycle where the individual incessantly identifies with their human ego as opposed to their energetic or spiritual form. The soul metaphorically gets trapped inside the body with no voice and little influence on the consciousness of the human ego. The soul becomes almost like an inmate locked up in a prison. Hence, they have fallen prey to themselves."

Damian liked my answer. I realized that I wouldn't have been able to explain it with that much eloquence if he hadn't encouraged me to tap into those early memories. I felt as though I'd tasted a sort of *super-consciousness*, like I was thinking with infinite intelligence pulsing through me. A door had opened in my awareness and I could see really far out into the ethers.

Pensively I asked, "as a child, how could I have so vividly known myself as spirit, only to completely lose touch with this part of myself as I grew older? I understand that I constantly identified with the issues of my personality to the extent that I neglected my soul, thereby creating an imbalance in my awareness. But why did this happen? How did I fall so far?"

His voice became powerful, "okay, brace yourself. Human beings are born with a gift called free will, but all that it is, is a choice to feel victimized by life or empowered by it. By knowing how to appropriately exercise this choice, a person will create an imprint in their psyche that will encourage their further 'spiritual' growth.

The overall result is essentially only a habit of perceptive focus driven by whatever choice is most consistently decided upon. This offers them the opportunity to continue using their free will to further unlock their potential, but if they neglect to use it, they stifle it.

If they don't know how to appropriately exercise this choice to expand their energetic awareness - or if they don't even realize they possess this capability in the first place - then by default, their psyche still gets imprinted. But when it happens by default; their psyche instead becomes imprinted with the lower desires of their personality.

The bottom line is, if an individual is not actively engaged in creating a habit of feeling empowered by higher spiritual frequencies - or more simply, the joy of life, then by default, they create a habit that expresses itself as victimized by lower, denser stress-based frequencies driven by the bodies survival hormones.

Those lower frequencies then plague their human personality, causing them to feel jailed, and can manifest as a feeling of separation from the source of life within them."

He went on. "As a person is dying, he or she will usually experience some level of realization of what we're talking about right now. But at that point, it's usually too late to embody the harmony of a unified personality and soul."

"What happens to a person's soul when they die?"

"Those who die before they die, do not die when they die. Do you understand?"

I didn't really know what he meant, and I said "no."

He nodded and explained:

"You don't have to physically die to know what happens to your soul when you die. That is because there is a field of pure potentiality that becomes accessible to you when you tap into the awareness of your awareness itself. The fact is if you can accomplish that, you can literally transcend any and all forms of death. However, there are strings attached.

If you do not go through this conscious death process before your physical body dies, then when it does, you will be subjected to an involuntary process where your gift of conscious free will is annexed from the equation. That is why it's imperative that you seek to awaken before that occurs: so you don't die when you die. Otherwise, it's gonna be a rocky road of reincarnation."

"So, you mean that I have to die to the part of me that's over-identified with my personality - my ego?"

He nodded, partially agreeing. "You're on the right track, but… there is a lot of work to do. A lot of rewiring."

"Rewiring?" I asked.

"Do you remember what I said about *programming* yourself to be in tune with higher spiritual frequencies?"

"Yes."

"Before this type of psychological programming can happen, you need to rewire the way you have become accustomed to viewing the world. The way you currently view it will inhibit this conscious death process, because of fear.

And because of fear, your human personality will resist it so much; it may sabotage taking any action to free itself for a long time, if not indefinitely."

"What does indefinitely mean? Years? Decades?"

Damian's eyes became really dark, and then he closed them.

"Lifetimes," he said, "perhaps countless lifetimes. As far as you're concerned - forever."

I heard his words, but more accurately, I could feel them. He meant what he said. I took a deep, slow breath.

Although I didn't have the frame of reference to grasp the magnitude of what he was sharing, I could still feel that it was accurate. But it was hard for me to imagine how something as dramatic as a conscious death process could occur by me *rewiring* the way I viewed the world.

"Please tell me how this rewiring works," I asked, " and give me all the details."

"Nearly everything that you think you know about the world has been taught to you, directly or indirectly, by others, who have lost all but the faintest awareness of their soul's 'motive.' So, the vast majority of your awareness has been redirected from the presence of 'divine' consciousness, and into recycled temporary thoughts, language, concepts, and images. The human body, with all its senses and functions, was designed as a living temple of the highest order. It's the place where a product of alchemical processes, rarer than the rarest of precious gems, has the potential to form, and to coalesce into a new species of human with a heart of pure gold: one that not only lives harmoniously aligned with the elements and laws of nature, but one that transcends them, and channels a force the human race may have never fully realized.

The human body serves as a link to the lower-level frequencies of this 'heavenly' source. But for most people, the body has become a deteriorating dungeon, a cage of the soul...a prison. The potential I just referred to has long been out of the equation, which is almost exclusively why the human race has suffered so much, and for so long."

Throughout the body runs nerve lines that are connected to the neural pathways in your brain, like fiber optics lines in a telephone communication center sending and receiving signals. As nerve current passes through the tissue in the brain, it leaves traces...grooves that eventually form a neural network or complex. To a large degree, these complexes determine your personality traits. Do they resonate with higher feelings or low stressed-based ones. That determines the frequency your energetic signature emanates out into the world.

Do you know what creates nervous current? Thought... The thoughts in your mind are derived from the energy that animates your being, and they're converted into a nervous current that is then dispersed throughout your body, dramatically affecting it for better or worse. You know the saying, 'You are what you eat?' Right?"

"Yes, I do."

'Though most wouldn't realize it, 'thinking' has far, far greater implications than what you eat, and feeling even more so. That's why you must work constantly to rewire your human perception - because you can reach a point where you begin to identify with reality, as it truly is, not just how you've been conditioned to think it is. Do you understand?"

"I think so."

"I'm teaching you how to identify with the energy that your thoughts are derived *from* - that's what comes before the thoughts themselves; it's your innate intelligence – the infinite energetic wisdom that animates your body and mind. When you have trained yourself to identify with that first, the thoughts that you will then be able to think from that place take on a powerful new dynamic."

"Wow, yeah. I can imagine that they would! How do you know about this stuff?"

"In our past lives, we have all been almost everything, each and every one of us. But like I said, most of this is common sense."

"What do you mean by common sense?"

"If you are as serious as you claim to be about wanting to know the reason for your existence, where do you think you would find it first; in the world that you see all around you, or in the source of energy that allows you to be able to see through your human senses in the first place?

"Okay, I think I get it."

My head felt like it was spinning in circles. But I decided to make a declaration. "I will do whatever I have to do to rewire my old ways of thinking, feeling, behaving and sensing so that I can program myself to be a living temple of divine energy." And, I meant every word I said!

This was all a tremendous amount of information to process, but there was one thing that really piqued my interest. With a smirk on my face, I asked:

" Earlier, you mentioned something about a *field of pure potentiality*. Is that a grassy field in some other dimension, or is it something else?"

His entire disposition softened. "It's very much in this dimension. However, it acts as a bridge to what might seem like other dimensions - but its source emanates from within your awareness. If you are able to successfully focus most of your attention on your awareness itself –without the distraction of your conditioned thoughts, this field will naturally and automatically become apparent. The potential of it is yours to cultivate within it."

I understood. It was a lot to take in. My mind was simultaneously reeling with possibility and fear...but the sense of possibility was much stronger than my fears. I didn't know how to explain it, but I felt there was a greater force supporting me.

I had no doubt that I was on my way to authentic self-realization. There was resistance to some of what he'd shared, but I wasn't going to allow it to derail my quest to know who and what I really was.

There were moments when I wondered what life might have been like had a chosen a more 'conventional' route, like what my parents wanted for me. But I also knew that if I chose what they or society wanted, I'd live a life of regret. From this perspective, the path I had chosen to walk was actually not a path. It was my life as it was meant to be - as I both wanted and needed it to be. What if the path to God was actually created by the neural pathways we consciously create in our brain and body? It made sense.

By the time March came around, signs of spring were starting to emerge. It had been nearly five months since I had bathed or showered. I'd been wearing the same clothes and snowsuit for about the same amount of time. I felt and looked like a 1700's frontiersman, barely surviving the frigidity of a long, cold winter. With spring in the air, I knew that we were going to make it out alive. But it was so much more than that; for the first time since I was a child, I started to truly and deeply love being alive. So much of that newfound love of life was tied to what Damian had been suggesting to me, and in the way that I processed it.

Toward the end of March, my parents showed up out of the blue. I had no idea how they'd found me, but when they saw how I was living, they were horrified. They begged for me to move back in with them, but I refused. They pleaded, arguing that I might die if I continued living as I was. But I had just turned eighteen; they had no legal jurisdiction over me, and I was certain of the choices I had made. I knew I was where I needed to be. I asked them to leave. As they left, tears were streaming down their faces. I felt tremendous empathy for them.

I wondered what kind of conversation they had on the ride home. It definitely broke their hearts, and even though I was able to feel compassion for them. I still hadn't been able to quite let it go of the things that had happened between us. I loved them, but I only wanted their unconditional love, and I just didn't feel they were able to provide that yet.

As the warm weather began emerging, Damian and I wanted to find jobs so we could afford to take better care of ourselves. But needless to say, it wasn't going to happen where we were living. I felt a change coming…

CHAPTER NINE

A Labor of Love

As winter finally turned into spring, it would have been an understatement to say that Damian and I were glad to have the cold behind us. For me, the past two seasons were a time of tremendous growth into the beginning of spiritual maturity. But I also knew I wanted to create a life that was not so wrought with hardship, a life that balanced all of my essential needs in a way that was sustainable to my single and most desired goal: to unconditionally be one with the universe.

The snows began melting, and the days became longer, but we were still hungry and emaciated. With few food stamps and very few places to spend them, our ability to get adequate nutrition was slim. Compounding the problem was our remote location, which meant that not many jobs were available. In all reality, we had just spent the last nine months almost completely isolated from the world. Aside from the infrequent trips into town for groceries, we were for all practical purposes in a state of hibernation. Interacting with other people was something we both tried to avoid. Now we didn't have much choice but to do just that. It was the only way we'd be able to provide for ourselves.

We decided Ian the farmer was our go-to guy. It wasn't a hard decision; he was the only person we could think of. So, on a beautiful early April day, we decided to visit him. We figured that employment aside, he'd probably like to know that we'd made it through the winter.

When we arrived at his farm, it was surprising, to say the least: it was busy. There were young men and women all over the place driving tractors, tilling up garden space, and starting seedlings in the greenhouse. Everyone there seemed cheerful. The place was teeming with life.

Ian was very happy to see us. He told us all about what he had been doing and what his plans were. Then he introduced us to all the people working there. Everyone was really nice. There was a sense of community amongst them that was welcoming; although it was foreign to the hermetic lifestyle we'd been living.

We explained our intentions to him: to get some work, eat well, and get better prepared for next winter. He just shook his head in amazement. He said that he couldn't believe we had been so far removed for so long, with so little. He also said that most of his friends didn't think we could make it more than a month or two living the way we were.

To him, the fact that we had toughed it out for so long was either a testament to our survival skills or our sanity. He half-jokingly said that he wasn't sure we possessed either. He mentioned that he almost came looking for us at one point because he hadn't heard anything about our whereabouts for so long; however, one of his friends spotted us on our bikes, so he knew we were alive. He also admitted that he informed my parents as to my whereabouts because they were so worried.

"What were you guys doing out there for so long?"

"We were looking for the meaning of life!"

My response made him laugh out loud. "Well," he said, still chuckling, "I hope you were able to find it because you had plenty of time!"

After the small talk and introductions to his workers, Ian let us know that he had all the help he needed. But he did know of a couple of places that were looking for laborers.

Ian brought us to meet Jen the herbalist first. She was - and still is - revered as one of the top herbalists in New England. As we pulled up to her place, there were children and various animals scattered about. Her little house was exactly what you might expect of an herbalist's abode: it looked like a hobbit's home, surrounded by colorful gardens and flower beds.

On appearances alone, she, Damian and I looked like birds of a feather. We all had long dreadlocks and wore patched-up hippie work clothes. We got right to work, spending the day doing manual labor and various farmhand chores.

Hesitantly Jen admitted that she wasn't able to pay us much. She offered to feed us, teach us about making herbal infusions, and help us to identify and harvest wild edibles. We were happy to accept her offer, but we soon concluded that this would not prepare us for winter. We decided to work for Jen part-time so we could explore the other potential employer that Ian had mentioned.

We then went and talked to a man named Preston who was, and is to this day, unlike any human I have met. A reclusive renegade outlaw, he truly walked the line between genius and insanity. It seemed that he started out as 'normal,' having received a college education with plans to make his soil study experiments public projects. After college, he'd gotten mixed up in a crime. The police had confused him with someone else. They tried to apprehend him, and he fled; he was warned to stop, or they would shoot. He didn't stop. They shot, and the result was a bullet lodged in his lower left buttock he'd never properly removed. He'd suffered immensely from lead poisoning.

There was no doubt this man had issues. One moment he would be speaking clearly and calmly; the next, he would fly off the handle. In a cartoon character's voice, he would ramble on about topics that were completely out of context to what he was previously speaking calmly about.

A few of the corners inside his house were covered in spider webs so thick he was able to use them like baskets to hold supplies. There were boxes, cans, and dishware resting in them. To this day I have never seen anything like it.

His greenhouses and gardens though were the proof of his genius. It's only a slight exaggeration to say that there were cucumbers the size of a grown man's leg, pumpkins the size of a chest freezer, and tomatoes as big as basketballs.

What impressed me the most though, were the marijuana plants. Some were literally twenty feet tall with whiffle bat-sized buds covering them. There were hundreds of them. The size of everything in his garden was so massive that it made me feel almost like I was a dwarf. An interesting side effect of this oversized garden was the dizzying concentration of oxygen. There were literally times I felt nauseous walking around in the greenhouse because of it.

To protect his garden from intruders both human and animal, nine fierce German Shepherds were placed around the border of the property line. Between the dogs, swarming hives of bees were positioned. The farm was a place of diabolical energies, obviously established by someone I assumed had a severe bipolar personality. At one end of the spectrum was a cornucopia of a garden - at the other were the killer bees and the hounds of hell. The fresh, lively garden meals he prepared were sharply contrasted against rotting animal corpses strewn about his property as dog food. They were mostly cows from local farms that had died and were hacked up via chainsaw. The contrast was truly diabolical. But the bottom line was, there was plenty of work to be done. With the copious amounts of cannabis everywhere we knew we'd get paid…and we assumed, very well.

However, what we didn't count on was that the marijuana growing there had such low potency that smoking it barely created a buzz. Even the most beautiful buds didn't have much more potency than the leaves. We soon figured out why. Preston was a soil specialist. He knew very little about marijuana strains and their potencies. As a result, he had collected many different strains from many different people and planted them all together over the course of a decade. This resulted in the cross-pollination of varieties that a skilled grower would never have allowed to take place.

After years of doing this, he'd unknowingly created his own strain. Yet it was one lacking in potency, and thus value. The people we tried selling it to were not willing to pay much for it, if at all. Even if we'd wanted to grow a single potent strain on his farm, it would have been impossible to maintain as the pollen from the male plants at this point was literally covering everything.

Another major issue on the farm was trying to effectively communicate with Preston about our work agenda. He was notorious for saying one thing, then doing another. He'd start us on one job, and then start us on a new one in the middle of it. It became chaotic and frustrating. I questioned whether this was the best work scenario for us. Yet when all was said and done, it was the only viable one available in the area.

While I was vocal about my apprehension in regards to Preston's farm, Damian wasn't at all. In fact, he didn't really question anything about it. Although he occasionally acted as a sounding board for my ideas and concerns, overall he maintained an even disposition no matter what life threw at him. From all outward appearances, he seemed to be fully accepting of every aspect of his life. I envied his ability to sustain such an even-keeled temperament and strove to embody the same for myself.

It was now the middle of summer. Since the past winter, I had personally evolved into a good place of mind, body, and soul. Life had become nourishing. I had a few friends, better food, and a clearer outlook of the future. Though I hadn't discovered the profound esoteric secrets of the universe that I so passionately sought, I was OK with that for now. Life was great as it was. It was the first time since childhood that I so deeply loved being alive and felt content with things as they were. I was truly grateful. But oh my gosh, if I only knew what was coming!

CHAPTER TEN

Cosmic Court

One morning as we drove to work, Damian talked about some of the projects he hoped to accomplish by the day's end. It was a pleasant car ride. The weather was perfect. It was a bright and sunny summer morning. The temperature was in the mid-seventies. The flora was lush, and the fauna was active. Life was teeming around every corner.

As he normally did Damian gunned the car as we pulled into Preston's driveway. Actually, it was more like a hundred-yard mud run than a driveway. The constant drainage of springs emptying into the watershed from the surrounding hills kept his grounds moist during the warmer months.

As we approached Preston's house, I became aware of a foul odor I had never smelled before. When we stepped out of the Volkswagen, a pile of over two hundred skinned beaver carcasses greeted us. It was a disconcerting sight, to say the least.

Seeing this many skinned animals in a pile brought great sorrow to my heart. Gory darkness penetrated my perception. Chills shivered up my spine as images of war-torn countries with rotting human bodies flooded my psyche. My heart was beating erratically. I slowed my breathing to a rhythmic pace as Damian had taught me, and I was able to calm down. I was surprised to have such an intense reaction like this, but this was no normal situation. There was a ghastly sensation of suffering present. For a few moments, I thought I could hear the spirits of these deceased animals as though they were crying out to me, but I convinced myself that it was just my imagination.

As I mentioned earlier, Preston took frequent trips to area farms. He would collect cows and other farm animals that had died and feed them to his dogs. It was the most cost-effective way for him to keep them fed. He also had an arrangement with local trappers. Instead of discarding the carcasses of wild animals that they had trapped, they allowed Preston to use them as dog food. All they wanted was the skins.

Before we pulled in, Preston had just gotten back to his place with the trailer full of dead beavers. The first chore of the day was to bring two dead beavers to each dog and then cover the carcasses with a bunch of tarps. After that, we were asked to spend the rest of the day weeding the garden. Damian and I agreed and got right to work.

Most of the dogs were good-natured. Their entire lives had been spent chained up and hidden in the woods, but they somehow still managed to be good-spirited and friendly towards me. Two of the nine dogs, though, were vicious. One was a man-eater. Over a year later this dog severely mauled me and bit two other people. As I walked towards this very dog carrying a beaver carcass under each arm, she began frantically circling at the end of her chain. As I got closer, she began violently barking at me, frothing at the mouth and psychotically baring her teeth. It was not an inviting situation.

I tossed a beaver to her and watched as she tore into it. Like a toy she heaved it into the air, jumping up to catch it, dismembering it as it hit the ground. The smell of aquatic rodent meat on my gloves and jacket was nauseating. I couldn't imagine how it tasted, especially because the meat was not fresh kill and had been festering, replete with flies swarming like biblical tales of locusts, and maggots greedily feeding on it, like drug addicts fiending for a fix.

After feeding the dogs and covering the carcasses, Preston took off for the day. He went to make his rounds collecting supplies and anything else of value. Damian and I headed into the garden to begin weeding. It was a project that, in its entirety, could never be finished. The garden spanned across acres, and there were only three of us to do the work. It was always a daunting, sweat-off-your-brow labor-intensive task.

Roughly twenty minutes into weeding, I began feeling dizzy. It got to the point where I felt so off-balanced I thought I might fall over. I walked to the edge of where the garden bordered the forest and sat down.

After a few minutes of deep breathing, I regained some semblance of normalcy, so I tried weeding again, but my heart began to flutter and skip beats. Then it felt like it was going to burst through my chest, sharp cardiac pains followed this.

It began to get so agonizing that I cried out and collapsed on the ground. My body was flush and sweltering with heat. I was sure it was a heart attack. Damian acted as though he had no idea what was happening to me.

"Bro, help," I desperately yelled, but he just walked away. I couldn't believe he did that. My whole body was cramping up, and I was stricken with fear. 'Why would he leave me here like this'?

As I lay there gasping for air, crying and screaming for help, the sky changed from a bright blue to a tense malevolent gray. Shadows that were eerily human-like seemed to appear from behind trees and out of thin air. It wasn't just me; the atmosphere was stricken with fear and anger. It was as though every living entity around had a problem with my presence. My heart was pounding like a jackhammer breaking rock: *THUMP, THUMP, THUMP*. I was losing control of my body. It was convulsing and thrashing about. Urine began to soak my pants, my bowels were trying to hold on. There was no way for me to stop any of it. I knew I was dying, and I was terrified to go out like this.

My consciousness began fading. I tried fighting every moment by hanging on to dear life, but I was slipping through the cracks. Staying in my body was not an option. I knew I was leaving this world, and none of my protests made any difference.

While fighting this battle, I somehow became aware of a reality within this world that I hadn't known before. I began experiencing dramatic visual and auditory hallucinations, but I hadn't taken any drugs. I could hear and feel individually, yet in unison, every blade of grass, every tree, insect, bird, animal, even the rocks, the water - everything - for what seemed like miles around crying out in sorrow. And paradoxically, they each cried alone and yet all together. Their focus was all on me. They lamented for what humans have done to the Earth and all her living creatures, past and present. Even more upsetting was that I was incidentally being blamed for all of this. The guilt I felt as I lay there was immeasurable. All I knew at that point was fear and treacherous guilt.

In the moments I was fading from consciousness, I found that it was not just biological entities that were crying out to me. The shadows that earlier were appearing out of nowhere, reminiscent of human forms, were becoming more human-like. They were weeping. I was able to recognize them as disincarnate souls. They, along with countless others, began circling me. It was like being in the funnel of a tornado comprised of disembodied spirits. In my already petrified state, I became even more so. The closer these spirits got to me, the more familiar they became. Although I didn't know how, a part of me knew who they were.

The spirit of a woman began to indirectly communicate with me. But before I could understand her, I was stricken with a pain I had never felt. A weak attempt to describe it would be like a colossal meat grinder churning my organs with the intent of total annihilation. I had never known such pain.

I knew this was it. My soul was being exterminated from my body. The last thought I had before I went out was, "*We're all gonna burn in hell for what we have done to this planet.*" With this thought, every human feeling and emotion that I had ever felt in my life was amplified to its highest possible intensity. Then the life force animating my body released itself, and "I" disappeared.

Every single bit of the person I believed myself to be, suddenly begun to de-molecularize into subatomic particles of electromagnetic energy. These particles left the foundation of my body and dissipated into the energetic dimensions of the space around me. Words cannot describe the intensity of how this felt. A visual analogy to this would be the way pipe smoke, after being lit, disperses into the atmosphere of a room. I went from a human being to a non-human energy form, and some part of 'me' was fully conscious of the whole process.

Once my bodily awareness had dissipated a new type of awareness formed. It metaphorically felt like my soul became one fiery drop of molten metal squeezed from the tip of a monstrous hypodermic needle and into the veins of a fleshy hell-bound machine. My awareness, free of its human identity was being processed, not unlike genetically modified meat on a factory-farmed conveyor belt. Yet this was occurring on a scale far too big for me to remotely comprehend or define. Not me, but the awareness of my 'soul's essence,' was in a zone that instead of being materially solid, was electrically pliable and porous. It was reflective of the same place my awareness entered through the scary fever-induced out-of-body experiences I had often entered as a child; the place that constantly fluxed between soft to comfortable, and hard to painful; that terrible place that left me screaming for my mothers nurturing. This was that times infinity.

I had become a ghost in this machine, subjected to discomfort that was dismembering. But it seemed the discomfort and devastation had just begun because now I was entering into some type of purgatory.

With my human ears, I had heard it said that, as you die your whole life flashes before your eyes. Wherever I was, there were countless lives flashing in front of whatever awareness was left of me. They seemed to be in rapid reverse sequential order. It started with my life, then to the life of someone I didn't know, then before that, and before that. It seemed to span back into infinity, far beyond and into the recesses of the collective human psyche. Then it went before the human species itself.

After the human element had diminished, it went through lifecycles of the animal, plant and mineral kingdoms, and even beyond that into fine electromagnetic particles that morphed between material and immaterial.

As these life cycles were being revealed, one preceding the next, there was the presence of another awareness looming nearby. It was acting as some sort of cosmic accountant observing and measuring each life cycle. Amongst the many measurements it accounted for there were specific aspects it sought to determine. The human experience measurements it sought were based on the levels of self-transcendence and universal awareness each individual achieved, or didn't, during their life. In the plant and animal kingdoms, it measured each life cycle's vitality, fulfillment of purpose and the levels of rudimentary self-awareness.

The fact that some part of my consciousness was able to perceive this was miraculous because the speed at which it was all occurring would have been inconceivable to my 'normal' human senses. I would have certainly melted down. It appeared to be occurring at light speed.

This infinite number of different identities that were being accounted for were so varied in their diversity that it seemed to include the composite for every possible type of human being. It was a molten amalgamation of every archetype of person who has ever lived on the planet and the sum total accumulation of each of their entire lives: the sperm, egg, gestation, birth, thoughts, behaviors, actions, virtues, vices and then their deaths. There were kings, queens, saints, tycoons, tyrants, mass murderers, thieves, peasants, children, babies—and that was just the human kingdom.

As it measured the animal and plant kingdoms, I witnessed not only the life cycles of countless species but also the origins of their genetics in exquisite detail. It went all the way before and through the epochs of dinosaurs and into the first single-celled organisms when the earth was covered by ocean, and it even went before that. Everything originated from tiny sparks of miraculous energy that emanated from the one and only source of all life.

As I relived all these life cycles in the presence of this universal accounting system, I came to realize my soul was being tried in a "cosmic court." It sought to determine the guilt or innocence of the person that my soul had become in this lifetime. This was based not only on the accumulation of this lifetime's "good and bad" deeds but also by how I reacted to the presentation of all these other lifecycles.

In lieu of this, it was clear that the scales of galactic justice were not tipping in my favor. Each life cycle I witnessed unleashed verdicts that weighed on the side of guilt. There were spiritual beings present in this "cosmic courtroom." Some were defending, but most were accusing me of guilt. It was all brutally and sonically deafening to my soul. The pressure of this was greater than one would imagine exists in the deepest trenches of the world's oceans. There were countless eyes staring at me in a spiral that spun into what felt like forever.

Just moments before an anticipated guilty verdict was to be announced the remaining vestige of my soul, without actually knowing the results of the final verdict, began to deny that everlasting hell was to be its fate. In its own way it declared that despite pushing the omnipotent scales of justice into the red, it was still "good" because it originated from "God." It pled its case honestly and fiercely, fighting for its survival. It acknowledged its flaws but that at its core, it was pure. It refused to accept this guilty verdict was to be its fate. It knew that when it all came right down to it, it was 'pure' because it came directly from the source. It petitioned that it couldn't be anything but...

The awareness that was once 'me' was worn out from experiencing such accused accountability of collective karmic debt. It was withered from trying to plead its case to a force that was infinitely bigger than it. It became so weak that it could no longer fight.

Everything became colder than an ice age. It was dark side of the moon cold, Pluto cold, and even that doesn't describe the eternal frigidity. There was nothing visible, but a kind of knowing became more and more evident. An endless dark night for a disembodied soul was imminent.

The cold began feeling like it had a gravitational pull. At first, it felt like a vacuum, subtly but forcibly sucking on my soul. This pull began increasing and then out of the deep blue something came into being. The nature of its presence felt like ground zero for evil incarnate. It was malevolent in its intent. I can only describe it as being surrounded by layer upon layer of ancient evil souls, and even this is a weak description. They were accusing my awareness of being evil. They wanted it to join theirs. If it didn't, they were going to make it join.

There is no way for me to explain how scary this was. In my human life, I had never known such fright. This wickedly evil force was having its way. It was sucking my awareness into it, but what was left of me refused to go. Like a cat clinging to a tree in the midst of a windstorm, my awareness clung to its decision that at its core it was pure, and from the source of life itself.

As this hellacious fire and brimstone cyclone slowly but eagerly pulled my awareness into it, parts that were 'impure' became consumed by it. The fear, anger, and guilt accumulated in these lives were the first parts to go. It then proceeded to consume every other sadistic part lingering in what was left of my essence: all of it. Eventually, all that was left in my awareness was the purity. It was all that remained, but it wanted that as well. Soon, the suction was so strong that even the purity began breaking up. This force was so big, and my awareness was so small. The remaining bit of purity in me was now beginning to dissipate.

Before I knew it, all that was left of me was one molecule of awareness: the smallest, most disconnected and seemingly inconsequential aspect of my entire existence in juxtaposition to this hurricane of ancient evil souls. But it wanted that last molecule as well. It pulled, but I held until I could hold on no longer…then I let go into the nothingness that spanned forever.

Out of nowhere, I opened my eyes…my human eyes, in my human body. It was inconceivable that I had returned back to the self I thought had died of a heart attack. It didn't seem possible.

As I felt my heart beating, my lungs breathing, and my hands gripping the Earth, bewildering confusion set in. I didn't know what was happening or what was real. Was that hell-realm real? Was this world in my human form real? Was either of them? Was neither of them? I was perilously lost.

Lying on the ground in absolute shock, I sensed that even though I was back in my body, something was wrong. Shaking like a leaf on a tree, I stood up, only to realize that I hadn't come back alone. I was possessed.

The hurricane of evil incarnate had crossed back over into this world. Horrible antagonistic spirits were circling me, filling the air as far as I could see. They were taunting, teasing, and tormenting me in wickedly deviant ways. They continued to accuse me of being evil. My field of vision was filled with vivid yet hazy, auras. They surrounded everything that I could see, no matter if it was a living organism or a car. In addition to these auras, there was also a sound emitted by them. But its message was one of urgency and dire distress. It preached doom and gloom in relation to the ignorant ways of human beings.

At this point, I thought I had managed to crawl out of the bowels of hell but that I was now cursed and would have to live out my days possessed by demons. To the outsider, unaware of what was actually happening, it might have appeared that I was suffering from a chronic case of paranoid schizophrenia. But on the inside, it felt way worse than this. I wasn't able to retain any composure. I would have been locked up in the padded room of a mental asylum in a turtle suit for the type of behavior I was displaying. I was screaming out, begging evil spirits to leave me alone, while flailing my arms as protection so they wouldn't fly into me.

I needed to find Damian. I yelled out to him, but there was no answer. As I hobbled towards Preston's house, I was swatting demons with my hands as though they were wasps, screaming in terror the whole way.

Stumbling into Preston's barn-like house, I found Damian sitting on a chair, cross-legged in meditation. My screams did not disturb him; he appeared to be in a still, deep pose.

Like a train coming off its tracks, crashing into chairs and tables, and knocking them over, I began interrogating him for answers.

"Please!!! What the fuck is happening to me? Please!"

He just sat there silently, unmoved by my query. The contents of the room around him looked as though they were spiraling into the whirlwinds of the Valhalla hurricane I had just escaped from. The air was riddled with devious spirit entities, engaged in a maniacal tongue. They were laughing at me while accusing me of guilt. I melted down and began screaming at full force. The frequencies emitted by the tormenting spirits and everything around me was so loud and extreme, it felt like I was at the epicenter of a magnitude ten earthquake. The ground felt like liquid metal under my feet. There was thunder booming from inside my brain.

The insanity of it all was so overwhelming that I felt like I was going to pass out again. My whole world was spinning out of control. Was this the curse of the Peyote theft crime that I was responsible for three years earlier? Because now there truly were evil spirits everywhere, "fucking" with me, as the peyote people warned would happen.

In this state of being, I had become a real zombie, the living dead. I could feel this hurricane of evil souls still trying to suck the life force from my body. Boom!!! I hit the floor. Again I had become too weak to fight. I was on the verge of surrendering to this evil force and letting it take my soul, but I couldn't. I knew that no matter what, at my core, I was good. I just couldn't believe that this is what my life had turned into. How could it ever have come to this?

Throughout all of this chaos, Damian did not flinch. In the periphery of my vision, I could see him sitting, eyes closed in meditation, like a Taoist priest. The intensity of this experience was bearing on my mind. My eyes began swelling and sealing shut because the deep oceanic pressure on my brain was so great. The demons were circling me like a flock of vultures, angry that I was still breathing, but eager to pick through the carrion of my soul. I couldn't hold on. I was going under again.

Somehow with the thunderous sounds in my head and the jarring frequencies ringing in my ear, I heard something resembling a voice, very lightly, say, "You know what this is."

In my state of infernal disarray, I wasn't able to connect to whatever meaning was associated with those words. I also had no idea who said them or where they were coming from. My whole being was toxified from an excruciating journey to the razor-sharp edges of the netherworld. As I lay there weeping, I heard those words again, but this time they were loud and clear.

"YOU KNOW WHAT THIS IS!"

This time I understood what they meant. My awareness lit up from the inside out as a silvery, ultra-luminous energy field surrounded my body. I did know what this is! I acknowledged it to myself, and out loud, **"I do know what this is!"**

Not only did I know what it was, I understood its purpose at the deepest levels of my being. At the drop of a hat, my entire awareness shifted from subjective fright to objective universal awareness. Once this shift had occurred, I felt like time had stopped in its tracks. Suddenly I remembered everything: all of it.

I picked myself up from the floor and stood on my feet. I was no longer dizzy, and at the same time, there was a feeling of rapturous bliss I had never known. All the horrible spirits who were accusing me were still there, but they were no longer horrible, and they were no longer accusing.

They were impossibly iridescent colored and benevolent, they were powered by universal love, potentiated by infinity. One by one in their own way, they introduced themselves to me, and I acknowledged them. When I looked into the eyes of these beings, I could see the faces of what appeared to be every human on the planet. At other times I could see animal faces. They were shape-shifters changing from one form to the next in the blink of an eye. They were similar to what I would imagine angels being like, but like nothing my imagination could have ever conjured. They were real, and they were alive, and they were communicating with me.

All they were interested in was making sure that I fully understood how much they loved me, but it wasn't a love that I have ever known. Up to this point in my human journey, nothing could have prepared me for this kind of contact. There was not one day I could have conceived that anything like this was possible…ever. It was more real than anything I had ever known.

In their direct presence, they loved me in a way that so completely transcended the human concept of love that it wasn't even on the map. Tears gushed from my eyes like Venezuela's Angel Falls. I began crying with such intensity that I was no doubt bawling as loudly as it was possible for me to do. But they stopped me from crying. They said there was much they needed to communicate, and that we needed to begin now.

They beckoned me to follow them through the gates of my consciousness. I lay on the floor surrounded by this vivid energy field and my awareness exited through these gates, or energy centers: the best way that I can describe this is through the analogy of a stargate that enables space travel, only this is for 'soul-travel.' These gates exist in every human being. To the uninitiated, this may sound like science fiction. But to those who have experienced it, it is more real than the reality we've been conditioned to perceive with our 'normal' human senses.

Once this energy field containing my soul had passed through the gate of consciousness, a type of divinely powered geometric seal would appear. It started out very basic, yet mystifying in form. I cannot think of any other way to say it, other than these geometric seals were "alive."

A specific seal would remain in my awareness until I acknowledged that I recognized it. Once I had, these "living" geometric forms would dissolve, allowing my soul entrance into a new dimension with higher frequencies and deeper revelations than the one before it. Each dimension seemed to contain countless universes made up of vast heavenly chambers. This process repeated itself through a few dimensions with the geometry becoming more complex with each "higher" dimension. My recognition of each geometric configuration was the metaphorical key that unlocked the gates into higher and more profound dimensions.

The geometry became so complex that it was becoming too difficult for me to recognize and identify with. Somewhere in the memory of my soul, I remembered having gone through this before. I knew these dimensions. I had dwelled in them for what seemed like eternity. But I also remembered my soul's evolution towards higher levels being - limited, due to my inability to recognize these perplexing geometric patterns.

Now I had arrived there once again. My soul's evolution was at its climax; only now, as I came to reach the top, something different happened. Like an implosion, my vital essence was sucked into something similar to a black hole that used all of its force to condense it. Just as in the purgatory realms when I had been stripped of all but a molecule of the goodness left in my soul, I was again reduced to such insignificance.

Here I was alone, as a single molecule. It felt like there was nothing alive near me for a trillion light-years. It was only mildly like being an embryo, trapped in a test tube with no escape. Just as the heavy vibrations of the purgatory world were deafening to my soul, so was the silence of this place. But the major difference between the isolation I felt in the in-between realm and the isolation I felt here, was that now I was able to gracefully accept it. After being released from the harsh judgments of the cosmic court, my soul was content with whatever the forces of life had in store for it. Now I knew the true meaning of love. Not only did I now know it, but I had also become completely reintegrated back into it. I always was, am, and will be a part of this 'love.' Everyone and everything truly is. It's just that humans have evolved thinking that they are consciously disconnected from it, creating an illusion that most believe to be reality. This has been going on for so long throughout countless generations that we actually believe that we are separated from it. We're not; we only think we are.

Now that I was able to accept such a state of aloneness, the opposite reaction of an implosion occurred. In a sense, the remaining molecule of my soul exploded for what seemed like forever. As this happened, I transcended all the dimensions that were still in front of me. The isolated sensation became enveloped by a sensation I can only describe as *the best feeling I have ever felt multiplied by infinity*. This feeling began permeating every bit of my soul to such a profound degree that I was able to actually glimpse and understand the basics of how miraculous life really is. I understood the beginnings of how the universe functioned, by witnessing the building blocks that created it. As this feeling continued to permeate my soul, I became aware of answers to questions that humans have asked since the dawn of our inception on this planet.

Just as witnessing countless lifecycles in cosmic court was an information download, but in an exhausting way, so too was becoming aware of all these answers, yet in an enlightening way. My awareness was downloaded with knowledge and information much too vast for my human mind so my energy field retained it and I could access it on-demand.

As this divine permeation neared completion, I came to rest in what I can only describe as the oneness of the universe. Everything that I ever needed to know about the true nature and meaning of life was there. In essence, everyone and everything I had ever known and loved was alive and intertwined within the fabric of this oneness. It was miraculous beyond anything that my human mind had the ability to imagine or conjure up. Never in my wildest dreams could I have imagined that anything like this existed.

I was able to recognize that every human on the planet will somehow, in some way, become aware of this oneness. My vision of this was filled with luminous sensations of colors and sounds. There were colors beyond the spectrum of what my human eyes had ever seen. It was filled with pitch, melody, and rhythms beyond anything my ears had ever heard. It was the most enlightening, super-sensual aspect of life that most people want to know exist, but have to experience directly to know that it actually does. Not in a trillion light-years could my human imagination conceive of such splendor. Words like Nirvana, heaven, bliss, ecstasy, enlightenment, etc., do not even begin to describe the nature of how this felt. It was ineffable.

After basking in this divine light and sound for what felt like forever, the angelic beings informed me that it all actually has been going on forever. Yet, they claimed, it goes way beyond what they have access to. They demonstrated that all they were, and all I was, were emanations of the source of life itself projecting itself through us. Each and every one of us no matter animal or human, individually and collectively, is expressions of incomprehensible creative projection.

Humans possess the advanced cognitive function of being able to self-reflect into the mysterious nature of their own existence. But the ability to self-reflect is contingent upon the individual's free will to do so and the free will to do so is motivated by their will power and their commitment to cultivating these states within themselves. There are many unseen factors motivating the individual's ability to effectively exercise their free will. The bottom line is, the more an individual soul desires to identify with the cyclical, or more accurately, *spiraling* forces of the spiritual world, the more their soul awakens, unlocking its co-creative potential as a human being, empowered by this unfathomable 'divine' energy.

The amount of information downloaded into my psyche is beyond the scope of this book. But, the fundamental root of it is that everyone and everything is created by and unified through a single energetic principle. The core of that principle is a source of *miraculous energy*, unlike anything imaginable. It's what quantum physics calls the unified field. The sooner an individual makes the pursuit of this discovery their number one priority, the sooner this unimaginable source of love will become self-evident.

After these angelic beings had finished giving me a non-corporeal tour beyond the universe, I returned to the consciousness of my human body. As I opened my eyes in my human form, after having been processed by this entire experience, I was jubilant, to say the least.

Previously, when I had returned back into my body after the trek into the hell realms, I thought I was forever cursed with the nightmare of being taunted by horrid winged demons. Now that I had gone through the heavenly realms, my return to human life was a blessed one. Finally, I had discovered 'what I was.'

The rapid transformation that I had just undergone was beyond belief. My psychic potential seemed unlimited. I was fully aware that I existed in many dimensions simultaneously. My clairvoyant, clairaudient, and clairsentient abilities were super-charged. The beautiful shape-shifting angelic beings (who I came to call the *iridescent guides*) were visibly and telepathically all around me. In those moments of my return to humanity, I knew who I was and what the point of my life was to be.

The iridescent guides informed me that because I had been reawakened, nothing in my life would be as it was. There was tremendous responsibility in how I chose to exercise my free will—my thoughts, behaviors, and actions—in this world. As a result of this entire *re-birth*, many psychic gifts and powers were bestowed upon me; however, the choice of how to properly use them was entirely up to me.

The iridescent guides showed me that by discerning how I conducted my thoughts, behaviors, and actions, I could prevent having to be subjected to the dense *lower* collective thought-form frequencies that are constantly being projected and enveloping our human species. These thought-forms enslave us, making it impossible to connect to the truth of what we are.

This discernment was easy to conduct after this awakening. In those moments, I was no longer living from the ego. It was way down the chain of command with my soul leading the charge. I was now aware that my awareness resided in many realms simultaneously, while at the same time, remaining in constant contact with my shape-shifting spiritual guides.

The guides then informed me in a very direct way about my future. They presented many glimpses of it; however, there was much that I didn't see. They showed that I would face many seemingly insurmountable obstacles, but as long as I maintained luminous conscious awareness, they would always be there to help me overcome these 'lessons.' These obstacles were supposedly for the benefit of my soul's evolutions towards more advanced dimensions if I could face them in this luminous state.

Glimpsing these future difficulties caused me to slightly protest, but the guides quickly quieted me down. They emphasized that this was for my greater good. After being told this, I was not able to comprehend, in any way, how serious these challenges would be.

But for now, none of these warnings about my future mattered. As far as I was concerned, I discovered exactly what I was desperately searching for. Not only had I discovered it, but also I did so in a way that I couldn't have ever imagined, not even on the most imaginative day of my life. The most beautiful words in the English language could not do justice to what happened. There was no way for me to describe the state I was now in.

The cries from my ego to my soul were blatantly obvious to my awareness. My ego declared that I was now a powerful prophet, here to awaken the people of Earth. But my soul would quiet this type of self-talk the moment it started.

Here I was, eighteen years old, the '*me*' that existed before was still there, but through this process of quantum expansion in my awareness, I had been transformed to an almost different species. It was nothing less than absolute divine consciousness. I was in my body, but I was no longer bound to it. Just as Damian had once explained to me—my body was no longer a prison of my personality, it was a temple for my soul.

In a grounded and balanced way, I was here, there and everywhere. My feet were solidly rooted in the Earth - my head was way up into the stars, and my heart was syncopated to the evolutionary impulse of the truest expression of higher love. In my vision were beautiful iridescent shape-shifting beings, amidst a backdrop of what looked like nebula pictures from the Hubble telescope. Tying it all together it looked like countless shooting stars, woven together with a bird's eye view of something vastly more splendid than the Northern Lights.

In my ears, I heard the subtle profundity of all the planets in the solar system, spinning around the sun. The deep bass sounds of Earths rotation combined with the high-pitched crackling of solar flares shooting from the sun created a symphony of celestial instrumentation. It became the accompaniment for the angelic voices of the celestial beings all around me.

Most of their communication was carried out in what could almost be described as a song. Ancient primordial rhythms intertwined with improvised harmony, inspired by the latent mystery of life's yet unknown evolutionary potential. To say this music was soothing to the soul would be a vast understatement.

But the most powerful sensation emanating from my new state of being was the feeling in and pouring out of my heart. Again, I can only describe it as the best feeling I had ever felt multiplied by infinity, like the feeling of a soul level orgasm times infinity! The combination of this feeling, intertwined with the vivid visuals and enamoring audio, allowed the illuminating energy field to radiate from within me, encapsulating my physical body. The more I concentrated on it, the brighter it became. This was the field of pure potentiality that Damian spoke of. It was clear to me that within this energy field, there was unlimited potential if I was able to harness it.

In the course of one Earth day, I had become reborn in a way that was supernatural. I laughed and cried over and over again. I couldn't believe it! I could not believe what the true nature of reality actually was. I never would have guessed, as this world is not at all what it appears to be. But the beautiful thing was—I no longer needed to believe or not believe in what the truth of life may or may not be. Now I had experienced it first-hand, but more accurately, I was able to remove my inner obstructions enough so that life was able to experience itself through me.

As I laughed and cried, I also remembered. Just as when Damian had me recall my earliest childhood memories in Concord, again these memories resurfaced. But now it was so much more than a memory because I could vividly re-live it. Though not nearly at the level I had just gone through, my childhood meditations were this exact same experience. I was flabbergasted that I could have ever forgotten my connection to the forces of reality.

But in the years after my awakening, I would come to find out how I had indeed forgotten. It is the human species dilemma. Beneath our personality is an energy source of latent potential; however, our consciousness is too focused on our personality to stay connected to its source. Because of this - all pay a heavy spiritual price.

But at this point in my journey, none of that mattered to me. I had become a young magic man, truly alive and well, in a magical super-conscious land.

CHAPTER ELEVEN

The Ascended Master?

Throughout this all, Damian was sitting cross-legged in a yogic, full lotus posture. He was seated in a chair towards the back of the biggest open space in Preston's house. I would call it a living room, but that's not what it really was. It was used mostly to store supplies.

At some point during this entire ordeal, a goat and two chickens had freely walked into the house. They were positioned around Damian relaxing, watching every move I made. Damian's eyes were now open, but it was almost as though he wasn't present in his body. It was reminiscent of looking at a life-sized wax figure. In a rare turn of events, he began speaking before I said anything. "You went far, however, what you just experienced was only the tip of the iceberg." The feeling of intensity he projected more accurately conveyed the meaning of his message than the words themselves.

"How far did you go," I asked.

"I've gone all the way around the circle, through the source and then back from there," he said in a slow, meditative drone as all of the iridescent beings circled into spirals all around and behind him.

"This is incredible, beyond amazing! I could've never imagined anything like this was possible! What I'm seeing, hearing and feeling is more than a miracle," I blurted out with elated enthusiasm.

I stared at Damian with a look of conflicted disbelief and joy. "Who are you? What are you? How did you become like this," I innocently and excitedly asked?

He surprisingly went right into it. "It's really difficult for me to explain because the depths of it are so far beyond what words can express. But I will try to summarize it.

During ancient times, when the world was younger, I was a human being that had a vision, an awakening. The energetic force that I truly was had awakened itself in my human perception. The contrast between the human personality I believed myself to be, and the energetic force that I'd always been, equally merged into my perception in that one lifetime. Later in that life, my physical body died, but my awareness remained conscious as it transitioned into another incarnation. It then reincarnated stronger and more consciously aware than it had been during that first awakening in the previous lifetime.

"And so it is…or rather was, that I continued to die, reincarnate and consciously evolve with the same soul, but different personalities. With every new life cycle, I would grow more consciously aware than the one before it, but then it evened out for a long time. With every new rebirth, I'd run into many of the same challenges, both personally and in dealing with other people.

Personally I would always struggle with my personality or ego, competing to overshadow my soul, and it usually always did. The challenge with others was that most cared too much about their own egotistical needs to even consider their true nature. I often took this personally, because it hurt me to see how they perpetuated never-ending struggle for themselves through their selfishness. Sometimes I would view the world through their eyes and take away their pain. At first, they would thank me, but then they began to fear me.

"Then, after hundreds of lifetimes of painful deaths and rebirths, something happened. I was born into a life cycle where my soul, my true self, enveloped my personality. It was the first time this had happened. This changed everything as it came with many types of abilities, powers, and challenges. But it included the ability to awaken other people's awareness to the source of their awareness itself – many call it God, but that's just a made-up human name. In essence, it's ego death, the rush and experience of physical death without actually dying. You know the rest."

I just continued to stare at him in disbelief. I knew everything happening was real, more real then anything I'd ever known in this life. Yet I also knew that had this not happened to me in particular, I wouldn't believe that anything like it was possible. It was so alien, yet so familiar.

So I asked, "What did you think was going to occur in this life, the one we are living in right here, right now?"

"In this life," he stated, "I have a choice to make." There was a long pause. "I believe that I am nearing the end of the line. Whatever will happen is based on this choice.

One option is to remain as the being I am with all my abilities and all my flaws, and then reincarnate one last time. I would then be reborn as something this world has not known. Something that could fully awaken the masses on a global scale." His words were heavy. They were filled with a gravity that made me feel as though I was anchored into the iron core of the Earth. I could feel the mind-blowing veracity of his message intertwined throughout his speech. In those moments, it was scary how real it all was.

"What is your other choice?"

"It's a choice I've never made in all my lifetimes." This time there was a really long pause before he spoke again. "I can remain as what I am, or I can pass the seed of my abilities into my first-born child."

His words were even heavier as he told me this. I knew I couldn't fathom the seriousness of what he had just told me, but I suddenly became aware of the purity that he possessed. It was the only way he was able to be the spiritual force of nature that he was. He was a virgin…and probably not just in this life. I assumed he had been since the first time his soul awakened in its human form, although I never asked.

All I knew was that on top of everything that had just happened, hearing his life story was completely insane. Had I not been in this elated state, I would have definitely questioned such a tale. But being in the state I was now in, it wasn't only believable, I figured it was probable. "This world is not at all what I thought it was," I thought to myself. My foundations had been shaken to the core, trying to make sense of this whole thing.

"What is supposed to happen now that I know and remember all of this?"

He continued to glare into what was formerly the unknown. "We'll just have to be wise and improvise because it's too complicated to say right now."

"How many lifetimes have you known this is what you are?" My questions were all over the place. I was completely blown away, and my composure was gone.

He gave me this tacit look that implied, *seriously*? He was one of these shape-shifting iridescent beings in human form, and he has known it for lifetimes. It was the reason he was always so quiet. It was why he always spent so much time alone. How could people relate to this if they hadn't experienced it? How would they relate to it even if they had? This was not an occurrence that you forget about and then move on from. It so deeply and fundamentally changed every aspect of every single thing that I ever thought I knew or imagined about my life or life in general. There was no way for me to anticipate how others might take this. But there was only one way to find out.

It was me that pushed the issue. After what I had just experienced, I was confident that if the masses experienced what I had - it would change the course of destruction that we all are headed towards as a species. I believed Damian had a gift the whole world needed to know about. His powers would change everything. There would be no more questions, just solutions for all - solutions that would eventually lead to a profound state of global harmony. The potential for change was beyond great, it was exponential, and it was quantum.

But of course, I was young and ignorant and having been newly awakened from lifetimes of slumber, I was unaware of the potential chaotic ramifications of wanting to awaken the sleeping masses.

Damian laughed at my proposal. The iridescent guides made me aware that all I needed to do was integrate all of the fundamental changes I had just experienced and develop my own latent potential. Damian said that he too needed time to figure out how I would fit into his immediate future. Because of all this, I decided that for the time being, I didn't have much of an option. The responsible thing to do was stay in the woods while learning to live in this rediscovered state of awareness. That's what I did for many months after.

To live and learn while being in such a highly illuminated state was nothing short of sublime. Now that I was aware of all this, Damian was able to reveal methods and techniques for harnessing this inner power without holding back. Most of this occurred through psychic transmissions that happened almost constantly. However there was a massive amount of physical, tonal and energetic techniques that we would implement to rewire all the neural circuitry of many different points, energy centers and ganglia of the body to receive and emit greater frequencies of information, energy and potential from the unified field. Essentially I was being guided to increase the size, coherence and potential of the field that animated my body.

Because I now knew a deeper level of reality, I was able to witness and take part in many things that before awakening, I would have deemed impossible or a miracle. The iridescent guides would superimpose images into my view, mostly geometric designs, causing my energy field to become stronger and brighter. The telepathic communication between the guides, Damian, and I was non-stop. Even at night while dreaming, I was in constant contact with these beings, learning, and training.

Almost daily, I would transcend the limits of my normal waking consciousness through expeditions of the soul and into dimensions near and far. I learned ancient secrets and routinely witnessed the impossible while celestial wonders of it all reached out to be seen and known. The miraculous profundity of it all became so normal that it was like dreaming with my eyes wide open.

My entire life experience had become that of energy, soul, and the deep exploration of it all. Once this began, a strange dichotomy started taking place. I felt the old me, the ego that existed before my awakening wanting to emerge at inconvenient and random times. These vestiges of prehistoric self were like the fossilized remnants of dinosaurs that wanted to break free of their monolithic casing for one last breath. I tried to ignore them, but I wasn't able to. Damian explained that eventually, I might be able to balance my soul and ego in a holistic way, although for now, it wasn't necessary. But my ego was stubborn. It didn't like being under the control of my soul. It wanted to be heard. It wanted to be in charge.

One day after months of existing in this state, we brought our car into the suburban town where I had been bullied, for repairs. We ended getting stuck there all day while the car was being fixed. Damian walked to his parent's house to get supplies. I decided to go to my parent's house for the same reason.

As I walked over there, I saw my old crush, Lucinda, from a distance. The iridescent guides urged me to keep walking. But, the memory of her waving a Carlos Castaneda book in my face while denigrating my character for being *unspiritual*, surfaced in my mind. Ignoring the guide's advice, I approached her with a slight smile on my face. Surprised to see me, she exclaimed, "Oh my God! I haven't seen you in such a long time! You look great, so bright and shiny. What happened to you?"

With her long wavy blond hair and her eyes bluer than the sky itself, I just couldn't hold back at all, so I blurted out, "Lucinda, something amazing happened! I've been changed at the deepest level. It felt like I was having a heart attack, then my soul left my body and went into some kind of purgatory where millions of lives flashed before my eyes. The purgatory was like a cosmic court that judged me. It said I was cursed, but then I pleaded my case and I was set free. Spirit guides brought me back to my body, and I awakened to the reality of what I really am! They showed me everything, and it is more amazing than I could ever imagine! That's why I'm glowing! If you come with me, you can find out! Please come with me!"

I saw grave fear and confusion in her eyes. It was the kind of fear one feels walking alone deep in the wilderness in the dark of night knowing that predatory wild beasts are all around. She took a couple of steps back and asked, "Find out what?"

I looked at her, smiled warmly, and said, "What you really are!"

Her face was puzzled. She looked down at the ground and said, "I believe you, but this feels really weird. I'm not sure I like it."

The iridescent guides urged me to walk away. The physical sensation of intuition felt like getting kicked in the gut. I got her point, but as I decided to leave, I became suddenly hyper-aware of many dimensions at once. Dimensions as perceived by the ego and dimensions as experienced by the soul. In those moments, they were all one and the same. The veil that usually seems to keep them apart was no longer there. I was lit up like a nuclear-powered Christmas tree. The frequencies emanating in and around me were oscillating relentlessly. The expression on her face went from fear to rage. She was not having it. Then all of the energy being projected from me started shutting down. The normality of the 'ordinary reality' appeared back into being. Lucinda gave me a piercing look with cold eyes, turned around, and walked away.

Conflicted, I watched her walk down the street. A piece of my heart and restless emotions followed her. Then she got into her car and drove away.

As soon as she was gone, I wondered if I had just committed sacrilege. Had I metaphorically tried to taste the forbidden fruit by activating this power when I was advised against it? My ego had two motives. It wanted retribution against her for denigrating my character due to its lack of spiritual awareness. But it also wanted to impress her, because somewhere in my heart, I was still in love. Sadly the outcome of this reunion with her spoke for itself.

The one thing that did occur as a result of seeing her was the discovery that my abilities could affect others. With this realization, I felt empowered, but I also knew that for all intents and purposes, these abilities were only to be harnessed with the utmost discernment for their possible outcome. Foolishly, in Lucinda's presence, I used no discernment, and I didn't heed the advice given to me by the iridescent guides. *'Right out of the gate and my track record is already in the negative,'* I thought to myself with my head hung in shame.

After Lucinda had driven away, and all frequency levels had been restored to normal, I began walking towards my parent's house. The guides did not reprimand or berate me. There was only silence. I knew what I had done. Using these powers to show off was as spiritually immature as can be. My ego was ashamed. My soul kept a low profile.

As I approached my parent's house, I saw their cars were there, indicating they were home. I was hoping they weren't so I could enter the house, grab supplies and leave unnoticed but I realized this wouldn't be the case. Emotionally, I braced myself for the worst. I was unsure how they would react to me in this intense illuminated state; however, I was more concerned about how I would react to them. After the incident with Lucinda, I was a hypocritical mixture of the soul's eternal love of and the ego's wounded love of narcissism. In addition to this, I hadn't seen them since the previous winter in Concord when they were horrified after witnessing my sub-arctic poverty-stricken lifestyle.

As I walked into the house, I saw they were happy to see me, but also seemed emotionally distraught. They asked how I had been. I remarked that I felt better than I ever had. They were surprised by my answer.

"What do you mean you feel better than you ever have?" they asked.

So I told them, and I didn't hold back. I described the feeling of a heart attack following my entrance into the purgatory that led to the cosmic court. I wasn't able to get beyond the description of cosmic court before they burst into tears.

My mother cried out, "I see parents with their teenagers, and they are normal and happy. Why can't we just have a normal teenage son?"

Hearing this hurt. I always felt our relationship wasn't good because of their expectations for me to conform to their standards. I didn't possess the passive attributes they desired of their offspring. This always created a power struggle between us. I wasn't interested in being possessed by them or anyone.

I looked at my mother and asked, "Normal?"

My emotions were heightened. This, in turn, caused my psychic frequencies to increase. At this point, the iridescent guides intervened and advised I tone it down. But as with Lucinda, I didn't heed their call.

I dropped the fifty-yard stare until I locked eyes with my mother. I peered into her soul and began speaking. "Normal? From my perspective, I don't believe you have a realistic understanding of what normal is! Is your definition of normal doing what others expect of you when you know these expectations are impeding the growth of your soul? Is normal living a cookie-cutter life and doing what society tells you the normal you are referring to? Even if it halts your spiritual development?"

She was hysterical. My father was holding her, and they were both crying. My father gave me a look that said *how could you do this to us*?

It was at that point that many different images of my mother's life began flooding through my psyche. I saw things that caused trauma in her life. While in a trance-like state, I started describing events that impeded her desire to develop the spiritual aspects of her consciousness.

She began screaming at my father, "How does he know that? Did you tell him that?"

The flood of images stopped flowing through my mind's eye. I realized my psychic prowess was having the opposite effect that I intended to have on others.

It was obvious my parents had no idea what just happened or how to deal with me. I felt bad seeing them so broken down. I canceled my plans of grabbing supplies and instead walked towards the door. As I exited the house and closed the front door behind me, it quickly reopened. I turned around to see my father standing there with a look of defeat.

"I don't understand what's happening to you or what you're going through and I'm not going to pretend I do, but…your mother and I love you very much, and we have always only wanted the best for you. I guess we just don't know what that is, but we were thinking…" After saying this, he paused. He was unsure about what he was going to say next.

"Yes, " I egged him on.

"If you come back home, your mother and I will buy you a really nice guitar."

After the emotional meltdown that had just taken place, I couldn't believe that he asked me that. With little compassion, I said, "Thank you, but no thank you."

As I headed back to the garage where our car was being fixed, I knew I didn't leave my parents in a good state of mind. That whole interaction didn't occur as I would've liked it to.

For the very first time, after what just happened with Lucinda and then my parents, I began having very human doubts about living in this world as an awakened being. Of course, the events that just happened were my fault for jumping the gun and not heeding the guides' advice, but I was too immature to take responsibility for that. This day marked the beginning of a lesson that I would learn constantly, over and over again - that the ego's resistance to the soul's wisdom is THE biggest obstacle I would need to overcome to maintain an enlightened disposition and grow into spiritual maturity.

As I walked to meet up with Damian, I thought deeply about the two incidents with Lucinda and my parents. I kept thinking that *here I was on my first trip into the world as an awakened soul and this his how people responded to me*? I was upset with myself for not handling it better, but there was a lot of energy surging through my body. It was hard to control; I kind of felt like a victim. What am I supposed to do with all these "gifts"?

When I made it to the garage, Damian was already waiting. He made no eye contact and hardly acknowledged my presence at all. I knew that on some level, he was aware of what I had just gone through. We paid for the car with what little money we had and drove off. He didn't say one word to me for the entire two-hour ride back to Concord. It was uncomfortably awkward.

When we arrived back at the shed, I broke the silence. "What was I supposed to do," I blurted out.

He snapped right back, "Control yourself a lot better than you did!"

But as soon as he said that, his entire demeanor shifted. He became calm and said something that sounded more like self-affirmation than a response to my question. "It's okay. It doesn't really matter. You did exactly what you were supposed to do. It was perfect."

I had no idea what he was talking about. "What does that mean?"

He wouldn't answer. I also knew he wasn't going to say another word the rest of the night. I thought about what his self-affirming statement might have meant. The iridescent guides were all around, but they gave no input.

Defeated, I climbed up into my loft and looked up at the stars through the little window with one pane of fragile glass above me. I went deep into thought—but as soon as I reached the depths, I realized there wasn't much to think about. *I did do exactly what I was supposed to. How could I have done anything else?* All that was left for me now was to consider the mistakes I made with Lucinda and my parents, and learn from them. In order to learn these lessons, I needed to be tested on them. Staying *enlightened* around other people would mean remaining vigilantly hyperaware. This would take tremendous self-discipline. But the lesson I learned was how quickly I could fall from grace. This was my big takeaway of the day. I made a pact with myself to follow the guides' advice before recklessly engaging my psychic abilities. I felt confident in this decision. I knew I was in the infancy of my spiritual understanding in this life, and that I needed to start wearing my big boy pants, so to speak. With that, I went to sleep.

The next day, Damian was more inclined to talk about what happened. He explained that since he didn't really expect me to have such a profound awakening, he didn't know what to expect in terms of not only how I'd be affected by it, but also how I would affect the world with it. He unremittingly reiterated that I had to be careful, that this energy was not something to play around with. He kept saying it was only to be used for one purpose - my own self-development.

Acknowledging all of this made me realize what a massive responsibility I had. In those moments, it became even more real than it already was. I had tremendous power in my hands, yet I believed I was responsible enough to man up.

CHAPTER TWELVE

Going Public

It was now late autumn, and I convinced Damian to go to a festival in Vermont. I had not left the state of Maine since I lived in Florida a couple of years earlier. I don't think Damian ever had. Why travel the Earth with your physical body when you can literally explore the universe with your soul on a daily basis?

Although I convinced Damian to go by suggesting that we needed a change of scenery, I knew that he knew what my real motives were. I wanted to see how people would react to this 'conscious death process.' I figured that a festival filled with partying hippies was as good a crowd as any to test it out on. Of course, Damian was apprehensive, but I kept egging him on "let's just see what happens!" In the end, I knew that he was actually looking forward to an adventure, regardless if I could get him to 'turn up the vibes.'

The drive to Vermont from Maine was eye-opening in itself. Even though they aren't far apart, the changes in the landscape are quite noticeable. When we arrived at the festival grounds, we were both surprised by what we found. This was no small event. There were at least a few thousand people there, and at first glance, it appeared to be a really fun time. There were booths with lots of arts and crafts, giant puppets and people who were as colorful as can be. Although it was mostly a hippie festival, there was a wide assortment of different types of people present. However, the crowd's pursuit of spiritual enlightenment didn't seem like an obvious priority.

I could tell that Damian was at first positively intrigued by it all. It was such a welcome change to the hermetic life we were accustomed to living. We spent the day walking around the grounds, checking it out and taking it all in. I kept trying to tune in to Damian, to see where he was 'at' from an energetic perspective. Every time I did, I knew he was in a good space. But then it got dark, both outside from the sun going down and in our vibrations as people started getting inebriated from various intoxicants, especially from drinking. Alcohol is referred to as *spirits* for a reason. The word itself is said to have come from the Arabic term "Al-Khul" and "Al-Gawl" which means 'Body Eating Spirit.' It was immediately clear to me that alcohol has been used as some sort of tool to keep human consciousness at a lowered state for thousands of years. The visible effects it had on the human energy field showed me everything I needed to know about it.

The primordial nature of nighttime is always a mystifying experience. The woods become dark. Nocturnal animals begin their hunt. One can look up into the night sky and know there truly is nothing between who we are as people and the limitlessness that we are a part of. To stare at the full moon, knowing that every human being with eyesight, who has ever lived on this planet since our kind began, has stared at that one moon. And then to consider how almost every single indigenous culture ever known, has accepted animism—the belief that natural phenomena are due to spirits and that inanimate objects have spirits—as self-evident.

I didn't take any hallucinogens that night, and I was pretty sure no one had drugged me. All I remember was people hooting, hollering and partying and then I opened my eyes, only it was daytime, and somehow I had ended up on the outskirts of the festival grounds almost a couple of miles from where I had been the night before. I was also the unhappy owner the worst headache I'd had ever known.

When I did open my eyes, I knew something dramatic had happened, but I didn't know what. I sat up and realized that I passed out and had been sleeping on bare ground. It was rocky and not at all comfortable. I was confounded. It didn't make sense. I felt a tingling but depleting feeling all through my body.

I got up onto my feet and started walking back to the festival area. As I got closer to the more populated areas of the grounds, I noticed a few passers-by staring at me like they'd seen a ghost. I questioned myself as to why. After a few more minutes of walking, a woman thanking me profusely approached me. "Thank you, thank you. I've never seen or heard anything like that. It was incredible; thank you!"

I stopped in my tracks even more confused than I had been waking up on a pile of rocks at the opposite ends of the festival grounds. As I looked at this woman, I knew she meant what she said, but I confessed that I had no idea what she was talking about because I couldn't remember anything.

She then explained. "Wow! OK! Everyone was partying and getting crazy, and there was a group of guys who were basically pigs, they were pushing me around, bullying others, robbing people and then openly joking about it. They were just bad guys, and they were big, and they were wasted. They were harassing everyone around. Then suddenly you were standing on top of a car next to them screaming apocalyptic threats at the tops of your lungs. Your voice kept changing, and so did the way you expressed yourself. One minute you were dancing around like an eagle, the next you were jumping up and down crying like a rabbit, and then you were speaking in different languages or tongues. Whatever you did, you got the attention of these dirtbags and they were freaked out by you. I mean they were really freaked out. They got in their vehicles and drove away completely wasted. There were at least a hundred people watching this, cheering you on! I knew that you were a medium because it was all so otherworldly. There was something magical going on, and I wanted to meet you and thank you, so again…thank you!"

I didn't know how to respond to what she said. So I thought about it for a moment, thanked her, and admitted again that I didn't remember any of it. Then I asked her a question. "You said that you knew I was a medium. What do you mean by that?"

She smiled and said, "You don't know what a medium is"?

"No"

"It's a human who is an intermediary between the spirit world and this world. The way that all went down last night I assumed that spirits were speaking through you. It was amazing!"

I really felt strange after hearing that because I knew that whatever happened was beyond my conscious control.

Following the advice and support of the iridescent guides was something that I knew was stable, but becoming unconscious and turning into a puppet for disembodied spirits didn't feel stable to me at all.

I really didn't know how to respond to this woman. I just told her that I was glad that she was all right and walked away. She asked me to wait because she had a lot of questions to ask. I was too freaked out by what she had already said. I told her I had to find someone and I wished her luck.

As I walked away, I felt paranoid. I thought that people everywhere were staring at me, so I started walking fast. I just wanted to find Damian to ask what happened and get the hell out of there.

When I didn't see him anywhere on the festival grounds, I ran to the car and there he was fast asleep in the passenger's seat, so I woke him up. He looked at me, gave me a disapproving look with a laugh, and then turned the other way. Frustrated, I just sat in silence for a few minutes and then he decided to speak.

"You put on quite a little show last night!"

"Yeah, but I don't remember any of it, what is that about?"

"What do you mean, what's that about?"

"Is that what's supposed to happen? I come around a big group of people who are all messed up, and suddenly I black out and become a puppet for the paranormal? Then I wake up the next morning, and I don't remember any of it? That feels pretty unstable to me!"

Then he laid the guilt on thick. "Oh, it does? It feels unstable to you? What did you expect? I warned against coming to a place like this since you started pushing the issue!"

Then he changed the tone of his voice from being accusatory to calmly explaining,

"Listen, let's put aside all of your good intentions for a moment because I know good intent is what you had in your heart when you wanted to come here, and I understand that, believe me, I do! But you have to understand something. Most people don't want to know what the purpose of their life is! They are far too content with their egoic megalomania. You are a minority, and I am not sure how small a minority that actually is. As we have spoken in the past, living harmoniously results from being aware of the energy that animates your human form, and then being aware of how that form exists within the cyclical flow of nature- *this* is the missing link that keeps humans from living harmoniously with themselves, each other and the environment. In fact, all of human consciousness at its core IS already aligned with it. It's just that we have generationally evolved by paying attention to the disempowering things, such as the distractions of the world, as opposed to our souls. Such behavior creates energetic obstructions within our perception of reality. These obstructions lead to an inner imbalance. We then go on to create an imbalance in the world. This is what most people are doing, and sadly, they are oblivious that they are doing it. So, yes, you are a minority. Very few alive are aware of the nature of their own awareness, and the rare few that do become so overwhelmed by what they're up against that they turn away from it."

"Yup, I can totally see why they would! Our species is so far removed from reality that they fear to confront it. It is very sad." I interjected like I had something of value to add to the conversation.

He continued explaining. "Most seekers become aware of these cycles, and how they operate in the world around us, we become aware of how they operate energetically within us. This awareness creates an alignment. Once an alignment takes place, obstructions are broken down, making way for a greater flow of universal consciousness. This cycle continues perpetually until a balance is reached. The balance occurs when your identification with ego and soul are on equal terms with each other. That's close to where you are now. To further develop your energetic potential, you have to work diligently at removing your own obstructing personality traits. These traits are really just distractions that keep you focused on your ego and not your soul. When you succeed at doing this, then your soul or energetic self will rise above your hopefully achieved parallel balance between personality and soul. At this point, a new balance becomes *manifest*."

"And what would that be?"

"At that point, your soul will be in alignment with the source of energy that has given birth to all cosmic order, great and small. When your perception is enveloped by this source, the possibility of what you're able to achieve in this world becomes uncharted territory with limitless potential."

I sat back and pondered his words. As always, they rang true. I understood what he was saying, but I also gleaned that I had BIG shoes to fill and filling them would take unprecedented discipline on my part. Overwhelmed, I felt that maybe I didn't have what it takes to live in this world with such intense hyper-awareness of the energetic realms.

So I asked, "Why do you think I had such a profound awakening? What significance does it have in this world?"

He laughed a little and then looked into the sky, and then he shut his eyes. "I have thought about and asked the very questions you just asked, and there's no definitive answer, other than there is a crisis. The human species is multiplying at an alarming rate while many other species on the planet are disappearing at an accelerated rate. We are in the midst of a mass extinction that our species is the cause of, but at the same time, the potential exists for a critical mass of great awakening. It's possible that somehow you will play a part in this."

"Somehow I will play a part in this? Here we are at a place that I was hoping would give me the opportunity to play a part in it and look how it turned out! If this is just the beginning of what it looks like for the world to wake up, I can't imagine what the future has in store! This was pretty much a nightmare!" I wasn't joking.

"I know that you are thinking you are in over your head, and you can try to turn back, but I think you will find you have gone too far at this point. You're always going to know the value of what's at stake."

He was right, and I knew it. Talk about feeling like you're carrying the weight of the world on your shoulders. I felt it. I knew it. I kept my head hung down and sighed.

"I wish I could just take a break and numb my awareness, at least for a little while so I can rest in preparation for the battle ahead," I said, feeling very overwhelmed.

His response completely surprised me. "Me too! Believe me, I have always and still do at times feel the same way. It's giant burden to bear, and I've tried to numb myself, and no matter how sedated I get, it doesn't go away. You might as well face it because if don't, you'll eventually have to anyway, so you might as well face it now."

He looked out the car windows at some women who were walking by. I sensed something happened to him last night while I was in paranormal performance mode.

I smiled and then said, "What did you do last night?"

There was a long pause. He attempted to speak but stopped. He did this a few times, but finally got out what he wanted to say. "I met a beautiful woman last night. We walked around for hours and then we talked for hours. There was lively chemistry between us. Then we started to stare into each other's eyes. I felt safe, so I started to reveal what I am. I showed her my soul, and she was in awe. Then she began to see, hear, and feel her own soul along with all of the obstructions that kept her from fully knowing herself as she really is. Once this happened, she became afraid and then asked, "Why did you do this?" Then she turned around and walked away. My soul retreated into the core of my body, and my heart sank. I've experienced this countless times with countless people throughout countless lives, that's why I prefer to go alone."

With that, he turned his head back up to the sky and looked out the window of the car. It was extraordinarily out of character for him to reveal his feelings like this. He almost always maintained a tough as nails disposition. I also could tell this affected him way more than he revealed to me.

We sat in silence for a long time, and then he repeated himself. "Because of situations like this and others, I've always, throughout many of my lifetimes, tried to numb myself, or intentionally subject myself to suffering, but it usually always makes everything worse…however, if I'm suffering, at least I know I'm alive."

The way he said it struck me like a right hook. It came from a desperate place of pain, of being hurt. It made me feel, *here is a man with all of God's love, yet he has been unable to share this love with another human being, for lifetimes.* I began wondering, *is divine love enough? Why isn't it enough for him?*

After that festival in Vermont, Dame and I both went into an introspective hibernation. We spent that fall, winter, and spring in a little rented cabin out in the woods of Clinton, Maine. Though it wasn't luxury by most people's standards, it was a big step from living in the arctic zone of Concord. Plus it had better heat, insulation, and running water, so it was luxury according to our standards.

I existed disproportionally in the spiritual realms much more than the human realms during that time period. I worked on balancing my perception through my awareness and by focusing on the source of energy that gave me the ability to be aware in the first place. The iridescent guides were always there to advise. I felt I had made good progress with personality corrections, which was great because I did evolve rapidly, but it was the calm before the storm. I had no idea how challenging life was about to get.

CHAPTER THIRTEEN

"Who Am I To Judge You?"

It was now summer in Clinton, and I was nineteen years old. It had been one full year since my awakening. The person I had become during this time was the polar opposite of the person I was before. From all outward appearances, my ego had become a wonderful servant of my soul, but inside, things weren't what they seemed. However, I had still managed to remove a lot of personality obstructions. These blockages once prevented my awareness of the universal intelligence that was constantly pulsing through my awareness.

Interestingly my intellect had grown in leaps and bounds. This occurred through the constant detailed conversations Dame and I shared in reference to what 'super-consciousness' could mean for the human species. I was able to understand, process, and explain concepts that before my awakening, I would have deemed unimaginable.

Even though we had been in an idle hibernation state, the inner and outer world had become a miraculous place to be. All was better than well, except for the part of my ego that wasn't content. It wasn't fully convinced that it wanted to be the full-time servant of an awakened soul.

Through all the conversations, I got to know the person that Damian was, in this life, very well. The thing that kept coming up though that always troubled me about him was how much he suffered as a human being. It wasn't just suffering that resulted from being a victim of circumstances. He intentionally went out of his way to create hardship for himself. To me, this seemed beyond hypocritical and in direct contrast to the exponentially super-advanced level of consciousness that he had attained. A level that allowed the energetic aspect of his existence to not only be enveloped by the infinite love of the universe but to also be so inexplicably linked to it so that he could channel and express it, directly through his physical being. Ironically he would frequently starve his body for long periods (fasting), *'accidentally'* get hurt and constantly deny himself of creature comforts.

I often questioned about why he did this. Sometimes he laughed it off and told me that suffering made him feel alive. Other times he became defensive and told me to mind my own business because it isn't anything that I'd understand. He was right. It wasn't something that I understood. How could someone who was able to shine so bright, in a way that had to be experienced to be believed, so recklessly create suffering in his own life?

Observing this sparked fear in me. I didn't want to end up like that. I had made myself an outcast and shut out by all the people in my life, leaving me feeling very alone, but he was at a whole other level with it. There was a wall around him so thick that it appeared as though no one would *ever* know the truth of who and what he really was. I had gotten close enough to him so that it not only allowed me a glimpse into the thick psychic barrier that surrounded this advanced spiritual entity disguised and living as a human being, but it allowed me to witness the complexities that living as such, has brought to him. In this regard, I was in way over my head. As free as he was spiritually, he was seemingly diabolically tortured in his human existence. Had he himself not come to terms with his reality? Was he losing faith in himself after being rejected by so many people throughout so many lives? Was he losing faith in God, Hashem, the light, Allah, Brahma, whatever human name anyone has ever called the source of all life, for putting him on this tiresome mission? Or was he losing faith in the source of all life for giving him the *choice* to embark on this mission, knowing the value of what is at stake no matter what choice he makes?

Whatever his dilemma, I knew his reasons were light-years beyond my level of understanding. I knew I might never know what deep knowing he lives every moment of every day, of every lifetime with, that causes him so much pain. But I thought I knew one thing—whatever it was that irked him, his inability to resolve it was the source of his perpetual suffering. My fear was that: if this was his *dharma* of being at such a highly evolved state, and since knowing that all life is connected, my own *dharma* might have such suffering in store for me. This seemed to be the direction my life was headed, but I just couldn't accept it. I knew I needed to be detached from these stories I was telling myself, but they were accompanied by a primal fear that made it difficult for me to do so.

However, I knew there was no turning back. I already became aware of way too much. Because of this, I wanted to temporarily numb myself to the intense responsibilities that I would inevitably face. More specifically, I wanted to sedate myself so that I could have one little break before I went to battle. A battle that Damian had fought for lifetimes… but how do I do that without suffering as he does?

I convinced Dame that we needed a dramatic change of pace, not forever, but just for a weekend. I wanted not just a terrestrial experience, but also a human experience and not just any human experience; I wanted a wild human experience.

The world-famous band, The Grateful Dead, was playing in New York City's Madison Square Garden. It was one of the last years they toured before Jerry Garcia passed away. At that time neither Damian nor I were fans of their music. But the counter-culture scene of it all definitely appealed to us.

We were told about this show by one of our cannabis contacts that interestingly was just an all-around terrible human being. A drug dealer/user, pimp, thief, criminal, you-name-it, this guy was into it. Before we decided to attend this show, our only interaction with him was to sell the little bit of cannabis we grew and collect the money for it. He was a stocky Frenchman with a short mullet and a nasally voice, who loved to fight. His name was Jimbo.

Why would we ever subject ourselves to a sixteen-hour round-trip car ride with someone like this? I really wanted a change of pace, a brief sedation from the realms of super-consciousness. I wanted to get high, or at least see if drugs were still able to get me high. Not to mention I was going stir-crazy from being so cut-off from the civilized world. On top of all of this, Damian actually wanted an adventure, and he felt like *slaying some dragons* in the underworld. So off to battle we went.

Within the first hour driving out of Maine with Jimbo, I knew we were in for a hell ride. All he talked about was what any degenerate of his stature talked about—druggery, thuggery, and skullduggery. Every other moment while telling his maniacal stories, he took his eyes off the wheel of his muscle car as we sped down the highway to look at

Damian in the passenger seat, or me in the back seat. Wild-eyed, wide-grinned, and with ample spit flying from his lips, he wanted to make sure we heard every word he said. I feared we would crash before even crossing the New York state border. It was a rock and roller coaster ride from hell right out of the get-go.

When we did arrive in Manhattan, we parked in a garage next to Madison Square Garden and began checking out the scene. Not more than ten minutes after we started checking it out, Jimbo got some LSD for the three of us to share. After ingesting more than a few hits, we were out of the parking garage and out on to the streets. Just the placebo effect from eating the acid was enough to not only make me feel high; it was enough to trigger my guilty conscience. Being as hypersensitive as I was, and eating acid during the day in New York City was nothing short of serious intensity. The iridescent guides, although not impressed with my choices, still surrounded me in the protection of the heavy questionable vibes being emitted from every person, place, and thing all around me.

As the LSD began kicking in, the three of us sat at the base of a tall building and watched hundreds of deadheads intermingling with hundreds of New York City street goers. Seeing businessmen, *normal* people, and the homeless interacting with the circus act scene of the Grateful Dead affirmed this was the wild human experience that I sought to find. To trip in such a place is eye-opening insanity.

Damian, Jimbo and I all started trading sketchy looks back and forth to each other. We were starting to get really high, to the point that we thought staying out on the street wasn't a good idea. We decided we wanted to hide out in the parking garage until after the acid peaked so that we'd be able to better compose ourselves. We were beginning to freak out!

Just as we decided to walk off a well-dressed normal-looking guy with short brown hair, glasses, and a geeky voice approached us.

"Excuse me," he said, "how are you guys doing?"

The three of us traded sketchy looks, while simultaneously thinking, *what the fuck does this clown want?*

I just looked at him and snarled, "Yeah, we're all right."

He had a huge grin on his face. Then he presented an invitation to us. "My name is John. I'm an English teacher. On the twenty-sixth floor of this building we're standing in front of I have a classroom with sixty immigrants from all over the world. They have noticed the streets are filled with many colorful people and they're wondering what's going on. Would you guys be interested in explaining to them what this is all about?"

At this point, the three of us were tripping so hard that it was becoming difficult to maintain any semblance of composure. Now we were really freaking out!

I looked at Damian. It looked as if he had no idea what to say to this guy; then I looked at Jimbo. He was shaking his head left to right while silently mouthing the words, *NO WAY!*

Suddenly Damian answered with, "Sure, we'll do it."

Holy shit, I thought, *here we go!*

The next thing I know I'm following Damian and this English teacher into an elevator with Jimbo in tow. Instead of going to hide out in a parking garage because we were tripping so hard, we were now going to speak to a classroom full of people about the Grateful Dead scene while completely losing our minds. Yikes!

At this point, the three of us looked like a circus act in and of ourselves. Damian and I had giant dreadlocks wrapped with beads, crystals, and other trinkets. We wore torn-up jeans and jean jackets ornamented with patches and other peculiarities. Our necks, wrists, and fingers were covered with colorful necklaces, bracelets, and rings. We looked like hippie elf frontiersmen.

Jimbo looked nothing like the two of us. But whenever he attended an event like this, he wore a costume he'd dubbed his *'colors.'* They were a fluorescent-colored tie-dyed hooded sweatshirt and pants. It was reminiscent of something a clown would actually wear. We were a motley crew.

As the elevator opened on the twenty-sixth floor, we walked down a hallway that led to a door. John, the English teacher, opened it, and sure enough, there they were—a classroom filled with wide-eyed immigrants who obviously were overly amused by their first glance of us.

John set up some chairs in the front of the room, and we sat down in them. He then went on to explain to his students that what they saw in the streets were the fans of one of the most successful touring band that has ever existed -The Grateful Dead. He then went on to say that the fans of the band were amongst the most loyal of any band there was, and that was who the three of us were: loyal fans. Then there was awkward silence as he expected us to start talking about how grateful or excited we were to be there, but none of us said anything. It was getting uncomfortable for everyone.

Finally, I broke the silence with, "Actually, we're not really fans of the Dead. We just came for the scene because it's so interesting."

Dame jumped in with, "We live a very reclusive, monastic type of lifestyle. We came here to observe human nature and hopefully uncover the common bond that fuses us all together."

One of the students said, "Yes, that's very similar to how we live in Russia!"

An Asian student answered with, "Yes, us too!"

Other students also agreed.

Jimbo decided to add his two cents (although it was certainly worth less than that). With his thick and nasally tone, he spat out "Yeah, well I don't live like these guys, and I don't believe what they believe. No one lives like that where we're from. They've completely lost their minds. It's not reality, and neither is this. I only dress like this when I come to shows. I don't dress like this in real life. I came here for one reason and one reason only…to party hard bro!"

Everyone in the room started booing him. I fell out of my chair and on to the floor because I was laughing so hard. Then the crowds booing instantly turned into laughter as they watched me in hysterics on the ground.

Damian straightened his back and launched into offensive mode against Jimbo's superficial remarks. "Actually, I believe what you call reality is quite insignificant when compared to the rest of the universe; human beings going against the laws of nature for their own selfishness and greed? From a rational perspective, it doesn't seem like your temporary version of reality would have much longevity."

The students all started to cheer. This triggered Jimbo to go right into his version of an offense.

"Ha! Yeah, whatever bro, there you go talking about all of your cosmic hippie shit! Who cares about what's going on in outer space? It has nothin' to do with life on Earth. All that matters here is getting fucked up and havin' a good time, and that's I came to do, so don't waste my time bro!"

Again, all the students started booing and laughing in unison, and Damian used this to his advantage. "Well Jimbo, it sounds like everyone here agrees with me a lot more than they agree with you, so which reality is more real? Mine or yours?"

The cheering went through the roof as most everyone stood up for a full standing ovation. I was high as a kite, but I recognized this as a turning point. *Immigrants with broken English agreeing with and rapturously applauding the universal truth's Damian had just spoken? Wow, hope is alive and well,* I thought.

But by now, Jimbo was hot. His blushed face was red with embarrassment, but it quickly morphed into anger. He stood on his feet and started yelling at everyone, "All right, bro" (he addressed the audience as bro). "You guys really want to know what this scene's all about?" It was so quiet you could hear a pin drop. "After this class is over go outside and talk to the hippie freaks you see everywhere and ask them to share a tab of paper with you, then you'll know what's really going on, bro."

After that, there was dead silence. People were looking at each other, but no one knew what to say.

By now Damian, Jimbo and I were tripping so hard that the line between fantasy and reality was blurred for all three of us. As I looked around the room, I noticed the students were now looking more like space aliens than immigrants. I began feeling like the classroom way up in this building was not a classroom at all. It was a spaceship flying through the air, and John, the English teacher, was its captain. He finally took notice that the three of us were on the moon and that it was probably time to get us out of there.

With a wild look in his eye, he said, "Class! Like I said earlier, the Grateful Dead has some of the most devoted fans on the planet and sometimes you never know who those fans are!" Then he unbuttoned his dress shirt to reveal a tie-dyed *steal-your-face* Grateful Dead t-shirt underneath. The classroom erupted into wild applause. By now, my face was melting. I had to get out of this spaceship that was parked on a skyscraper before it took off for a galaxy far, far away.

"Thank you, everybody. This has been more fun than you could imagine," I said and then headed for the door. Dame and Jimbo were right behind me.

"Holy shit! What was that" I said to my two cosmonaut companions once we made it into the transporter room—I mean the elevator.

"Oh my God, bro, I'm tripping so hard! Get me the fuck out of here," Jimbo cried.

All I knew was I had to get somewhere to hide out until I came down. The city that never sleeps had awoken to an entirely different dimension, and it was a bizarrely intense one at that.

We made it into the parking garage, but by then we were so far gone that we had no idea where we parked. The effects of the acid were so strong that even in broad daylight, I couldn't see very far in front of me. The sights, sounds, and scents of this crazy counter-culture atmosphere all blended together into a kaleidoscope of sensual psychedelia. I began experiencing vivid audio/visual synesthesia where colors are *heard,* and sound is *seen.* Then there were voices laughing and talking at me, while strangers' hands were grabbing my body. I was so high that I had no option but to just completely *let go.* The kaleidoscope of psychedelic sensuality became my exit out of this world and my entrance into the next. My soul went beyond time and space to rest in the oneness of it all that is while this lysergic chemical worked its way through my body.

Later in the evening, I started coming to. I could feel my body. Wow, I'm human! I didn't open my eyes yet. I just felt around with my hands; there was some fabric, maybe a shirt or a dress or something, a baseball, a tire. A tire? I opened my eyes to find I was in the trunk of someone's car. *What the fuck?* The trunk hood was open, but I had no idea whose car this was.

As I lay there, spun-out from the acid hangover, I looked for the motivation to get out of the back of this car. *Oh man. I am wasted. I feel so tired…Hmm; it sure is noisy out there. I wonder why there is so much yelling?*

When I arose to my feet, I was shocked by what I saw. Police in riot gear and DEA agents were in every direction I looked. Twenty feet from where I stood a blond dreadlocked girl was trying to get away from a cop who was trying to handcuff her. As she struggled to get away, the cop pulled out a can of pepper spray and shot it in her face. This caused her to let out blood-curdling screams. Out of nowhere, her boyfriend came running at full speed, jumping onto the cop, knocking him into the pavement with a thud. As they wrestled, police with clubs showed up and started beating him. Similar scenarios were playing out all around me.

I ran over to the edge of the parking garage to assess the scene in the street. There were cop cars, police on horses and on foot swarming all over. It was a full-scale raid.

As I stood there at the edge, still reeling from the acid trying to decide what my next move would be, I watched an NYPD patrol car pull into the parking garage I was in. As he pulled in, the gate in front of him had not fully opened yet. The blue lights on the top of his car smashed into the partially opened gate, ripping them right off the car. Then all kinds of on-lookers erupted into deep guttural laughter in unison. This caused the police to become even more aggressive.

As a result of everything happening, a riot broke out in the street. Lots of skinheads and punks were involved with rocks, bottles and who knows what flying through the air. I watched a bottle smash a cop's head as he sat on top of his horse. He fell on the ground. *I gotta get the hell out of here,* I thought, bearing witness to all of this.

By now, I had returned to earth enough to remember where Jimbo's car was. I ran over there, but neither Jimbo nor Damian was around. By now, I was getting ready to scale the side of the parking garage to get away, but I took a few deep breaths calmed myself down and looked at it objectively. What was I worried about? I didn't have any drugs or pot on me, and clearly, this was most likely a drug raid. *Ok,* I thought. *I'm just going to walk right out of here and as far away from the violence as possible.* And that's exactly what I did.

I walked down many flights of stairs and out onto the street. Holding my head down, I walked like I had blinders on, making no eye contact with anyone. My plan was to walk into the front door of a store with the goal of exiting its back door onto a street without chaos. But a cop interrogating me interrupted my plan. After a lot of questions and a thorough frisking, he walked me to a barricade and let me go.

After all that, I walked to a small park that was five or six blocks away, sat down on a bench, and considered what my options were. I decided I had had enough of this wild human experience and was ready to head back into the woods of Maine, even though I had only been gone for the day. I also had no idea where Damian and Jimbo were, but I needed to find them.

A half-hour in that park was all that I could take. Being in New York City, I was already out of my element. Being there while tripping as hard as I was made me feel like a bioluminescent deep-sea fish out of unexplored ocean depths. The shadows all around spooked me, so I started walking.

Once I got near Madison Square Garden, off in the distance, I saw Damian and Jimbo walk into a bar on the side of the street. I walked in to find them. The bar was lit up. It was a microcosm of the Grateful Dead scene. Carlos Santana was blasting over the sound system, and everyone was dancing and partying.

Jimbo saw me and came running over. "Bro, are you all right," he asked.

"Yeah," I yelled over the music. "I woke up in the trunk of someone's car!"

"Listen, Bro." His eyes were shifting back and forth. He kept looking around with extreme paranoia. "Listen, we gotta get out of here, there's cops everywhere!"

Paranoia aside, he was actually right. They were everywhere.

"So what are you thinking," I asked inquisitively. By now, Damian had joined us.

"I bought some acid, Bro. If you help me get it out of here, I'll share it with you guys." Jimbo said with paranoid intrigue.

Considering what he just told me, I asked, "What do you mean by 'get it out of here'?"

"Bro, I don't know if you've noticed, but the cops are everywhere."

"Yeah, I've noticed."

"I'll give you this shit, Bro. You leave now and take a Greyhound. Dame and I will pick you up in Boston tomorrow morning, and we'll all head to the show." (The Dead were headed to Boston next).

Through the desperation of wanting to get out of this city and the desire for extra cash, I decided to accept this knowingly preposterous offer. It was absurd because on top of the fact that I was still tripping hard, visually I stood out like the poster boy for hippie drug use with my dreadlocked elf frontiersman looks.

On a whim, I said, "Okay, I'll leave now and see you guys tomorrow."

Damian had no input for this plan whatsoever. The three of us walked to the closest bus station. There was a bus leaving right away, and it arrived at Boston's South Station at roughly 3:30 in the morning. I bought a ticket, took the LSD that was wrapped in plastic, stuffed in under my shirt and boarded the bus.

"We'll leave now, and we'll be waiting for you before you even arrive," Jimbo tried assuring me.

"All right. See you guys in a few hours."

As I took my seat, I started wondering what I had gotten myself into. It was a careless not-at-all-thought-out plan. I was still tripping out of my gourd. The iridescent guides and all my psychic awareness began surfacing. My energy field seemed to repel weird transient spirits who were unknowingly trapped between worlds. Being so high made my communication with the guides spotty at best. I was beginning to feel claustrophobic. *Holy shit…it's gonna be a long strange trip.*

When the bus finally arrived at South Station, I couldn't wait to get off of it. Like all the other groggy people, I shuffled my way off as soon as they opened the door. Once outside, I looked around for Damian and Jimbo, but they were nowhere to be found. *Dammit,* I thought.

Now I was starting to get paranoid. The few people on the bus with me had all cleared out of the station, and now the place was completely empty, aside from a few orderlies who occasionally wandered by. This left the giant pink elephant in the room, me, sticking out like a sore thumb. I wasn't sure how much jail time I would be facing were I to be caught with this acid, but it would've certainly been a lot.

I found a little bench snuggled into a corner, sat down on it, and shut my eyes. It hadn't even been twenty-four hours since I left Maine and I had already felt like I just survived through a war. I decided to lie down on the bench to see if I could just catch a little bit of sleep. I opened my right eye, just to make sure I was still alone. I didn't want to be surprised by any police. Out of the corner of my eye, I saw some thuggish-looking guys off in the distance, but I paid no attention to them and tried to relax.

Just as I started letting my muscles soften, I heard a withered voice, "Sonny, whatcha doin'?"

It was a little old man. I sat up and looked at him. I wasn't sure if I was seeing him clearly or if it was just the acid, but his face looked mangled.

Suddenly his voice started to boom. "Sonny, if I was you I'd keep a close eye on my money. You know what I mean? I'd keep a close eye on my money!"

As he was saying this, he kept slapping his pant pocket to give me the visual indication of a wallet. Since I didn't say a word, he probably wondered if I spoke English. Out of exhaustion, I just sneered my lip and made a low rumbling, growling noise as if to acknowledge, "Ok, thanks."

He then disappeared as quickly as he appeared. *What the hell was that about* I thought as I lay back down.

Not more than sixty seconds after I lay back down, the distant thuggish guys I saw out of the corner of my eye came walking toward me really fast. *Oh fuck,* I thought, *they're gonna roll me."*

These guys were big, mean-looking; gold chains…perfect representations of stereotypical ghetto thugs. As they got within ten feet, they split apart with two coming on my left and the other on my right. *What am I supposed to do? Guides, please help me!*

Like a volcano shooting molten lava rocks thousands of feet into the air, I burst forth with emotion. A force came through me that was not only fearless, but it was comprised of the desire to inject itself into my muggers. With fire in my eyes and a voice sounding like I had been gargling broken glass and ignited gasoline, I jumped to my feet and spit words like bullets that were charged with 'the fear of God.'

"Bring it on! I've been to the other side, and I know what I've got coming! If y'all had any idea what you were facing, you'd be on your knees begging for forgiveness every moment until the curtain closes! Kill me now and watch me smile until I'm gone because the difference between you and me is that I know what I've got coming and I know that you don't!"

They all stepped back. None of them knew what to do. With the looks they were trading back and forth, I knew my reaction wasn't part of the plan.

"Let's go," one of them said. Then they split.

That was close, I thought.

After that incident, I was so exhausted that I actually fell asleep on that bench. At 7:20 a.m. Damian and Jimbo awakened me.

"Where the fuck have you guys been? I was almost killed here last night!" I was pissed off.

Jimbo's reply was, "They searched every car in that garage, Bro. We didn't get out of there until 3 a.m.! C'mon. Let's get the fuck out of here."

But the trouble had only just begun…

CHAPTER FOURTEEN

You Can Run, But You Can't Hide

After leaving the bus station, we soon made it to the area in town where the deadheads were all waiting for the night's show. The scene at these concerts always replicated a microcosm of what I imagined the hippie counter-culture of the '60s to look like. Of course, that was only at face value. While most went because they were fans of the music, an overwhelming number of non-fans went in an attempt to milk concertgoers for money or drugs.

I was strung out from the crazy day and night before. My brain, like a sponge, was still saturated with LSD - making it hard to relax. All my psychic awareness surrounding these other dimensions that I had been steeped in for the past year was going haywire. I really wanted to sedate my conflicted mind and build up a thick egoic barrier to deflect my awareness of all these energetic realms, at least just this one time, or at least until I made it back home to the woods.

So while Jimbo and Damian were checking into a hotel room, I decided to walk into the Grateful Dead parking lots, to see what I could find. While my illuminated soul put on a protective shield, my ego was on the prowl and up to no good. The inner conflict I carried was in full battle mode as I walked through this over-indulgent and hedonistic playground.

While looking for trouble, I saw a guy with a look on his face. It was a look that said, *I feel so good right now that nothing in this world can bother me.* Whatever drug he was on, I wanted to be on as well. I started talking to him, and upon closer examination; I could tell that whatever it was that he was on, he had completely numbed himself into oblivion. In a moment of desperate unconsciousness, I just came right out and said, "Whatever you are on, I want some!"

My words only so very slightly startled him as he suspiciously eye-balled me. He realized I was sincere. So he cracked a huge toothless smile and said, "You're no cop," and then started laughing. He gave me a small bag of white powder. I paid $15.00 for it. He told me to snort just a little bit.

I saw a row of port-a-potties and made a beeline for them. Just before I opened the door to the portable toilet, the iridescent guides let me know they were watching. I started second-guessing myself. *What was I doing? Why would I want to put something so horrible into my body?* But then I convinced myself against my clear better judgment. I just needed a little break from the intense frequencies that were permeating my awareness at all times, because I was becoming confused by how to live in this material world and countless other dimensions at the same time – I didn't know how to integrate it so that I was balanced. *Really, I needed a break from this intense energy-based being animating a human form that I had become.* I demanded that the iridescent guides allow me this one break from it all. I was only going to do this once. In their own way, they were upset with me.

I closed the port-a-potty door, took out the small bag, dumped some of it into my hand, and then snorted it. I walked out of the port-a-potty and down the sidewalk. Within a few minutes, I felt the rush of opiates flooding my brain for the first time. After a few more minutes, I realized I was floored, completely wasted. It was so strong that I began feeling dizzy. Then I threw up all over the sidewalk with people everywhere, grossed out by the sight of me doing this.

The floodgates of my stomach had opened, seeming to release buckets of vomit. I pulled myself together, took a few more steps, and then did it again. Concertgoers all around me were rushing to get out of the way. I repeated this process a few more times until all the contents of my stomach had been expelled, and after that, I continued to dry heave. After about a half-hour of this, I started to relax. The first thing I noticed was that all the psychic transmissions that I normally received and emitted, seemingly had been shut down. For one brief moment, I felt relieved. It felt that for once I had numbed myself into oblivion. The iridescent guides appeared to be gone, and so was any thought related to the energetic aspects of my soul. The thing most noticeable to me was that I was very grounded and aware of my physical human body. It was the first time in a very long time when being 'human' had felt so good. I had spent so much time since my mid-teens trying to get out of my body and then after my awakening, living in the spirit realms - that doing heroin was the first time in years that I'd ever felt so grounded.

I could still see all of the auras and energies being emitted by everything, but I no longer cared about it. Then I realized I had a smile on my face. It wasn't just a smile; it was an ear-to-ear face-splitting smile that said, *I feel so good right now that nothing in this world bothers me.* It was the exact same smile the guy I scored the H from was wearing.

I lay back on the dirty, filthy sidewalk and enjoyed watching people walk by. Every now and then I would dry heave and as sick as it sounds, I almost even enjoyed that because it was such a grounding biological function.

I've done it, I thought. In these moments, I was numb to the world.

I was only partially surprised when Damian appeared out of nowhere with his hand open telling me to "give it to him." At first, I thought he was going to throw it away, but then I realized he had seen the smile on my face. I gave him the little bag with the rest of the H in it. As I gave it to him, I thought *Most of my suffering has been in this life. He's been suffering forever for all I know. Why wouldn't he want to do this?*

Damian took off with it and a couple of hours later, after I was able to walk with some stability, I found him under a park bench passed out. There were no frequencies or any signs of vitality this time though. There was only numbness like a dead zone in a polluted ocean. It was a desolation of bliss.

Now we had both done it: a complete 180-degree turn from super-consciousness to near unconsciousness. I had dumbed myself into oblivion while Damian had found another way to suffer in this life. While the next few hours were spent in a state of blissful stupor, I had the thought that for me, *all that matters right now, is the way I feel.* I needed a break from it all. Unbeknownst to me at the time, I had opened the door to tremendous suffering in the years to come. But in those moments of being high, I was clueless about even that. I could've cared less about the future.

As evening came around, we decided that we were going to drive back to Maine. Jimbo, who suddenly claimed to have standards, refused to try the heroin and thus was sober enough to drive.

As we were walking back to the car, we saw someone we knew from Maine. He and a big group of others were going back as well. He told us they were all going to a big gathering in Maine's western mountains and that we were invited. Since we had nothing going on and were still high, we decided to go with the flow.

The ride from the Dead show to Maine, aside from Jimbo talking to himself, was spent in complete silence. Neither Damian nor I said a word to each other, and neither of us wanted to say anything. We both knew what we had done and while we didn't care at all, paradoxically at the same time we cared deeper than we could ever imagine. We allowed the dark side to take over, and we both did it in each other's presence. I justified it by thinking it was a one-time thing. I also didn't judge Damian for it at all. Even though I had spent years learning and meditating with him, I also knew that I was the one person alive who remotely understood the burden he bore. Having such a profound spiritual connection and living in a world where humans are deeply imprisoned by their egos is a lonely place for a being like him to live, and now it was for me too. Though I now had an idea of what *knowing what you really are for lifetimes might be like,* in all reality, I knew I was just an amateur. Discovering it in one lifetime was hard enough, countless lifetimes was incomprehensible. It was a complex situation in a world that was seemingly even more so. And at that point, the simplicity of it all eluded me...

When we finally arrived at the gathering in Maine, we were delighted to find a big group of people welcoming us with big smiles. Everyone was high as a kite, but so were we. Because of this, the energetic aspects of my consciousness had become temporarily disarmed. There were no spirit guides giving me warnings or advice. The visible energy fields and varying audible frequencies being emitted from everything in my awareness had been dulled to where it was no longer my primary focus. Even though I was drugged, I felt like a normal human being without the social anxiety that came from being overly protective of my psychic self and its influence on those who weren't ready to confront that part of their own consciousness.

The guy who owned the house was a lunatic, but flamboyantly charismatic. He had long brown hair and was actually wearing a purple wizard outfit with big embroidered stars sewn into it. His name was Ward, and I could see a peculiar glare in his eye. He immediately honed right in on Damian and me, offering us a mirror with lines of cocaine on it. We both did it without thinking twice. As we sat down and started talking with him, it didn't take long for the cocaine high to kick in. It was the first time I had done it since living in Florida a few years earlier. Ward then took out a bundle of ten bags of heroin and asked if we'd like to try it. We politely accepted his offer. After we snorted the heroin, we sat around with him and thirty of his friends talking, laughing and snorting cocaine. It was the complete opposite of the type of lifestyle I had been used to living.

"What are you guys all about," Ward asked.

I looked over at Damian, but he gave me no eye contact, so I said in a joking but semi-serious way, "You wouldn't believe me if I told you!"

He was like, "What do you mean?"

Then Damian chimed in with, "We just fight the good fight while living in hell brother."

Ward nodded, then agreed. "Yup! It sure is hell out there!"

Jimbo had nothing of substance to add to the conversation. As we sat there higher than satellites orbiting the planet, I began having tremendous waves of guilt crash into me. *What was I doing,* I thought. Doing hard drugs like this is completely insane and in absolute opposition to the laws of higher consciousness that had become my primary state of perception. I felt my face get white, and then I just kind of shut down inside of myself.

"Are you okay," an attractive young woman said to me as she touched my arm. I looked into her eyes and saw serenity, but as our stares locked for a few moments, the serenity that I saw became chaos.

"Excuse me, " I said as I jumped up onto my feet and ran outside. Once I made it out the door, and my feet actually touched the earth, I collapsed onto the ground. Tears started streaming from my eyes. My inner thoughts started racing. *What have I done? What is this completely insane rollercoaster life I am living: Sky-high super-consciousness to the devilish realms of hard drugs?* Then, as these poisons were seeping deep in my stomach, I began feeling violently nauseous. The next thing I knew I was on my hands and knees, dry heaving so hard it felt like my stomach was going to emerge from my mouth. My eyes were bulging out of their sockets. My whole being was swollen and toxic. Everything hurt. The numbness of the opiates was not enough to mask this type of pain. It was light-years beyond the physical. It wasn't only my body that was rejecting these drugs; it was my soul. It felt like vampire blood had begun streaming through my system. There is nothing on Earth that can numb the pain of a newly awakened soul whose body had been self-poisoned. That is, nothing other than generation after generation of unconsciousness and ignorance, much like the collective condition of the human species. Damian was right when he said that trying to numb it only makes everything worse. It felt like an entire galaxy was dying inside of me.

As I lay on the ground in this state, I began to weep in a way I never had. I felt human sorrow I never knew. I had already experienced severe soul sorrow that transformed into a beauty beyond all of my knowing. I also knew that I was evolving, metamorphosing into something else, an expression of energy more beautiful than I was able to comprehend through my intellect. But I had poisoned myself to the degree that I had at least temporarily halted this inner alchemical process. The tears that I shed felt like blood weeping from the marrow of my bones. The sorrow I could feel was like that which I had always felt coming from the Earth. It was like the sorrow of being mortally wounded by the ones she has so graciously given life to - us. Similarly, just as the Earth has been wounded by her own inhabitants—the stewards who she herself gives life to—so to has my soul been wounded by my own ego—the ego that should be taking care of the soul and body that gives it expression. This was not a wound inflicted by accident either. It was a choice I made. Just like we as a species choose directly or indirectly, to inflict the Earth with our destruction, the motherly source of life that nourished our individual and collective physicality.

While I lay there weeping after this cathartic episode, I felt a warm hand rubbing my face and another on my forehead. I turned to see the same girl, who inside the house a few minutes earlier, asked if I was okay. Her name was Florence, and she kept whispering, "Shhhh," as she rubbed my face and forehead. All of the tears and mucus that I had excreted all over my face and neck didn't bother her one bit. She just continued to lovingly and graciously comfort me.

After fifteen minutes of this, she helped me onto my feet. Then she took my hand, and we walked towards the house. She walked in front of me, and the sway of her hips was so graceful, yet suggestive of her mood and intent.

We walked into and through the house of wild and wasted people. She kept turning around to reveal the flash of her bright eyes while gently biting the side of her lip. I was dumbfounded because I felt so unsexy being covered with drool and dried tears. I didn't understand what she saw in me during those moments?

We went into the bathroom, and she locked the door. Once inside, she helped me take my shirt off and then started washing my face with a wet towel. It was such a polar shift from feeling mortally wounded. I felt like she was an emissary of all that was good, sent to help mend my wounds. After cleaning my face, she started kissing me. I was surprised, but I went with the flow. It was the first time that I had been sexually aroused in a long time. I was on fire. As she was kissing me, she began rubbing my crotch. My heart was pounding against my chest. The temperature in that bathroom was rising. We both began devouring each other with our tongues and then she all at once stopped kissing me, turned around, and began to forcibly vomit into the toilet. Watching her do this, in turn, triggered the same response in me. I went over to the bathtub and bent over the side as I began successively dry heaving. It was so absurdly anticlimactic that it became comical!

After we both pulled ourselves together, we started laughing crazily. I guess we couldn't expect much while completely smacked out on heroin. The whole episode was morbidly funny, and it did kill the mood, but after a little while, I began to feel that there wasn't anything even morbidly funny about it. It was actually terribly pathetic. I did my best to not feel guilty about it by continuously telling myself that after we left this party house in the mountains, I would get back on track and serve the needs of my soul. But I still had a nagging feeling that I had done some serious celestial damage to the core of my perceptive faculties.

As the night went into the wee hours of the morning I finally fell asleep from all the heroin in my system. I woke the next morning to see Ward passing around a mirror with more lines of H cut up on it. I didn't want to do it, but they passed it to me while close to ten people watched. Feeling a little pressured, I snorted a line, and the madness started all over again. Damian and I stayed at this house and did this for almost two weeks. Jimbo took off after a couple of days, but we stayed. Ward had what seemed like a never-ending supply of drugs. It was complete insanity. Another girl cuddled up to me, but we were so high that neither of us was very stimulating to each other.

Someone handed me a guitar because I mentioned the night before that I played, but my creativity was gone, and my fingers wouldn't move on the fretboard at all. A few people started laughing because it sounded so bad.

"I thought that heroin enhanced creativity," someone jokingly mentioned. I had always thought it did as well. But as I came to find out over the next few years, that statement couldn't have been any further from the truth for me or anyone else I knew who became an addict. Every drop of creativity in me evaporated as did any knowledge or care about super consciousness. When I was high, I felt like I could relate to people instead of feeling like a biblical abomination of a preacher constantly being stoned by naysayers shouting blasphemy.

The only reason that we left the heroin den house after two weeks was because the seemingly never-ending supply of drugs did actually come to an end. In school, we had all heard stories about how addictive heroin was, but between knowing the hypocrisy of the system and none of us being exposed to heroin addicts growing up, we didn't know firsthand how addictive it really was. The entire group of us at the heroin den did know one thing though, once we ran out of it, we all definitely wanted more.

A car full of us took a ride to Massachusetts to visit one of Ward's contacts, a guy called Grandpa. He was a Vietnam vet who had been addicted to heroin since the war. It was the first time I had ever seen anyone shoot up. Our clan was only snorting it. Florence grabbed my hand in horror as we watched this guy shoot a speedball of heroin and cocaine into his arm. The amount he injected was quite substantial compared to the amateur amounts that our group was doing. After the contents of the syringe had been emptied into the scarred remains of what Grandpa had left of his veins, his body started convulsing, and then he nodded out. Ten minutes later, he awoke, and then he put crack rocks in a few pipes to share with all of us.

Our group from Maine stayed there for hours snorting heroin and smoking crack while pooling all of our money together so we could buy as much heroin as possible to take home. Once one of Grandpa's runners returned with all of the heroin, we drove back to Maine. This trip was the first of many.

After a month of spending most of our time at the heroin den, Damian and I were so addicted that even one day without it was unbearable. We started selling a lot of pot so that we could afford our habit. This was the beginning of a downward spiral in my life that continued for years.

During the first month, when I started using, I could snort a quarter of a bag and be high for twelve to fourteen hours. Six months into the addiction Damian and I were each doing massive amounts every day. It was outrageous how quickly we both became addicted to it. I was in way too deep.

Due to the volume of our marijuana sales, we were able to maintain high volume habits. We used as much as we desired. It was such a diametrical, bi-polar extreme to go from living as super-conscious monks to feeding ravenous junked-out monkeys living on our backs. Both lifestyles were characterized by the pursuit of seeking joy; only the latter was temporary, destructive, and above all incarcerating, while the former had the potential to forever transcend all that was temporary. I would come to find out it was clearly my "dharma" to go into the darkness of human despair after having been immersed in such beautiful soul light. It was the only I could understand the value of super consciousness. And, it was the only way for me to understand how easily a state of awareness deemed as super consciousness could be lost. Not just for me, but for all. But, by choosing this route, I had set myself up for a world of pain.

The effects I immediately and continuously noticed, as the result of flooding my system with heroin was nothing shy of extreme toxicity. It altered my entire body chemistry to the point where my metabolic functioning began to dramatically malfunction. Most of my bodily functions became muddled, but the desire to constantly get high took precedence over the sickness that it left in its wake.

It didn't take long for our friend Ward who aside from his addiction was actually a decent guy to get arrested and end up in prison. He spent many years on that bid only to eventually re-emerge and then go back for another ten years. And it was all because he was a drug addict. Everyone who we were involved with during that time period, even the ones who weren't severe addicts either died, went to jail, stayed addicts to this day or became so psychologically messed up that they were unable to function in any productive way.

Once Ward was in prison, Damian and I began leading group trips to Grandpa's twice a week. A different group came down with us each time. We'd spend most of the day smoking crack. Then we'd drive home with as much heroin as we could afford. Our appetites were so insatiable that it always left us taking the long trip from Maine to Massachusetts hurried and recklessly.

One day while in Maine, we ran out of heroin. Our car was leaking transmission fluid all over the place. We drove it down to Grandpa's anyway. It was a two-and-a-half-hour drive. Smoke billowed out of the engine compartment as the leaking transmission fluid poured all over the heated engine block the entire way down, creating an unnoticeable scene. Every car we drove past stared at us in disbelief. We were so possessed by our addiction that we just didn't care.

Another time during the dead of winter, we were so desperate to get down there, that no risks were too great to take. The roads were completely iced over, and it was snowing. I was going way too fast in a frantic frenzy to get our fix, and I lost control of the car on I-95 in Massachusetts. The car did a complete 360-degree circle and then straightened itself out on an eight-lane highway with traffic all around. I saw the horror in the eyes of people driving beside us as they thought we were going to collide with them. Then a couple of miles down the road we got pulled over. I had drugs under my seat. The state trooper made everyone get out of the car while he searched it. The only place he didn't look was under my seat. I would have certainly gone to jail for that. I used to wonder if that would have stopped my addiction, but that obviously wasn't my fate. Much darker things than going to prison in Massachusetts were coming my way.

CHAPTER FIFTEEN

I'd Rather Rise in Love, Than Fall in Love

The lease on our cottage in Clinton came to an end. A friend told us about a cheap cottage for rent in Hallowell, Maine. Hallowell was a little hippie town, filled with galleries and bars. The cottage was a dingy little place covered with lead paint both inside and out, but it was an appropriate place for us to hide from the world and feed our raging and ravenous habits.

Next-door was a man who became an interesting friend and a great inspiration to me, someone I would come to adore at the deepest levels of my being. He was a singer/songwriter/comedian who in 1963 was the second most famous person in America. His name was Abbot Vaughn Meader. In 1963 he released an album called *The First Family*. He was able to do a spot-on impersonation of John F. Kennedy's voice. The album sold 7.5 million copies, which at the time set a new record even the Beatles hadn't broken. He was propelled to meteoric fame for about a year, but after Kennedy was assassinated, Abbot's career was over. People during that time period said that it seemed like a ghost followed him everywhere he went. By today's standards that album would be considered ultra-conservative comedy, but nonetheless, it was a true masterpiece. Whenever I listen to it, I can feel how important it was in its day and it is still staggeringly relevant even today.

Abbot experienced a level of fame that very few ever do, but then it all completely crashed overnight. It was an intense bi-polar wake-up call that left him questioning the meaning of his own life. He gave away everything he owned, including all of his gold records, and headed to California with the hopes of finding himself after his career abruptly ended.

After being in California for a while, he had what he described as a religious experience, though for all his intellect, he wasn't able to describe it with any clarity. He struggled with the roller coaster ride of his life and ended up becoming drunk and destitute in Hallowell, Maine with his wife, Melissa. Although Melissa refused to live directly with him, they shared an upstairs/downstairs apartment building where she lived on the top; "Ab" was on the bottom.

Dame and I were terrible addicts by that point, shells of the beings we used to be. All the energetic vibrancy I had acquired was now flickering like a lone candle in the wind. And the place we were living in was so messy that it looked like a bomb went off. Disharmony abounded.

Abbot's personality was iconic. He was truly a historical relic who was filled with wise words and unbelievable stories. We had epic conversations about every topic imaginable. We eventually formed a friendship that was built to last.

After becoming close to him, he began expressing concern for our well-being. He used to say he saw so much potential in us, and he couldn't understand why we would want to risk dying every day at such a young age. His concerns were appreciated and well placed, but were in deep. Even a few hours without a fix was too long for us to wait.

One day Abbot asked if I could get him some LSD, for which I said yes. I got him ten hits of fresh acid, and he put it in his freezer. Abbot spent most nights of the week at a bar in Hallowell where he would perform for the locals. A few days after I got him the acid, he went to this bar and got roaring drunk, as he often did.

The next morning his wife Melissa showed up at my door frenzied and in panic. She told me Abbot had lost his mind. He was screaming and yelling and mumbling all kinds of gibberish and she didn't know what to do about it. I asked her to calm down and said that I would check in on him.

When I got to his door, he was going off with behavior that could only be described as hysterical. I walked in and said, "Hey, Ab, what's going on?"

He had no idea I was even there. He was lecturing all of the chairs in his kitchen that were perfectly lined up in front of him. The speech that he was delivering made no sense at all. The sentences he spoke were all jumbled together. Just as something started sounding coherent, it quickly shifted into incoherent or absurd. He was using Kennedy's voice and saying things like, "Yes, Mr. President, I fully commend you to deal with these government subsidy ghetto children, we cannot let Mr. Nixon know what has happened, yes, Mr. Bunny. Bunnies, bunnies, bunnies." He was all over the place! A month earlier, he had told me that a blue bunny was his spirit guide.

The whole episode was fascinating, but it was clear to me what was happening. He was having a mish-mashed flashback of all kinds of events in his past. I assessed that even though he was losing it, he was not a danger to himself, so I decided to leave him alone.

Later that evening, I heard a knock on my door. There he was, standing with his eyes wide open. He had just been through the wringer, but he was inspired. He told me he went to the bar the night before and put on a great show – singing, playing and entertaining. He knew he drank a lot because he had a tough time walking home. He remembered opening up the freezer door where the acid was kept, but he didn't remember actually taking it, and then he went to bed. He then woke up a while later thinking he saw stars through the ceiling and that's all she wrote.

When he finally returned to earth the next afternoon, the acid was no longer in the freezer. He realized he had eaten all ten hits. He then said a few things that stuck with me. The first thing was about the trip itself. He said, "I don't remember every detail of what happened while I was away, but I'll never forget it."

I followed this with, "All you'll ever really know is that you'll never really know."

He answered that with "Those who say don't know, and those who know don't *say*."

I replied, "Ain't no way anyone can say what's right or wrong for anybody anyway and if they do, it's so untrue!"

We then both cracked up laughing. Then he gave me a nickname, "Space", and he said, "Space, when you sing put all of your heart and soul into it!"

At the time, I didn't sing or ever think I would. But I smiled and thanked him for his advice, and then I said: "Ab, we've been fightin' to enlighten' since the day we were born, and I think it's time to surrender because that might be the only way we will ever win"!

He became very contemplative for a moment, then chuckled and said, "fightin' to enlighten. I like that!"

Abbot told me that while he was tripping, he felt like he was channeling healing energy into the U.S. government's past, present, and future. He believed that at some level, he had succeeded. He also remembered lecturing the Senate advisory committee about the importance of doing enlightened community service by helping inner-city youth understand the spiritual aspects of the universe. Then he mentioned rainbow-colored spirits helping the Senate advisory committee become enlightened. They couldn't see these spirits, but he could. After he told me this, I excused myself as a sharp pain pierced my heart. I went into the back room of our grungy lead paint infested house and started weeping. I had completely lost touch with all the luminous spirituality in my life and look at me now. I was a morbid disaster, a zombie. What was I doing? All I could think about was heroin. I had fallen so far. After ten minutes, I pulled it together, but Abbot had already gone home. Damian was sleeping on the couch.

This one acid trip was like a renaissance in Abbot's life. He felt renewed. What happened to him after that was quite exciting. Long-lost friends, many of whom were well known national touring musicians, started flocking to see him from all over the country. He became a sort of guru to us all. Lots of good times and great music came as a result of this trip that Ab had taken. I learned a lot about performing and playing music through all of my time spent with Abbot and his friends, but in the meantime, Damian and I were getting deeper and deeper into addiction. We hadn't just numbed our spiritual abilities at this point; we had almost completely shut them down.

There were many times when we both realized how out of control we had become and that we needed to stop. But our level of dependency was so extreme that one-day without H would initiate brutal withdrawal symptoms. The only way to stop these withdrawal symptoms was by doing more heroin. This created a vicious never-ending cycle of getting high, coming down, going through debilitating withdrawal (that left us physically incapacitated because of the pain) and then needing to do more heroin just to be able to function. It was a miserable existence, morbidly miserable.

A year and a half into our addiction, really harsh things began happening. We took them as obvious signs to get clean or suffer a terrible fate. At that time we were living in a trailer in the woods outside of Augusta Maine.

The first major sign came through our association with Jimbo. He had dove headfirst into extreme freebase coke addiction and had entirely lost his mind to it. He was the complete antithesis of someone who cared about pursuing inner peace and awareness. But since Damian and I fell off the boat, Jimbo somewhat resonated with our brand of sickness. He used to come over frequently and spend one to three days at a time cooking and smoking free-base cocaine in our house. His girlfriend, Brandy, would always be in tow. He had no qualms about pimping her out, and she often encouraged it. He even offered her up to us once – we adamantly declined. They created a filthy scene everywhere they went.

Jimbo would basically hold us at ransom in our own house by getting us to participate in his free-base rituals. We would go into the bathroom, and he would lock the door (at our trailer deep in the woods with no neighbors anywhere nearby). After a few hits, Jimbo would get so paranoid that he would have all of his cocaine on a piece of cardboard sitting on the edge of the toilet. Every hit he took out of his clear crack pipe stem made him so paranoid the cops were coming that he'd put one finger on the flusher and another underneath the cardboard. This way if the cops did show up, he could safely dump the cocaine in the toilet. While he did this, everyone became completely silent, and then he stared each one of us down. If someone were breathing too loud, he would stare that person down until they became quiet. Of course, the entire ritual was an act that he would play out again, and again, and again throughout the course of every night. We participated in this quite a few times. After a while, though, we decided we weren't going to tolerate this anymore. We were mellow heroin addicts who did coke and meth for entertainment. Jimbo was the opposite, a speed freak who did sedatives to mellow out from his high-octane entertainment.

Damian decided to call Jimbo and tell him we weren't going to do this anymore. At first, he got real defensive and threatened to not buy weed from us, but then he calmed down. We were still moving an enormous amount of weed to support our habits. We didn't see or hear from him for weeks after that.

A day came three weeks after Damian last talked to him when I was counting the money that I owed to my pot dealer. There was a lot of cash laid out on the floor. Suddenly the front door of our plastic-panneled heroin trailer was kicked in. In comes Jimbo and ten of his thug minions all wielding baseball bats, crowbars and other assorted blunt objects. The timing for a situation like this is never good, but at this point, it was just plain awful. Chaos erupted as guys started grabbing the money I was counting while at the same time smashing windows inside of our house. Outside others were bashing in the windows on the Volkswagen Golf and bus we owned.

Jimbo started screaming at Damian, accusing him of breaking the windows of his Camaro, which was untrue. He then swung his bat at a 55-gallon fish tank with fish I had raised since they were babies. It smashed, dumping the contents of the tank, with all the fish, all over the floor. Then he started destroying everything in sight. I grabbed about a third of the money that the other guys didn't grab and started running outside. Just before I made it out, I saw Jimbo and another guy beating Damian with their bats. I wanted to save what money I could because I knew that my dealer would not respond well to me losing it all. Jimbo yelled at me as I took off, but they didn't chase me.

I waited a half-hour until I heard their cars squeal off and then I went back. I couldn't believe that no one had called the cops. When I went into the house, it looked like a tornado went through it. Damian was lying on the floor in a pool of blood, fish were flopping, and everything was broken with piles of shattered glass coating everything everywhere.

Damian was still conscious, so I helped him up then I put all the fish into one of the last unbroken containers left in the house. They all died anyway.

The gash in Damian's head was massive and definitely needed stitches, but we weren't the types to go to the hospital for anything. We always told people that if we overdosed, we didn't want anyone to call the paramedics. We reasoned it would be easier to die than to deal with the legalities that would ensue as a result of a drug overdose. A testament to how reckless we had become.

Once Damian cleaned the wound to the best of his abilities, he said, "The reason this happened is obvious. Clearly, it is a message for us to stop what we are doing or to expect much worse."

I couldn't have agreed more. When ten guys show up at your house stealing and destroying everything you have, while severely beating your friend, you tend to take it as an impetus for change. We didn't interpret this as random. There was a clear message behind it. The sad thing about this incident is that it deeply changed Damian. It seemed like it erased whatever sanity he had left, plus he became way colder than he had ever been.

However, we needed a game plan. We knew that our level of dependence was severe and that the withdrawal to actually kick for good was going to be a long and brutal trial requiring every drop of will power we had. We didn't want to kick at our Hallowell house because it was now a target for those psychos to hit again. It would be stressful to anticipate them showing up while we would be going through some of the worst times of our lives. We needed a plan. But more graves "signs" were coming our way.

CHAPTER SIXTEEN

Glacial Blue Skin

I put in a bunch of phone calls to see if there was somewhere we could go to detox. No one knew of anything, but a few said they would look into it. It was now almost winter again. Everything was frozen, we didn't have any substantial snow in the lowlands, but the mountains were covered.

The invasion we sustained really shook me up. It made me deeply consider the self-destructive trajectory I had been on. The problem was that even when something hardcore shakes your foundations, and you realize serious change needs to be made, the monkey on your back demands your attention, thus diverting your newly discovered motivation. After that happened, we made a pact only to do as little heroin as we needed just to get by until we were able to find a place to kick. But that damn monkey is always hungry with an insatiable appetite that needs constant feeding. It can never be satiated.

In the midst of all this self-deception, I decided that I wanted to be alone in the woods even though it was now really cold. Since I was a child, it was the one place I could go to feel safe.

I drove out of town to where hiking trails were, and I parked my car. The parking lot was empty, and I saw a pond through the woods covered in ice. I walked over to it and saw that the ice was thick. I threw a few boulders onto it and determined it was indeed quite solid. It was at least thick enough to hold up my weight. Like a little kid, I wanted to run on the ground and slide across it. I did, but as I slid way out onto the pond, the ice started cracking. Growing up, I had always known better than to put myself in a situation like this, but I wasn't thinking clearly at this point in my life in any manner.

The ice broke under my feet, and suddenly I was waist-deep in water. Every time that I tried climbing up on top of the ice, it would break. This kept happening all the way to the pond's edge. Hypothermia was setting in so fast that I could barely move. My body wanted to stop as I felt a sensation like sleep; only it was so strong I could hardly keep my eyes open.

I remember saying to myself: *I'm not going to die like this. I'll fight with all I've got to survive.* And that's what I did. The ice cracked all the way to the shore. It probably took close to 15 minutes for me to get out of the water. I was yelling for help, but I knew no one was there. When I made it to the land and out of the water, my legs were so cold they couldn't hold me up. All I wanted to do was make it to the heat of the car, but I couldn't walk. I started crawling, but even that was too hard. Out of nowhere, I felt people on either side of me, lifting me up, and at that point, I passed out.

After passing out, I became aware of a sensation similar to the car accident I was in at the age of fourteen. It was a relatively painless process as my spirit just dissipated from my physical vessel like smoke. It was on its way to immersing itself more fully into the oneness of the universe, or so it seemed. As quickly as this energy left my body, it returned back. The process of dissipation reversed itself as my soul populated the cells of my body, immersing itself into my physical being as opposed to the oneness. Once this process completed, I didn't awaken to a 'normal' state of consciousness. I remained sleeping in an almost comatose state.

When I awoke in my body, I came to with a gasp. I was in a bed in someone's house. I recognized the photographs of people on the wall. I got out of bed and felt terribly weak. I called out *hello,* and a few minutes later a woman I knew came into the room. She and her partner were friends who I sold pot to. They said that they heard someone yelling and ran over and discovered it was me. They pulled me up and brought me into the car. My whole complexion was frigidly blue. They debated as to whether or not they should bring me to a hospital, but the woman's partner did EMT work and decided they should slowly get my body temperature up, but quickly take action as opposed to keep me waiting on the long ride to the hospital. They put me in a bathtub of warm water fully clothed; my pulse and all readable signs were normal. They took off my wet clothes, left my underwear on, and threw me in bed, loading it with blankets. I slept for almost thirty hours.

It was surreal to hear all of this. Just like that I almost died, it was a shock that I wasn't able to fully come to grips with because I was so dope-sick. It had been at least thirty-three hours since my last fix, and I was going through harsh withdrawals on top of the weakness from the near hypothermia. While these people were talking to me, they noticed how badly I was fidgeting and shaking. They didn't play dumb either.

"Based on your behavior it looks like you've got a serious problem."

I just burst into tears and told them how terrible this addiction was. I also told them about our recent home invasion and how I interpreted it as an obvious sign to make serious changes. They agreed, and they also commented on how this incident with them could also be viewed as a sign that I am at the edge of my life.

They understood my dilemma of not wanting to kick in the home that I had been using in. They happened to know of a place that was available, and they were going to look into it for me.

I thanked these people the best that I could. They saved my life. At the time, everything about me was an emotional disaster, so I felt incapable of truly expressing how grateful I was. Eventually, I lost touch with them.

While I was sleeping, they went back to the hiking trails parking lot and got my car. Thank God they weren't pulled over because there was heroin in it.

After I thanked them, I ran to the car, cooked myself a fix, and relieved the withdrawal pain I was in. I waited for fifteen or twenty minutes while the rush of opiates flooded my being, then I drove back to the trailer. Once I got back there, I cooked another fix.

I told Damian what happened and he responded the way that he always did, with no emotion and very little to say about it. I sat on the bug-infested couch that came with our plastic-paneled trailer and nodded out from the strong fix I had just administered. When I awoke, the realization of what just happened hit me hard. *Oh my God, that was so close,* I said out loud. I thought that the iridescent guides had left me a long time ago, but somehow I was saved by the skin of my teeth. In those moments, one thing was certain to me—this latest incident was a very clear signal advising me to change now. After almost freezing to death, I realized that I was actually closer too the edge of death than I had any idea of.

CHAPTER SEVENTEEN

Frozen Turkeys

The beautiful people who saved me from nearly freezing to death, my human angels, had found a place in Bryant Pond high up on a picturesque mountain where we could kick this habit. They gave me the landlord's number. I called him and arranged to meet at the place. The area was beautiful, but the cabin had no running water, no electricity, very little insulation and giant picture windows in the front that sucked out all the heat. However, he only wanted fifty dollars a month for the place.

"We'll take it," I told him.

After looking us over, he probably decided we were out of our minds, which we were because winter in this place wasn't easy living even by a mountain man's standards. The place was so high up on the mountain that there was already three feet of snow everywhere, even though it was just the beginning of winter. We paid him fifty dollars for one month, and we stayed there for sixth months. He never came back to get any more money for the rest of our stay. I'm sure he didn't expect us to even make it through the first month.

We brought what few possessions we owned and moved in. We kept our habits going until we were settled; otherwise the move itself would have been impossible due to the painful withdrawals. The one good thing about the cabin was there was plenty of dry wood to burn, even though there wasn't much insulation to hold the heat in. We were way out in the mountains with only two mom and pop convenience stores and strangely enough, an organic vegan bakery that became our primary source of life-saving nourishment. Winter in Maine is brutal, but winter in Maine high up on an exposed mountain while kicking heroin cold turkey is an entirely different type of brutal. The onset of a high altitude winter in an unforgiving environment was about to set in, but this was mild in comparison to the unforgiving inner turmoil that Damian and I were about to face.

Once moved in, we immediately kicked our habits. After two days, the withdrawals were so tortuous. In my head, I had started making plans to score some dope with the hopes of lessening the severity of the detox symptoms. Damian stopped me by saying, "No way, we need to ride this out." He was right because heroin is not a drug that you can wean yourself off of. As soon as you do a little, the withdrawal process starts from the beginning. The only other option we had back then was the methadone clinic in Portland, but we knew better after seeing what others went through being addicted to that. In many ways, it was harder to kick a dependency to methadone than it was to kick heroin.

By day three, we were in excruciating pain. Every single cell in every part of our bodies was crying, aching, begging, and screaming for a fix, and there is nothing that can remedy the pain except for more heroin. Aside from having your limbs ripped out of their sockets or being skinned alive, I couldn't imagine anything hurting more than heroin withdrawal. Every part of you - physically, mentally, emotionally, and spiritually suffers in a way that conjures images of hell itself. It is only mildly like having your entire body and face wrapped in cellophane. No matter how badly you want to breathe, you cannot, but the agony continues because you haven't died, you are still alive. It's like being trapped in a frozen lake, under the ice and you cannot break it, but you don't drown either, you just suffer on and on. You can hardly walk, talk, eat, drink, sleep, breathe, or perform any other biological function your body may require. If you had a loaded gun, you would be holding it to your head for days on end pondering whether or not to pull the trigger, and you probably would accidentally do it anyway due to the excessive and uncontrollable shakiness of your hand. The only way out is to metaphorically stare the Devil down, directly in his eyes for weeks on end until you convince him that you are stronger than he is. But even if you succeed, you will still feel defeated for many months due to the havoc it wreaked on your mind and body.

Only those who have gone through this process cold turkey with little or no support or even with a lot of support can understand how hard someone has to fight for their life. People who don't understand why their loved ones cannot stop using have no idea what they are up against.

By day four, we were falling to pieces. We became so desperate to relieve a little of the pain that we had a hare-brained idea to try eating some ecstasy. We convinced ourselves that we had heard that taking ecstasy (MDMA) while going through the withdrawal process helped to lessen the severity of the symptoms. While there may or may not be much truthfulness to this, it was certainly an incredibly dangerous experiment to undertake while already holding on for dear life.

We had these big wafers called peppercorns that were a derivative of MDMA. They were giant horse pills, and we knew they'd be dehydrating to our already dehydrated bodies. We decided to take half each because that might have been all we were able to handle in our current state of decrepitude. After about an hour we thought we might be feeling the effects, but it was hard to tell due to the agonizing pain we were in. In our typical take it over the edge fashion; we ate another whole pill each.

I decided to go upstairs in the cabin while Damian stayed downstairs. As I lay down in the bed, I thought I could feel a fuzzy tingling sensation rippling through my body. It was a welcome feeling amidst the unbearable distress. I could hear Damian mumbling something, but I didn't know what. Laying in my bed shaking violently while whimpering and looking at the cross-section of this dilapidated hand-built cabin, I prayed the ecstasy was going to help.

Before I knew it, the cross-sections of the building were disappearing into nothingness. My slipping mind couldn't figure out what was happening. I felt like I was convulsing. Then there was sheer pain as I came to the edge of self. My soul forcibly started disconnecting from my body. The pain dial was set at maximum. As the last remnants of my human senses began disassociating from my physical form, I knew I was dying. Like a shotgun bullet leaving the barrel of a gun, my soul rocketed from my body. The last thought that I had was, *I can't believe this is how I died.*

As my spirit floated off, it began the process of dispersing itself into the oneness of all that is. The soul aspect of my being knew what was happening to it, and it was, for lack of a better way to explain, *happy* about what it was becoming.

As this energy got closer to the source, it felt the peace that it longed for. As it began merging with this ocean of energy, all of the geometric alignments making this transition possible began setting in place. But then something occurred that never happened before. My soul was denied entry into its birthplace. There was a moment where it was actually rejected by it. The source of all life is ineffable consciousness itself. It consciously denied my soul integration with it. Discombobulated, my soul began its descent back to my body.

As my soul made its return to my body, the agonizing sensations of heroin withdrawal became at the forefront of my awareness. But the pain of my soul being rejected from its collective source was way more powerful than my already tortured body. It is like being rejected by your parents when you were a baby times infinity. Returning to my tortured human form after this created a sensation of pressure on my whole being. It was so heavy; it felt like my whole body would crumple like a tin can. I couldn't believe I was still physically alive. How did I survive through that? I was in shock, serious shock.

"What just happened," I yelled out to Damian downstairs. Was he still alive? He didn't answer. I used what little strength I had to pull myself up and get down the small staircase to see if he made it through. As my foot hit the first stair, I slid all the way down the staircase smashing my tailbone on each step before finally landing in a pathetic pile of human pain on the floor below. I could see Damian lying on the floor, but he wasn't moving. I attempted to lift myself from the floor while spying a jug of water sitting on the counter in front of me. I was so parched. I needed to drink that water. As I feebly withered towards the counter, my legs, like Jello, were weakened to the point where they were unable to hold up my physical frame. In a desperate attempt, I reached out to grab the water. Only one of my fingers touched the gallon jug and knocked it off the table, spilling water all over the floor. Damian came to from whatever state he was in.

"Bro, did the same thing happen to you? Because I was sure I had died, but obviously I made it back," I said as my parched voice trembled with frailty.

He affirmed, "My soul was there, our work isn't done. Otherwise we would have stayed. It doesn't want us to enter after what we have been doing to ourselves. <u>You</u> especially need to purify yourself." I could see how bad of shape he was in, but at the same time, he seemed almost to enjoy the challenge. He then said, "Just be happy you're alive. This pain will go away. You're a warrior; you can do it."

From the time I'd eaten the ecstasy and left my body, until the time I returned, over thirty-six hours had passed. While the entire experience seemed to last a few minutes, it took over a day and a half to revolve through this trial. For me, this was pretty hard to comprehend, but beyond the surface of reality, time, and space cease to exist. I was beyond lucky to have survived. The truth truly is stranger than fiction.

We stayed in that cabin for two weeks while the most severe symptoms started to work through us. The pain was absolutely unbearable, and we got no sleep at all. I eventually just surrendered to it, knowing that *this too shall pass*, and that I truly loved my body and soul regardless of the fact that I did this to myself. I couldn't see them, but I thought that I could feel the iridescent guides watching over me. I believed that they too loved me and were helping me to overcome this. I did the only thing that I could do at this point…endure.

Weeks turned into months, and I started getting glimpses of being healthy and *normal* again. After about four months, I started feeling halfway decent again, but the headaches persisted for a while longer.

Right around the six-month mark, I felt like I had pretty much made it through. It was summer, and at that point, I didn't really have any desire to do heroin or any white powders again. But by then, heroin and synthetic forms of it like Oxycontin and Roxicodone, were everywhere and many, many people who we knew, were doing them.

At first, we were telling everyone we encountered who were on these drugs they should stop as soon as possible because they wouldn't want to go through what we did. But people are like robots in many ways. Once they become programmed to certain behaviors, it is easier to constantly engage in those behaviors than it is to change their programming. These drugs made for powerful programming. They were such an addictive momentary escape, no matter what someone's level of consciousness was.

One day in mid-summer while hanging out in an apartment in Portland, more than seven months after we had kicked, Damian and I both relapsed. Someone who had been using for a long time, but not daily and not injecting it convinced us that if we just snorted it we could enjoy it occasionally as opposed to becoming addicts again.

How could we ever forget the brutal agony we caused ourselves in the past two years because we chose to do this substance? We didn't forget, but we hadn't been clean long enough to resist the allure of the most addictive of all drugs. With some hesitation, we both snorted a little bump. Wham! Then, ahhh!!!: the return of the fire-breathing serpent. At the time I used to say, "If the devil actually exists, the first place to find him is in white powders.

After a few days, we did a little more and then again after a few days. Within a couple of months, we were back to being full-blown junkies. With self-deceptive loyalty, we returned to this drug, and it returned itself to us, consuming our every waking thoughts, desires, and motives. Like puppets on strings controlled by the Devil's hands, we explored hell on Earth with wicked wonder, but there were lines we wouldn't cross. We would only sell weed, not heroin, to pay for our habit and unlike some junkies, we didn't rob or hurt others to pay for it. Sometimes people would say to us, "Well, maybe you aren't hurting anyone directly, but your friends and loved ones will suffer as a result of your choices." This was true, but at that time, we felt abandoned by, and we intentionally abandoned all of our families and loved ones, so we didn't really care what they thought. Plus we didn't see them very often, if at all. We were truly toxic at that point in our lives.

Already weakened physically, mentally, and emotionally from the long bout of destruction the first time around, this time, the life-negating effects of the addiction began eroding my body much quicker than the last time. The most noticeable effect was my inability to not withstand overdosing. The big doses I used to take now caused me to frequently suffer indomitable bouts of vertigo. It felt like my brain was actually spinning around in my skull. Every time this happened, I would hit the floor and often throw up. But even this did not deter me from doing large doses. Damian seemed to be able to handle it better than I did.

Almost seven months after we relapsed, two events happened in less than twenty-four hours that I took as clear signs to stop now, once and for all or suffer a seemingly eternal fate of torture that was becoming more decadent for the Devil by the hour.

The first sign came as I was driving to a house I stayed at in Portland from Unity, late at night on Interstate 295. Because I didn't have any drugs on me, I was speeding back to Portland as quickly as possible. I was jonesing for a fix, hard! The highway was empty, and I was recklessly speeding down it a 2 a.m., at 90 mph in an older Saab 900 turbo. Fog from the ocean started rolling in, and visibility became obscured. I thought I saw something ahead of me, but just as I was about to hit the brakes, a deer came running directly at me. My car hit the poor creature with tremendous impact. The collision was so forceful that it triggered a brief out-of-body experience that, like the car accident when I was fourteen, caused me to see my skeletal structure and then led to almost alien-like transmissions being received and sent to and from my brain. As soon as I realized what had happened, the car came skidding to a halt on the side of the interstate. Smoke was billowing from the front end.

Completely freaked out and out of breath, I jumped out of the car to find the deer lying in the road and the front end of my car completely smashed in. I started panicking because, in addition to hitting an innocent animal, I was starting to go through withdrawal. This was before the days of cell phones, so I wasn't sure what to do. As I stood there staring back and forth between the deer and my smashed car, I noticed two cars approaching on the interstate. I waved to them with the hope that they might stop and assist me. The first car drove right by without stopping. I had a bad feeling about the second car that was approaching. It was swerving a little bit, and it looked like it might crash into my car and me. I ran off to the side of the road as fast as possible. The car ran right into the dead deer. As the front tire hit the deer's midsection, the pressure of the animal getting crushed by the weight of the car caused its innards to project from its face and its rear. After the driver hit the animal, they swerved to avoid hitting my car and then kept driving. They had to be drunk and didn't stop for fear of getting arrested.

Watching this entire thing take place was like watching a real-time scene in a movie play out. It didn't seem real. In a moment of a split decision, I opened the back end of my car while conjuring Herculean strength. Then I grabbed the deer, dragged it to the car, and threw it into the back. I tied the trunk shut with bungee cords. Then I got into the front seat of the car. The thing miraculously started even though fluids were leaking out all over the place. I drove back to the house where I was staying in Portland, and the car literally died as I pulled into the driveway.

The next day I called the game warden, and he told me to keep the deer. It was so badly damaged from getting hit and then run over, that it was inedible for humans. Damian fed it to his dog.

The whole incident was insane, but the deeper meaning of it was clear. Slow down, get clean, or get hit hard and die. I felt certain the deer took some of my junkie karma and died for me. I thought it helped buy me some time to save my own life and I gave thanks to this animal that sacrificed its life for me.

The second obvious sign came the morning after I hit the deer. I got high and it hit me so hard; I didn't think I was going to survive it. The vertigo it induced was so strong; it caused me to hit the floor and pass out. When I awoke, I was covered in vomit and urine. A voice in my head kept saying, "Stop getting high or you will die!" It echoed endlessly in my head for a long time. I was lucky I didn't aspirate by choking on my vomit while passed out, something that sadly happened to one of my closest friends, a beautiful brother. I was shocked when I heard of his passing but I still was getting high after I heard of his passing.

While I was fully aware of how hard it was to kick, I knew I wasn't going to let this habit kill me. As I summoned what little will power

I had left, I told my greatest teacher and only friend, Damian, that I needed to kick, this time for good. He agreed and said he would join me as well.

So here we were once again, totally strung out and caught in the inert lifelessness of winter in Maine. We didn't want to go through another withdrawal detox that instead of being called *cold turkey* could have been seasonally referred to as *freezing to death turkey*, so we discussed migrating somewhere in the southern hemisphere. But we had no idea where. After being in Florida, I decided it was too hectic of a place to be while clinging on to dear life.

I talked to a friend in Boston who I had a lot of respect for. He was a really interesting guy who actually seemed to care about Damian and me. His name was James. He was a white Rastafarian who had eleven children and one giant dreadlock on his head that wasn't even a foot from reaching the ground. His kids all had long dreads as well, except for the two youngest who hadn't developed any yet.

After explaining the situation to him, he suggested going to Jamaica because it was warm, cheap, and we could lie around on the beach and smoke weed while we battled our inner demons. *Wow*, I thought. *That actually sounds like a good idea* "What part of Jamaica should we go to, "I asked.

His response was, "I don't know, man, I've never been. But I do have a phone number for some people who live there. You should give them a call to see what advice they have for you."

I considered calling the people he mentioned, but I was such a mess that I didn't want to project my dire situation on to someone I didn't know. I didn't think there were too many people who would know how to give a couple of *cosmonaut* junkie's advice on how to survive heroin addiction withdrawals in Jamaica, but I kept the phone number in my wallet anyway.

I decided to give AAA a call. I wanted to see if they could book a trip for us. They reserved a hotel in Montego Bay on the beach for $40 a night and a flight through Delta, but we had to wait a week to leave. I was so desperate to start the withdrawal process with the hopes I could get clean, stay clean, and reclaim a life of spiritual integrity. But we kept our habits going full-force right up until the hour that we boarded the plane for Jamaica.

During the week we waited for our completely unplanned wellness journey into a land of what we had no idea of what to expect, Florence stopped by. We had stayed in touch throughout the entire time I was an addict. She remained one as well. She was heavily addicted. It was sad seeing such a beautiful young person so messed up. We hadn't been lovers the whole time we knew each other, but she wanted to be. I was way too complex to be available to anyone sexually or intimately, but in her trademarked approach of sexual prowess, she wrapped her arms around my neck and slapped her body against mine. We embraced each other tightly and began kissing passionately. We landed on my bed. But nothing happened. I was excited mentally, but I wasn't physically aroused. I was too unhealthy to be.

She peeled herself off me in disappointment. "Why are you not attracted to me?" she said, feeling rejected.

"It's not you at all," I quickly retorted. Then I realized something that had or rather, hadn't taken place since I started using heroin. "Florence, I just realized something. I have not had an erection once in the past three years.

She gave me a very perplexed look. "Well, look at how you live your life. If your junk doesn't work, then you must be dying, because that's where the life is!" She said that half-trying to be funny and half-seriously, but in all reality, she was more right than not.

This drug was killing me. My body had fallen apart in more ways than one since I started using. It was really scary when I put it into perspective. I was a train wreck that was rusting.

"It's okay," she said. "I've always liked you, and I've always wanted to make love to you and I probably always will!" Then she put her arms around me again and kissed my cheek.

Then I hear, "Ewwwww," really loudly in my ear. "You have lice! Disgusting!"

She was right. They were all through my dreadlocks and scalp. Damian had them as well. He was way more infested than I was.

"No wonder my head always itched," he said.

We both decided to cut our dreadlocks off right then and there. Florence helped us. Years of growth, gone just like that.

When you hang around scum, you attract scum, and eventually you become scum. I knew that I needed to heal myself and get my vibration up. I was a being of life, not death.

Shedding my dreadlocks was actually very therapeutic. It was out with the old, in with the new. That's what I needed to do with this addiction.

We had no idea of the hell ride we were in for kicking cold turkey in a third world country like Jamaica. We were about to be culture-shocked while hanging on for dear life

CHAPTER EIGHTEEN

Jamaica's Got Soul

We took our remaining supply of heroin to the Portland Maine airport. We parked our car in the parking garage and did the last big fix of our lives. After getting high, we threw all of the incriminating evidence into a trashcan and walked into the airport to begin boarding our plane. I was so high that I could hardly walk or carry my luggage. Once we had finally boarded the plane and were getting ready to take off, I knew one thing for sure…by the time that the plane landed in Jamaica, six hours later with all the layovers, we would be jonesing for a fix big time.

After a long layover in Miami, we were on our way to Montego Bay. While I was excited to experience a new culture and get a fresh new start, the reality of the decision we made—to kick in a foreign environment—was actually very impulsive, stupid and recklessly risky. We had been so strung out, that we weren't able to foresee how to plan this trip accordingly in a way that best served our dire needs. Our only goals were getting to a hotel that we knew nothing about so that we could get to a beach that we knew nothing about so that we might have a chance at detoxing as smoothly as possible. The entire thing was orchestrated and improvised out of sheer desperation. No one we knew had been to

Jamaica, so we had no idea about the locals, the culture, or their way of life. It wasn't until we landed that we found out this heavily over-populated island was not friendly to white tourists.

Through talking with tourists at the Jamaican airport, we discovered that most of the white people who visited this island stayed at exclusive resorts. Most had prison-like fences and guards to keep the tourists safe from certain segments of the locals. We found out on our own that to just show up and explore this island freely is likely to get you robbed or worse, especially at night. We also learned that to survive it, you must act crazier than the craziest of locals. We also didn't realize that more than a few Jamaicans were heavily biased towards those they perceived to be white Rasta's, which we weren't, but some of the islanders felt differently.

The second we got off the plane in Mo Bay, Damian and I were both ravenously jonesing for a fix. A high-budgeted heroin addiction like ours needed constant feeding. Two hours without a fix was too long. Six hours was downright torture. Aside from that, the hot Jamaican sun felt like a divine gift. But after stripping my outer layers down to my t-shirt, the visible horror of what I had done to my body through incessant drug use became glaringly obvious. We were scarred and scabbed up white ghosts so skinny that we'd fit through the eye of a needle. Anyone who looked at us knew something was way off.

Before we even made it out of the airport, people were offering us weed, coke, and crack in ostentatious marketing displays that resembled the New York stock exchange floor during a bullish market. They were all over us. We bought a little weed and refused everything else, and then we grabbed our luggage and got in a cab heading towards our hotel.

Getting into the cab was like a quick breath of fresh air from the hustle and bustle of the airport marketplace. But as we got settled into our seats, I noticed the cabbie eyeing us like a hyena, licking his chops as though he'd discovered a new find of old meat.

"Wha' g'wan? Wha can a git you," the cabbie quickly started questioning us.

"Uhhh, nothing man, we are all set, but thank you."

He didn't even hear me. "You know dem I got a cuzin who git anyting u wan."

"Yeah, I think we are all set, we just want to get to our hotel so we can chill out. It was a long flight!" The withdrawal anxiety was really brutal at this point, and we just wanted to be left alone, but this guy couldn't sense that.

After five minutes we arrived at our AAA-booked hotel that was supposedly on a beach, but what we didn't realize that because Jamaica is an island, it is subjected to constant erosion, leaving very few natural sand beaches. This hotel was literally right on the side of the road, and its "beach" consisted of rocks, sharp broken shells, and broken glass. It wasn't a spot anyone would want to lie down and catch some rays on.

As we were checking in at the front desk, the hostess was eyeing us in a salacious and provocative manner. It was all too obvious what she was thinking. The cold shivers were really pulsing through my body even amidst the tropical heat. I just wanted to get the hotel key and get away from these people. Once we had gotten it, we walked out the front door and proceeded to bring our luggage to our room. On the way, we noticed a giant of a man. He had huge muscles, thick gold chains, a pant leg rolled up, and reptile eyes fixated on us two white boys who were so pale from sickness that we were translucent-white.

I made no eye contact and went right into the room. It had been very badly abused. It wasn't a healing sanctuary or a place that was going to be comfortable for the sheer agony we would soon be in.

Not more than a minute after we closed the door, the giant thug-looking guy started knocking on it to see if we needed anything. He said he worked for the hotel concierge services, but I was sure the hotel had no such thing.

"No, we're all good, but would like to buy some water, if you have any."

He cracked a wide smile that visibly showed off his mouth full of gold and diamond-encrusted teeth. "Water, huh? How about this?" He opened his hands wide to reveal a mountainous pile of crack rocks that barely kept from toppling over each other.

I took one look at Damian and knew he'd seen enough. "Look, man, we don't want any of that fucking shit. If you don't have water, then get the fuck out of here!"

Oh shit, I thought to myself, *this didn't look like the kind of guy to piss off,* but before I knew it, Damian was right in his face, again telling him to leave.

The guy was surprised, but he backed off nonetheless. "Look, man," he said, "my cousin is working the front desk, and if you're interested, she will come visit you for $50."

Damian just pointed his finger at the door and said one last time, "Get the fuck out!"

"Okay, okay," the guy acquiesced as he shuffled back away from the door, closing it behind him.

Damian and I looked at each other like, *what did we get ourselves into?* This wasn't even remotely what we expected.

At this point, the withdrawal symptoms were becoming unbearable. Due to the heat, the plane ride and being harassed by almost every person that we came into contact with, I felt like I was going to collapse.

"Let's take a walk and see if we can buy some water," Damian suggested.

I reluctantly agreed. The shape that I was in did not afford me much defense in dealing with whatever mayhem might be lurking outside of this hotel. It was a culture that was the polar opposite of what I was used to.

Like two senile old men, we began walking down the street outside of the hotel. It became glaringly obvious that we were the main attraction for every drug dealer, prostitute, and fruit salesman in our path. Before we knew it, we had an entourage trailing behind us, incessantly trying to push whatever it was that they were selling. Some of them got within inches of our face. We just ignored them like we didn't understand a word they spoke. Every car that drove by would stare like they've never seen anything like us in their entire lives. It was king of embarrassing, but even more than that, trying to remain cognizant of my surroundings was becoming very difficult due to the deeply penetrating pain resulting from the lack of opiates in my system. The combination of getting constantly harassed, while trying to find the strength to stand, was taking what little energy reserves I had left.

Finally, we made it to a fruit market that looked like it might provide us with the hydration that we so desperately needed. The market was composed of two rows of shanty-like structures with little sections separated by tapestries where different vendors would sell various items. The first thing we saw were two green coconuts that had been cut open by vendors, so we guzzled them immediately. For a second, I felt life in my body, but it wasn't nearly enough. I could've easily put down five of them myself. However, we only brought a little bit of money because we both sensed we might get robbed. After drinking the coconut water, a little old lady grabbed our hands and brought us into her section of the market. She tried selling us sandals, t-shirts, and other beach-made crafts. As we looked over the items on her table, another old lady hastily grabbed our arms and brought us over to her little commerce section. This went on and on until we saw everything that this market had to offer. Every person's little section of commerce offered basically the same exact things, only in different colors and only slightly different designs. It was a first-hand look into how limited the resources these people had to work with actually were. Their desperation to sell this stuff to us was a testament to the level of poverty they lived at. This island suffered so greatly from over-population that these people had to make the best of what little they had, and the competition was fierce.

Once these ladies realized we weren't going to buy anything due to a lack of funds, they began getting aggressive. One woman along with her friend and some kids demanded that Damian give her the shirt of his back and she meant it! Smiling, he reluctantly turned it over to her. After that, the same posse badgered me until I gave them the sneakers off my own feet. At first, I refused, but then they started yelling out to their sons and husbands to assist them. While they were doing that, I took them off my feet and said, "Here you go." We smiled the whole time because even though the assault was absurd, we saw how impoverished they were to so desperately rob us like this.

We let them take what they wanted, and then we hightailed it out of there. Bewildered and dope-sick as hell we retreated back to our hotel. As we hobbled back towards our room, a car pulled over. The driver was covered with gold chains, and he revealed a handgun to us. Then he demanded that we get in his car.

Damian said, "No thanks, man, we're all set!"

Then he started screaming at us, demanding that we get into his car. We ignored his demands and just kept walking towards our room as he sped off. When we finally made it back to our hotel room, we found that our bags had been searched and all of our money was stolen. Here we were, experiencing culture shock while holding on for dear life, and now we were broke. I cannot begin to describe the sensation overload my nervous system was being subjected to as a result of all the stimuli going on inside and outside of my body. It was all so confusing.

We had come to the crossroads, and we made our decision. This place was not at all what we expected it to be. We had to leave. The sun was setting. Based on what had happened so far and our current state of decrepitude, we began thinking that if the withdrawals didn't kill us, a murderer would. We figured we had a better shot of survival going back to Maine than staying here and getting killed by a crazed drug dealer.

With no money left, we started collect-calling people in Maine to see if someone could help us get some tickets home. But no one was able to. At this point in the withdrawal process, my hands were shaking so badly that I could hardly hold the phone. It felt like the bad spirits were closing in all around me.

Damian desperately suggested calling the people in Jamaica that our Rastafarian friend in Boston had given us the number for. There might be a chance they could help us get off this island. Besides, we had no one left to call, so I gave it a shot. It rang and rang and rang, and just as I was going to hang up a woman with a soft English Jamaican accent picked up. "Hello?"

"Hi, a mutual friend in Boston gave us your number. He told me to ask for Abu. Is he there?"

"Oh, okay. Hold on for a minute."

After a few moments, a man with a well-spoken Jamaican accent, free of the thick dialect that most people we'd spoken to thus far had, answered the phone. The tone of his voice was very soothing and optimistic. "Hello, Mon, we been really looking forward to meeting you."

I went right into it. "Aw, thank you, but we've decided that we are going back to Maine because we had no idea what we were in for coming here. So far we've been robbed, threatened, and hated because we are white. On top of that, we are both gravely ill, and we feel like we might die. We have to go back!"

He responded to this mad rant in the most lovingly fatherly voice. "No, no, no Mon, you must wait der my son, and I come and get you, you c'yan leave!"

I was surprised by his response, so I put it to him bluntly, "Look, we are really sick, I don't think our health will permit us to stay here. We would be a terrible burden on you."

He gently but adamantly put his foot down. "Mon, stay right there! My son and I will get you."

I looked at Damian. He was shaking while sweat was dripping off of his face, and I told him what the man said. He threw up his hands and said, "Fuck it. We're here. Let's ride it out even though we may not make it out."

I bowed my head down because, in those moments, I felt almost certain that I was going to die on that island as the pain train of heroin withdrawal was really starting to burn my soul as fuel. "Okay, we'll be waiting right here at this hotel in Mo Bay."

"Yes, Mon, don't worry 'bout a ting. We will come get you and take care of everything. We will be there in six hours."

"Okay," I reluctantly agreed.

Damian and I looked at each other and thought, *Six hours?* We didn't realize this island was that big. I crawled into my hotel bed, soaking in cold sweat that penetrated deep into every aspect of my being and pondered if the island of Jamaica would be my grave. Damian said nothing.

We were still profusely dehydrated and needed water so badly that we were forced to wander out into the Jamaican night to score some water. We had one dollar left that Damian had hidden in his shoe. With that, we conjured up what diminished strength we had left to find some water. I was barefoot. The hostess told us there was a small market just down the street opposite of the direction we walked earlier that had water.

As we practically crawled in a near rigor mortis state to the market, cars whizzed within inches of us. Many people drove with their high beams on all the time. It was always blinding when trying to look down the road to see where we were going. When we arrived at the market, we found that they did have water for sale. It was $.45 per bottle, so we bought two of them. While standing in line to pay for them, a young girl about the age of ten was pulling her mother's arms while laughing and blurting out, "Oh my God, mama! Look at how white those white dudes are!"

Her mother, the cashier, and everyone around them started laughing and pointing at us. The chain reaction of laughter caused me to snap, and I yelled out to the entire store, "It doesn't matter what color my skin is, we all share the same heart and soul! As long as everybody around the world thinks skin color matters, then my world, your world, our world will not get any better. Why don't you look at us as human instead of white!"

All the laughing stopped immediately, and no one in there looked at us again. We made it back to the hotel in so much pain that it was unbearable. The night was filled with visions of abominable terror.

Early the next morning, Abu and his son Ibn came just like they said they would. Like Gollum from *The Lord of the Rings*, we sluggishly approached them dry heaving and dripping with sweat. I cannot even imagine what we looked like to their eyes. Much to my surprise, they greeted us with open arms and loving embrace.

"Welcome to Jamaica. We are so glad you guys are here!"

Hearing this was comforting, but I couldn't express it. "We are really sick," I cried.

"Shhh, don't worry, we will take care of you. This is my son, Ibn." Ibn was a little younger than me, burly and rugged, but very warm.

At first, it felt like rays of hope were shining through, but I had no idea how they would respond when they saw how violently ill we were about to become. In addition to being white, I was sure that high-budgeted heroin addicts initiated in cold-turkey withdrawals from the States were probably a pretty rare minority in Jamaica.

This family was about to witness two young men going through some of the hardest times of their lives. I was afraid for them.

They helped us get in the back of their white pick up truck as they put our two backpacks, the only things we brought, in the truck as well. I hesitantly got in, and I realized I had no choice but to surrender and allow my fate, whatever it was going to be, rest with the Divine.

Other than our greeting, we didn't say much else. Suddenly we were driving down the road in the back of the white pick up truck with a metal bed and no cushions, driven by people we didn't know, bringing us somewhere that we never asked about.

Most of the Jamaican roads are one lane, and all the vehicles drive with two wheels on the road and two wheels off. This made it a rough ride that caused us much discomfort in our already direly uncomfortable state.

As we drove off from Mo Bay, the tourist area that we had first been exposed to in Jamaica quickly degenerated into a third world country. I saw people living in shanties without running water or any westernized amenities for miles around. This was the first time I had ever seen so many people living like this. The combination of culture shock intertwined with being on the brink of death was incredibly overwhelming. Again, this combination made me feel like this island would be my grave. It was a desperate and desolate feeling.

The ride seemed to go on for hours, but it was broken up by many different stops. Abu would stop the truck, get out, and talk to the locals. One of the times that he stopped, he stood in front of the truck and talked to a guy for almost an hour. Damian and I were squirming in the back of the truck. Every breath was a fight just to survive.

Clinically we should've been hospitalized. I spent the entire ride holding myself back from breaking down and telling these people that I felt like I was dying and to please bring me somewhere for medical attention. But we were in a country with draconian medical care, where doctors use dull scalpels to do C-sections. There was no telling how or if anyone had treated heroin addiction withdrawals. I'm sure they didn't. We had no option but to just man up and to try not to reveal how bad of shape we actually were in. Feeling this close to death while being in such a crazy place was a terrifying and surreal experience.

Our hosts told us that they were bringing us to some huts that were down on a private beach for a couple of days.

When we arrived at the place, I was aware that it was quite beautiful, but my vision was blurry from the detox symptoms. It was hard to see beyond our own suffering. We spent two days and two nights at this place they called *Ital rest*.

I tried to allow the sounds and smells of the ocean to help soothe me, but there was nothing other than the heroin that could soothe this type of pain.

There was someone bringing us food and water, but we couldn't consume anything. The person tending to us saw what we were going through. He decided to not communicate with us. I was begging God, the universe, anyone, or anything that would listen to have pity and save my life. The morning after the second night, Abu came and got us. He acted like nothing was wrong with us, behaving like a coach, motivating us into action.

It was still early morning when we arrived at his home. It certainly was a sight for sore eyes. They had a lush farm with gorgeous coconut trees, papaya trees, and vibrant gardens filled with abundant food and herbs. The backdrop of their property was the famous Blue Mountains of Jamaica.

At the entrance of their property were a couple of hand-built mosques where prayers were made five times a day. They were devout Muslims of a derivation related to Sufism. It soon became apparent that our arrival on this island was no accident. My view began wanting to slowly shift from seeing it as a grave to it to be a divine blessing that might actually save us from death.

The first thing they did was bringing us into the mosques. Damian and I were at the peak of the most unbearable moments of physical pain. We were so beat up that we could hardly move our bodies. We were whimpering with pain and deathly discomfort. Our friends by now recognized the seriousness of what we were going through and helped us get out of the truck and into their prayer temples.

The second I was in the temple I lay down directly onto the floor and listened to them pray. Their chants and rhythms helped to moderately soothe my annihilated mind and body.

This was the first time since landing here a few days earlier that I felt hope emerging, hope that I was not only was I not going to die here, but there was a chance for some sort of deep healing to take place.

Somewhere in the dismal recesses of my mind, I remembered my soul and the iridescent guides, and I thought, *"Wow, I remember wanting to do heroin to numb out all of my psychic abilities, and I succeeded, but look at what it almost cost me....my life.*

It was a godlike feeling to realize that people who I didn't know, were more than willing to go completely out of their way to save two people's lives they didn't know anything about. That is unconditional love – serious selfless service. They never once asked what caused our sickness, but there was no way to hide the scabbed track marks all over our arms.

When I got up from the mosque floor, there were children all around. They were laughing and filled with joy. Abu, the father of this beautiful clan, told us that the next day was his son, Ibn's, eighteenth birthday and that we would have a big feast.

They had us staying in a small room with two beds that was separate from the main house. We spent the rest of the day in agony, just lying down in these beds.

As night came, this beautiful family made their prayers and then went to bed. Sleep was something that Damian and I wouldn't get to experience for many weeks. The copious amounts of heroin we were using made it impossible to sleep until our bodies had purged the most violent effects of the drug. I began having horror-filled hallucinations so scary, that at times, I couldn't tell what was real and what was imagined.

When we stayed on the beach, we could only hear ocean sounds, but our first night in the countryside revealed something to our ears we'd never heard before.

Once the sun goes down, you can hear every animal for miles around wailing like they are in pain. At moments it sounded like every donkey, horse, cow, chicken and wild animal in the surrounding mountains were screaming bloody murder! I couldn't tell if they were doing it because they were relieved to be out of the sun or if they had a deeper significance. But then I remembered my awakening at eighteen years old when everything around psychically cried out to me. Being so ill, what I heard them doing sounded painful. I could relate to it. It wasn't just a personal pain; it was collective. Humans have bashed this island and most of the planet for a long time. The animals are hyper-aware of this at levels that humans couldn't even begin to imagine.

The flip side to these agonizing animal screams was that on the weekend the island's main radio station, *Irie FM* would echo throughout the hillsides for miles because it is the station that mostly everyone listens to. Hearing all of the individual radios that people had blasting coalesce into one symphonic reggae concert that could literally be heard from every mountain top brought only a very slight smile to my wearied face.

The next morning Abu's wife Isha started to notice how badly Damian and I were suffering. She began nurturing us with round the clock care. She forced us to drink water and eat nourishing medicinal foods, infused with herbs and other healing plants that they grew and wild harvested. At one point, she was holding me up and spoon-feeding me because the pain I was in was so crippling.

It was so humbling to have someone you just met taking care of you like that. There were moments when I was suffering so badly that I felt I might not be able to hold on, yet her angelic presence would always help to ground me.

While Damian and I were praying to live, Abu's family was running around and getting ready for the feast. They brought out a giant kettle known as *the pot* and then filled it with coconut water and got a fire burning underneath it. The kids were very excited, and they begged Damian and me to come and sit by the fire with them. Like two very old men, we slowly hobbled up the incline that led to where the fire was.

Abu and Ibn came walking over, leading a goat with a rope around its neck. They tied the rope to a tree, hoisted up the goat and then slit its throat. As the blood poured out from its veins, I felt like the blood was running from my veins as well. I sat there and watched the entire process until he had bled out. I allowed myself to feel what the goat might have felt like. As the goat sacrificed its life to provide a feast for Ibn's initiation into manhood, I let the addict in me die. It was a ravaging addiction, wrought with nothing but pain and hardship, but most of all, numbness to the soul freedom of the authentic nature of my awareness itself. But this wasn't the temporary numbness I originally wished for. This numbness ultimately led to one outcome and one outcome only… the bitter physical death of the body.

After the goat died, they took his body down from the tree. Damian helped them skin it because they weren't sure how to. They then took most of the meat, organs, entrails, and innards and threw them into the *pot* to make soup.

You've got to be kidding me, I thought to myself. *Eating that in my state of dis-ease?* As it was, I had no appetite, but I especially didn't have an appetite for that!

After the soup was done cooking one of the kids suggested that they "let the new guys try it first!" I didn't hear that, but before I knew it, a paper cup containing soup was in my hand. Everyone looked to see my reaction to the taste. As I slowly brought the cup to my lips, the smell of it triggered a reaction of dry heaving. I tried to keep it concealed, but they had to notice. Then I manned-up and did everything in my power to taste this food. I didn't want to offend these people who had gone considerably out of their way to care for us. As the soup went down my gullet, I chewed on things so rubbery they wouldn't break apart, but I managed to get it down without vomiting.

After it slithered down my esophagus, I quickly declared, "It's good!"

Everyone cheered, and then an interesting phenomenon occurred. It was almost like time slowed down. The second that everyone stopped looking at me, I took the cup of soup and threw it over my shoulder. I was relieved that I didn't have to eat it but dismayed because small animals—cats, dogs, and chickens—appeared from the bush to scavenge the discarded food. I tried shooing them off, hoping no one would notice and somehow no one did.

After the goat coconut entrails soup, the curried goat dish was ready. That was much more palatable but still very tough to get down in such a nauseated state. At the conclusion of this feast, Abu stated that for the most part, he and his family were vegetarians and the slaying of the goat was a ceremony specifically for his son's feast.

After the feast, Damian and I sat on a patio outside of their home. Abu brought out a big plastic tote filled with ganja and told us we could smoke as much of it, whenever we wanted, with no need to ask. While smoking didn't rid of us the intense pain, it definitely brought tremendous relief, and it gave our minds something to focus on other than the constant suffering. Clean cannabis, with all of its phytocannabinoids, terpenes, bioflavonoids and amino acids is undoubtedly one of the most powerful natural remedies on the planet. Despite the widespread demonization of it on so many levels, but especially in regard to cannabis being declared a gateway drug that leads to harder drug use – nothing could be further from the truth. Cannabis isn't a gateway drug that leads to hard drug use. It is a medicinal substance that offers an exit path away from hard drug use. But it can also be it's own addiction if we let it be.

So smoke we did, one big spliff after another all day and night. The ganja was so fresh, and it tasted great. It was able to help soothe a substantial part of our battle-ridden nervous systems, and it was a major catalyst for us to heal.

We stayed on that part of the patio the rest of the day, and as night came, we went back to the small room with our beds in it.

The morning finally came after another painful night of cellular agony with no sleep. We were still alive, but our nervous systems were still needing lots of repair that the love our caretakers, the ganja and the healing foods were providing. We made our way back to the patio, where Isha forced us to eat a bowl of plant porridge for breakfast. It was the first time that food tasted good in a very long time. It was also the first time that Damian and I had a real conversation with Abu and Isha since we had met them. They wanted to know who these two tortured souls they were caring for actually were. Abu started telling us a little about himself, his travels, and struggles. He was a world-traveled, world-cultured, highly intelligent spiritual man who had overcome great adversity in his life. He had gone on to create a beautiful paradise that we were sitting in. He was also a philosopher and a deeply critical thinker who could quickly discern what another person's hidden or visible motives might be.

He then looked at us and said, "What are you guys hiding from that you would do this to yourselves?"

Damian and I were shaking like leaves on a dying tree caught in a tornado. Sweat was beaded up all over our bodies. We felt reserved, to say the least. We weren't able to open up at first, but Abu kept beckoning us.

I kept making excuses. "I am really sick. I'm sorry."

Damian said a few things, but nothing much.

Then Abu asked about our mutual Rastafarian friend in Boston, James, who originally suggested that we come to Jamaica.

"Yeah, he is a really good friend. What a beautiful family," I murmured.

Then Abu got very serious with us. He said, "Mon, do you think that Haile Salassie is the Son of God?" He sort of assumed that we were white Rastafarian wannabees because we were in Jamaica upon the recommendation of our white Rasta friend.

Damian then replied with, "I think he is a part of God."

Abu then got upset and declared, "That thought has created years and years of Christian/Muslims warring."

Damian then reiterated his statement, but this time, his words conveyed energy. "I think he is a part of God in the same way that everyone and everything is a part of what is called God."

With those words came a feeling that touched the four of us simultaneously. The feeling of connection and oneness overtook us all. We sat in silence and awe. Everything in and around us had melted into unity.

Isha declared, "Wow, this is beautiful! It all is one!"

Abu had a huge smile and said, "You guys are all right!"

Though no out of body traveling or deep, insightful revelations occurred none were needed. So much was energetically conveyed between the four of us in those moments that we all felt our coherence with each other.

Abu recognized who we were and why we had suffered so greatly. He only wanted to be an inspiration in our lives, showing us that love for all was alive and well in the hearts of humankind.

The next few weeks were all about integrating us into his family by providing unconditional love and support. Damian and I were in really rough shape the whole time, but we fought to overcome our condition by being receptive to the give and take that occurs in such a large family atmosphere. The love that this family shared with us chiseled away the ice that had formed around our cold hearts. It was ice that had formed through self-inflicted abuse and the lack of self-love.

Another thing that happened to me during the moments of coherent connection that we all shared was that I felt my need to do heroin disappear, and ever since that day, I never did it or desired to do it again. I didn't need to be sedated. I just needed to feel love in my heart simply by choosing to, and share it with the world. Now I remembered that love. It was the love of the soul, the love of the body I was blessed to be in, and the love that was shared with other humans.

Although the pain was great, and it lasted for quite some time, we shed our old skin and were renewed. We were reborn. Abu and Ibn drove us all over the island country of Jamaica. They showed us so many thought-provoking sites. We saw beautiful things, and we saw terrible things. There was a bit of love and a bit of hate. We saw where Bob Marley grew up. We met devoted spiritual people, overflowing with love and abundance, and we met destitute murderers. Driving into Kingston the day the Jamaican tennis team played the US, almost led to our demise on a few occasions.

The thing that most struck me about this place was the effects of overpopulation. To me, this place was a view of how most of the planet will soon become if we as a species don't change our ways. There were people almost literally everywhere. Even in the sections of the island that were declared *pristine*, it was still overrun by people. I walked into wilderness areas thinking I was alone to pee, only to find people randomly hanging out, like that were where they actually lived.

Trash was another huge issue. It wasn't just candy bar wrappers and plastic bags; there were generations of trash buried deep into the ground. I first noticed this in an uprooted tree. After finding trash that was at least fifty years old, I began digging in a few spots across the island only to find the same thing. There were spots with so much trash that there was more trash than there was topsoil.

The issue of diminished resources was another problem that hit home for me. Aside from the lush gardens that some individuals were blessed to be able to grow, practically everyone across the island was eating the same things. This basically consisted of rice, beans, curried goat and small, dehydrated ocean fish. With so many people and so few resources, the general mentality of the people was not at all based on abundance. Jamaica is also the halfway point between Columbia and the United States. Because of this, cocaine is plentiful and cheap. This has greatly contributed to the low morale and desperation that is widespread there.

Damian and I had no idea what we were in for when we decided to kick our destructive habits in this country, but we were both blessed with an outcome that neither of us anticipated before we left Maine. We made friends with a family who became a part of my life to this very day. I am eternally grateful for this brutal but love-filled experience. Jamaica saved our lives.

CHAPTER NINETEEN

To Resurrect

When we finally made it back to Maine a month later, we had already been through the worst of the withdrawals, but the harsh side effects still lasted for many months. At 22 years old, my body chemistry was so altered that even when I made big strides in getting healthy, there were aspects of my health that didn't improve quickly at all. My nervous system felt like it was fried, and in addition to that, the production of serotonin in my brain and gut seemed like it was reduced to a small trickle. It was some time before I could truly feel 'normal,' much less experience sustained wellness.

In addition to all of my psychic abilities, my emotions had also become numb. For a long time, it was almost as though I could feel nothing. When I would consciously let go of the pain, the energetic aspect of my soul would heal the negative and fragmented sections of my mind and body. But in order for this process to work, I had to constantly and consciously engage in the act of being aware of my awareness itself, and then from that observational place allow the 'light' of my soul to guide my mind to the parts of my body that needed healing.

This was not always easy to do, because the world appears to be set up in a way that distracts an individual from doing this deep inner work, but I was persistent and eventually I was able to reach a place of moderate balance. At first, it was a process of mind over matter, but that was just the beginning. Once I was able to shift my focus from feeling *off* to not just believing but actually *knowing* the energies that animated my body would heal me, just as they would a wound, then I was able to heal rapidly with very little, if any, conscious input. It was like I had to trick my mind into focusing primarily on this animating principle of my consciousness itself, but once I did, a powerful energy took over and did the rest.

Now that I was clean, I had a great interest in health. I wanted to be vibrant in every way I could. I began educating myself in every form of natural health and healing that was available to me.

Often I would drive to Hallowell to visit Abbott, and on one of these drives, I noticed a new sign on a building that said *Kundalini Yoga and Meditation School*. After attending one class, I was hooked. I began attending three to five nights a week for the next year and a half while becoming very friendly with the people who ran it. They taught me about Ayurveda and shared incredible stories about their many trips to India, where they trained to become the teachers that they were. Their Kundalini techniques definitely activated aspects of my previously super-conscious awareness that had gone dormant for a while, but never disappeared.

I was now growing in leaps and bounds. My mind and body were becoming strong, but I still had issues. The spiritual vibrancy that I possessed before I was addicted to heroin had not even remotely returned.

In my mind, this was good and bad. My goal before the addiction was to numb out my energetic abilities so that I could be a functional human being in the modern world as opposed to being primarily an energetic multi-dimensional entity perceiving the world through human senses. Now that this was the case, I felt incomplete. Not just incomplete, but damaged. I feared that the addiction might have hurt me in ways that rendered my hard-earned spiritual abilities inert. The constant communication with the iridescent guides that used to be a cornerstone of my heightened awareness had become so clouded that it almost seemed non-existent, to the degree that I began questioning myself to discern if it ever really happened in the first place. In response to those issues, I did constant energy arts practices (e.g., yoga, meditation, qi-gong, nutrition) with the hope that I could restore the damage that the heroin did.

Whenever I talked to Damian about these issues, he'd just give me this expression that said, *so what,* and he'd say almost nothing about it. This type of response frustrated me. While we were addicts, the entire pursuit of spiritual/energetic development did not occur. Heroin was the only pursuit. But now that we were clean, I felt ready to embody that aspect of myself in a sustainable way.

Damian was now bothered by my inquiries into these realms. From my perspective, he had changed a lot. I knew the heroin really messed him up, but the beating he withstood from Jimbo's home invasion was what hurt him the most. From the moment I found him lying in a pool of blood, he had never been the same. After that event, he became even quieter than he already was. It was almost as though he had taken a vow of silence, but it was more than that. Something was troubling him deeply, and I knew that he had no interest in sharing whatever it was with me.

A mutual friend of ours named Chad always questioned why we never had girlfriends. He did it so often I began to step back and think about this. Yes, years of my life had been spent developing my energetic awareness, and then the heroin addiction really threw a wrench into the works. I'd been so all about soul that I never made *myself* available to anyone and on top of this, I'd never known true intimacy with another.

Here I was, almost twenty-three years old and for the most part, I'd led a very reclusive, monastic type of life for the past seven years, despite the dark contrast of drug addiction. Could something as dirty and brutal as a heroin addiction be likened to the *clean* image that a monastic type of life conjures? Maybe not, but it was absolutely a spiritual struggle nonetheless, and if anything positive at all came out of it, it was that I knew I had tremendous inner strength. I was on the front lines of the soul's battlefield fighting tooth and nail for my life while seeking truth. Damian was the only other person I knew who had made it out of one of the most deadly of addictions. Every single one of the people that we had gotten into it with was all still doing it, including Florence. I begged her to stop. I told her that I'd help her and be with her if she was able to, but she didn't want to stop because she felt like she couldn't. You have to be ready to stop. You have to want life more than you want to get high, and unfortunately, I've met very few who wanted to choose life over addiction. It was a choice that required serious determination and will power in order to succeed. I realized that at some point I would really help those who want to get clean be able to do so.

Chad's constant inquiries into my self-chosen celibate life did make me consider why I was choosing to live the way I was. I was a little gun shy because I'd witnessed firsthand how people would respond to the intense psychic frequencies that Damian could emit. Though nowhere near his level, I was afraid that if I got close with a woman, she too would flee once she felt how intense of a being I really was.

At this time, I met a woman. It was one of those instant connections that you see in the movies. I felt the energy between us and really wanted to explore it, but the circumstances of our life didn't match, so I let it go for the time being. However, I couldn't stop wondering about her.

Later in the spring of 1998, my parents invited my brother and me on a family trip to Alaska. I decided to go. It was the first time I had been around my family in almost seven years. At first, it was awkward, but then it became very healing for all of us. It was the first time since I had left home at such a young age that I realized how much I loved and missed them despite the conditioning of their unconditional love. I also saw how much they loved my brother and me. They had no idea of the extremes I had been through during that time. As soon as I mentioned anything about it, they would shut down. It hurt me really badly to see how much my choices hurt them, but at the same time, they had no idea how lucky they were that I was alive and in front of them. They had no idea how many times I had come within moments of death, and the seemingly countless near-death experiences I had sustained. It could have been so tragic for them if I had actually passed, but miraculously I didn't. When they became sad about how my life had turned out, I tried explaining why they should be grateful, and they were open to that, but they still were not able to confront their own guilt in regard to how my life appeared to have turned out to them. Regardless, as a family, we had all reunited, and we all were happy about it despite their inability to confront their own wounding.

It was also on that trip that all four of us had the idea to start a business selling hemp oil body care products that consisted of lip balm, healing salve, and massage oil. We called it "The Maine Intellihemp Company" and not long after it got started, it blew up, as I was able to get placement for the line in almost a thousand stores across the country. Aside from the hemp shoes I sold in my teens, this was my first official and legal cannabis company. In the year 1998, hardly anyone even knew what hemp was. Our company helped educate a lot of people!

Meanwhile, summertime brought news of a giant Phish concert in northern Maine. Phish is known as a *jam band* that attracts a very festive hippie circus type of environment. The music is like special effects Rock and Roll. It had the potential to be a very fun scene, but dangerous fun. There were lots of drugs and non-Phish fans who attended these shows to exploit any opportunity in their path. Often the unsuspecting fans became prey for these predatory *opportunivores*.

Regardless of the shady elements, it was sure to be a good time. Our friend Chad took the entire event all too seriously. He had an oversized RV stocked with food and party supplies as well as a big entourage to follow us up there. One of the members of his entourage was a guy from California they called *Crystal Dean*. His name was fitting for his interests and his talents. He could go into areas around the world known for crystal and gemological activity and become a *human dowsing rod* of sorts, able to detect pockets of gems and crystals.

Dean made frequent trips to Maine because it is regarded as one of the most geologically diverse and abundant areas in the world, with world-class tourmaline crystals. Over the next few years, he taught me how to unlock my own gem dowsing abilities, a gift that has brought me many incredible discoveries. It is a practice that has invoked in me a deep metaphysical connection to the Earth. The first time that

I discovered and opened up a pocket filled with crystals on my own, space, and time ceased to exist.

Being deep in the woods as the first person in 250-300 million years to discover a chamber of crystals entombed in rock since way before the dinosaurs existed is an experience unlike any other. To reach your hands into one of these pockets that have been sealed in darkness for hundreds of millions of years is indescribable. To feel with your hands, the perfectly smooth geometric faces that crystal possesses and then to take a vividly colored crystal out from its ancient resting place is sublime. To know that not only is it the first time this wonder of nature has seen sunlight but that it is the first time it has ever felt a human hand, it to experience the sacred in a way that cannot be described. Next to building a solid state of internal heart-brain coherence or selfless soul-filled lovemaking, it may be one of the most direct ways for a human to physically connect to the divine. For a consciously aware human being, it is not a process to be taken lightly. The first time that it happened to me, it so deeply rocked my world that I couldn't imagine experiencing it again, but over the years it continued to happen, again and again many, many times. Great reverence and gratitude are always paid and displayed by me whenever it does.

When we all arrived at the concert grounds, we discovered that it was being attended by tens of thousands of people. The energy of it all was overwhelming. It felt claustrophobic. Since coming back from Jamaica, I had limited my cannabis smoking only for the medicinal effects and cut out drug use. At this concert, I decided to recreationally use some MDA, a derivative of ecstasy, only to conclude that I was absolutely over the temporary rush of drug use that brought harsh long-term side effects. It created way more pain and negative consequences than it was worth. At that point, the only reason I could justify doing drugs for was ceremonial purposes like peyote, Ayahuasca, and other sacraments, but in all reality, those were not really drugs when done with sincere intentions to know one's self.

Damian came with us to the festival, but he was quiet the whole ride there. When we got to the grounds, he didn't hang out with our group very much at all. He was like a ghost. You'd think you were seeing him around, but upon closer examination, he wasn't there.

Even though we both still lived together, we didn't spend much time with each other, and when we did, we'd hardly say a word. I gave him the space he needed to process whatever it was that he was going through. The whole teacher/student relationship had pretty much ended once we became addicted to heroin, but after the beating he took during the home invasion, it became non-existent. Like I said earlier, I wondered what on earth he could be going through, but I didn't want to pry.

The first night at the Phish concert was an all-night party for 70,000 people. It was as wild as anyone would expect a drug-fueled party that size to be. When that many people get completely wasted like that, suddenly they don't seem like people anymore. They become something else. The dark psychic vibes that go through a party that size, where so many people were so high, are intense, exciting, sometimes fun and at times gruesome. But there are always random pockets of goodness.

By the time morning came it looked and felt like a bomb had been dropped on the place. There was trash and hungover people everywhere. I was sitting in front of Chad's RV asking myself what I was doing there when I noticed two bright figures walking through all of the funky scents, sounds, and sights of this tie-dyed atmosphere.

Upon closer examination, I realized that it was Damian and a very beautiful woman. As they got closer, I could see that this was a woman unlike any other. She was angelic, but very grounded and real. She had long, brunette hair and a radiant smile. I knew upon the first impression that this was literally a match made in heaven. They appeared to be each other's equals. I had never once since I'd known Damian in this life, seen him so happy and smiling so much. Love circled them both like a magnetic field. When they stood next to each other, the aura was so bright that it was practically blinding. *What does this mean*, I asked myself.

Now I understood, or at least I thought I understood what he had been going through. He was conflicted because on some level he may have known that he would soon meet her. He probably felt like he had a choice to make. I wondered if this was a choice that he was challenged with in every lifetime or if this was a singular event. He could live alone, as a virgin, continuously advancing the supernatural powers he'd developed over lifetimes of accumulating this godly energy or he could choose to share these powers directly with this woman who as far as I could tell, possessed the spiritual capacity to *get* who he truly was. In those moments, I realized that for him, the risk was not so much in having a lover it was the choice that having a lover presented.

If I was able to even partially comprehend what he had explained to me after my profound awakening at the age of eighteen, it was that he had a choice that was at the top of any decision that any person could ever make. That choice was to live as a supernatural being in a human form, ceaselessly cultivating his energetic potential through countless lifetimes, growing stronger every time that he was born, becoming more god-like, or he could pass this self-developed evolutionary potential to a child with a fresh *blueprint*. A child with a brand new soul and body free of all the trial, error, and suffering that he himself had been subjected to both intentionally and as a victim of evolutionary circumstances.

After years of training with him, I learned the secrets of my own evolutionary potential that I would have previously believed to be impossible. But at the same time, while I had no way of knowing how serious his choice of choices actually was for him or what it entailed, I had no reason not to conclude it was far more serious than I was able to comprehend.

His angelic counterpart walked up to me and introduced herself. "Hi! My name is Izabella. Damian told me that you are his closest friend!"

In a very cheesy gesture, I took her hand and kissed it like a sixteenth-century nobleman. *Why the hell did I just do that,* I said to myself, but I quickly followed this up with, "This is true! It's wonderful to meet you. I see almost like a bright halo around you!"

She started laughing, and I felt kind of stupid for saying that. "Well, it looks like you had a good night!"

"Ha! I wouldn't necessarily say good, but I had a night!"

Damian than introduced her to other members of our group and then they walked off. Once they were gone, Chad immediately came over to me and said, "Whoa! I never thought I'd ever see the day when Dame met someone!"

I didn't say anything, but I thought *I was sure I wouldn't ever see this day,* and I was resisting it. However, as soon as I felt resistance to it, I stopped myself and asked why I felt this way. The reason why was that I was afraid to lose him as a friend and a teacher.

Once I acknowledged that, a flood of compassion poured through my heart because deep down, I had nothing but love and respect for him and his choices.

I crawled into the little tent that I had set up, and I began to meditate. A flood of images was streaming through my mind. I saw what seemed like a hundred past lives where Damian and Izabella had met. Their faces and bodies were always different, but their souls were the same--life before life before life. They had come together and met up many times, but they never fused their souls together. I couldn't get clarity as to what might happen with them in this life but based on those images I saw in my meditation, I knew that whatever their 'dharma' was, it was powerful beyond my limited awareness. I shuddered and tried to shake those images out of my head because they were intense. But it was difficult to do.

I kept asking myself, *If they keep meeting then isn't this an obvious sign that a child is supposed to come out of their union? Or is it like Damian said - a choice that he alone has to make? Is Izabella just a test for him to overcome in an attempt to prove to the universe that he is a worthy soul who deserves to keep developing this otherworldly power unfolding inside of him? Or is she his equal other half, designed by the divine forces to bring through a new soul who is far more pure and advanced than the both of them combined? Was Damian being selfish and resisting this opportunity to create a truly divine being? Even though the energetic potential he has developed was not from him originally* (it came from the source of divinity itself) *had he begun convincing himself that it was indeed his own? He had worked so hard at developing it through so many lifetimes, was he suffering because his own ego was getting in the way, fooling him into believing that he was a god and not just a blessed vessel through which this energy worked? Like cosmic-consciousness megalomania?*

I may never know, but meeting Izabella and seeing Damian with her was not just a random occurrence. It was like a rare celestial event that happens once in millennia, if that. And even through all these unanswered questions, the compassion I felt in my heart remained.

CHAPTER TWENTY

A grand mystery

Damian and Izabella were spending as much time together as they were able to. She lived in New York State and was making weekend trips up to Maine. When they weren't together in person, they were talking on the phone. There was no doubt in my mind, or anyone else's who knew Damian that he was over his head in love with her. It was really refreshing to see this, but it caused me to ponder in the deepest of ways what this could possibly mean for this insanely supernatural path he had walked for lifetimes. He remained a good friend to me while he was courting Izabella but not once uttered a word about the energetic potential of the soul, and he gave me no advice about personality corrections. I couldn't help but wonder what he was thinking or planning, but from all outward appearances, their relationship was a serious one. Izabella and Damian were all about each other. They couldn't get enough.

During this time, I discovered I was really good at selling our family's hemp products as they were now in close to 1500 stores across the country. It was really funny because at one point a friend called me and told me they were in the middle of nowhere in Northern California at a gas station, and they found our hemp lip balm from Maine there!

I loved the response that the store owners I sold to had when I told them that the first American flag was made of hemp, the declaration of independence was printed on hemp as well as many other industrial applications during America's earlier days. Not only had I become passionate about it, but I also became an advocate for it and literally envisioned the day when hemp and cannabis would become legal in the US and then the world. At that time no one said it would ever happen, at least not in this lifetime anyway.

I also found a love for using and selling potent nutritional supplements because of my devout interest in them. I had been taking products from a company that had a big line of herbs and products based on traditional Chinese medicine. I found these products to contribute to my wellbeing in a powerful way. Because of this, I learned a lot about health and longevity herbs. As a result of this interest, I was able to generate a really good legitimate income that was also supplemented by selling high-quality cannabis as well.

When late autumn came around Damian wanted to have a meeting. He told me that he and Izabella had gotten a loan and were buying a house in Lovell, Maine. Both of their families were helping to make this a reality. He told me about the house and their plans for it, and then he dropped the bomb. "Bro, I have something very important to tell you."

"OK, what is it?"

"Izabella is pregnant.

Oh my God, I thought. It took my breath away. "Yeah?"

"You are more than welcome to come visit, but do not talk to me about, 'turn up the vibes' or ask any questions regarding anything that happened or anything that I taught you ever again. It's over. The abilities I once had are gone. You're on your own with it. It's the end of the story. Okay?"

He told me all this in a very direct and stern manner that didn't give me any room to ask a single question at that moment. I just agreed, congratulated him and said that I'd honor his request.

From that moment on, the Damian that I knew was gone. Someone who had been my mentor, and my one true ally, had left me. It was hard to explain what this meant to my inner core; after all of this time, I was on my own with all of this.

Personally, now that I was getting healthy, I wanted to learn how to integrate all of the lessons that I'd learned from Damian into my psychological make-up in a balanced way. I wasn't expecting him to teach this to me, but I hoped that he would. I kept vacillating, going back and forth in my mind telling myself that I am ready to do this on my own, and then I'd doubt I was ready.

After Damian told me this, I began to really question life on a whole other level as the lines between fantasy and reality were becoming hard to distinguish. The entire thing was like fiction, science fiction, really. Was it really like this, or was there something wrong with my perception of it all? Was the reason that the experiences of my life were more like fantasy as opposed to reality because I was losing my mind or delusional? But then I centered myself and remembered that the truth is stranger than fiction and that life *is* a miracle, regardless of how few are truly aware of it. I felt I wasn't delusional, not overtly anyway. I was just overwhelmed with living in two worlds at once. I knew myself as spirit and as a human, but I had not yet achieved the balance allowing me to sustainably bridge the gap between the two worlds.

I saw Qi-gong and Yoga as absolutely helping me to achieve this equanimity, but it was a slow process. I had awakened very fast, at a very young age and then built a "Chinese wall" around my awareness to block it out. This wall was challenging to deconstruct on my own.

Having Damian cut me off made me feel very alone and unsure how to proceed. Since I had gotten addicted to heroin, my capacity to focus the bulk of my awareness into the energetic realms became weakened to the point where I began to identify more with the limits of my ego as opposed to the limitlessness of my soul. I knew that I had to tip the scales back towards the limitlessness of my soul, but the dysfunction of my ego made this difficult to do. With Damian out of the picture, I needed more information.

I spent a lot of time at bookstores in Portland trying to learn more about the experiences that others had in relation to this inner energy. There used to be a health food store in Portland called The Whole Grocer. One day while looking through their books, I found something that grabbed my attention. It was about a spiritual healer in Brazil named Joao de Deus or John of God. The book told about the type of healer that he was. It said that he would be there as the person he was one moment and then out of nowhere, his body would become inhabited by one of potentially hundreds of different *spirit entities*. The entities were the incarnate spirits of people who were once living as doctors, healers, scientists, and even philosophers. These entities would use his body to perform *miracle* healings on the sick and elderly. After the healing work was completed, the entity would leave his body, and Joao would wake up not remembering anything that had happened. I resonated with this deeply. I thought about the festival at age eighteen when I went unconscious and spirits used my body to ward off the belligerent men who were threatening everyone. This wasn't a medical healing, but it seemed that spirits were definitely using me for what I'd say was good, plus I did not remember any of it happening when I came to.

Reading this book inspired me to want to study with this man. There were no doubts in my mind that I had paranormal abilities, and from what I read, they might possibly be an undeveloped form of the abilities that he supposedly had. The book was a pretty old printing. It claimed that after a long flight and a 36-hour bus ride through mountains, hills and plateaus the seeker would arrive at the *Casa de Dom Ignacio* in Abadiania, Brazil, where Joao de Deus held his practice.

I bought the book, walked out to my car and then I sat in it to meditate. I could clearly see and feel myself at this place in the presence of Joao and all of the entities. I felt that what I'd read was authentic, even though the reality of it all was way crazier then I could have ever imagined. I made the decision to go no matter what it took and that I needed to leave as soon as possible.

After some research, I discovered that after the flight to the capital of Brasilia, Abadiania was only an hour and a half cab ride, not a grueling, but potentially exciting 36-hour bus ride through the jungle. I was slightly relieved to hear this, but also a little dismayed. The idea of the journey to the place felt like it'd be just as rewarding as reaching the destination.

After getting the contact info of people who led trips to and from Abadiania, I was able to rent a *posada* near the healing center. The people who led these expeditions all verified the information in the book was mostly accurate. They claimed to have witnessed many miraculous healings take place during their visits to the *Casa*, as they called it. I told them that I didn't perceive myself to be physically ill and that I felt called to make the journey for spiritual fulfillment. They said that I would not be alone. There were many people who go for similar reasons.

I let the people in my life know my plans. Everyone, for the most part, was very supportive, though some were afraid that I'd disappear into the jungles forever!

I showed Damian the book that I bought and told him about my plans. He had absolutely nothing to say about it other than, "Looks good. Have a great trip." At that point, I guess that was all I could expect from him.

CHAPTER TWENTY-ONE

John of God

(Disclaimer: since I wrote this book, the global media has accused John of God of horrendous crimes against woman and children. The accusations are so severe that if they're true, I hope justice is served swiftly and to the full extent. However, it was really hard for me to believe what he is being accused of, especially when the media outlets attacking him are known to be the most corrupt in the country of Brazil.

But these accusations against him were even more difficult for me to believe when countless people with illnesses that span from moderate to inoperable have been able to heal after visits to the Casa, even though there were many people didn't experience any healing whatsoever.

With that said, I was fortunate to have met many people who have successfully healed in the presence of this man. It was definitely a reality for many. People were healing in a way that most cannot explain with any modern scientific justification. Again, it just didn't make sense to me that he would have been involved in such heinous crimes, but I don't know what is real and what is being fabricated in his arrest.

And, in this case, the conspiracies against someone who is bi-passing the modern medical industry make more sense than the crimes he's been accused of, but who knows, because I've also spoken with many people that have tremendous integrity who claim to know for a fact that the accusations against him are indeed true.

I visited John of God at the Casa De Dom Ignacio in Abadiania Brazil in 2001 long before Oprah Winfrey, and others made his works world-famous, and again, what I did witness was many people healing of inoperable diseases while I was there, and a medium who seemed to be precisely tuned in to what ailed people. The healings that took place there that I personally witnessed far exceed any literal explanation as they're beyond the minds ability to understand.

But again, if the accusations against him are true, then may he be punished to the full extent of the law. If they are all false, then let those who have made these accusations fully experience and process the karmic implications that would incite them to make such accusations so that they do not continue to hurt the innocent).

The following was my experience with John of God.

My flight was long on the way to Brazil. Once I had landed, the *posada* where I was staying at had a cab waiting for me. The ride from Brasilia to Abadiania revealed a plateau-like country how I would envision the plains of Africa to look. Like Jamaica, there was a lot of the poverty that was evident.

After arriving at my *posada,* I was brought to see the healing center. It was almost exactly how I envisioned it to be, but I didn't detect any paranormal activity that was beyond the norm. For a moment, I felt slightly discouraged, but my host told me that Joao was out of town and would be returning tomorrow. I let go of my anticipation and decided to remain open-minded and hearted.

All around the Casa de Dom Ignacio, there were new age pictures and paintings. They had an area where wheelchairs and crutches were dropped on top of each other into a heaping pile. This was from all of the people who had experienced miraculous healings from being crippled or paralyzed. I was told that they left this stuff behind so that new arrivals could have faith in their own healing taking place. It was all certainly very interesting. Most everyone who I met around there that day whole-heartedly believed in the power of John and the entities, thus enhancing the placebo effect and positive energy of the place.

I was brought back to the *posada* for the night. When I awoke the next morning, my head was ringing in a good way. I could sense paranormal activity.

When I arrived at the healing center, there were hundreds of visitors from all over the world. While most were there for health reasons, others were not. Many people were medical rejects. They were people whose doctors had given up on them. They came here as a last resort, praying that John could save their physical lives.

Before anyone got to meet John, an *energetic soup* was given to all of us. It was a simple vegetable/bean broth with some spices that had been spiritually energized by *the entities*. After the soup was eaten, the attendees began filing into what they called the *current* rooms. John, while *in trançe,* was sitting in front of these three rooms, directing people to go into the specific room that was being worked by entities tending to certain ailments. Before going in, we were told to sit where John asked us to and under no condition were we to open our eyes while we were sitting there. We could open our eyes once we were informed that it was time to leave.

When I stood before John, his English interpreter told me to sit in the second room. Once seated, I shut my eyes and began to meditate. It was really hard for me to concentrate because on top of all the commotion. The experience of being here had me very excited. I tried to just go inward and focus.

As I was sitting with my palms up, I felt someone place their hand in my left hand. I knew that I wasn't supposed to open my eyes, but I couldn't resist. I had to see who was holding my hand. I opened my left eye and peaked towards my left hand. What I saw made tears gush from my eyes and caused every goosebump on my body to swell, because there was no one visibly there! Not anyone in human form anyway.

Not being able to see anybody there, yet still be able to feel a physical hand holding and gripping my own caused me to melt down. I couldn't control myself at all. *Was this really happening?* Maniacal crying and laughter began to project from my whole being. I jumped up from my seat and ran out of the meditation rooms and through a back door. I saw a knoll behind the casa, and I just kept running towards it. When I reached it, I just collapsed onto my knees and cried my heart out. It was a very cathartic type of release, but it was infused with joy. So many negative memories surfaced that I was able to shed. I let go of a lot of the agony that I'd created through my self-inflicted drug addiction. I stayed on this knoll for over a couple of hours while purging all of these emotive memories from my being. I kept thinking, "*What a crazy life.* Once I pulled myself together, a giant incandescent blue butterfly flew by me. Its beauty made me consider that on some level, I had just been transformed.

That one event in the Casa's current room was so powerful that it provided a tremendous healing force to enter my body. I acknowledged that this man, John, and his casa represented the coming together of the physical and the spiritual realms. It was a clear balance between the two worlds that I had hoped would provide the equanimity I sought for my own life experience. In my heart, I thanked John and the entities, and then I walked back to the casa.

When I got back there, I felt like I was living in heaven on Earth. I was so grateful and so in love with life that I wanted everyone to feel the same way, but I soon realized that many people there didn't feel like I did, they were definitely a minority. There were people there who were terminally ill. They didn't have such healing like mine take place yet. Most had hope, but it was obvious they'd been let down many times in the past, leaving them skeptical of the possibility of getting well here. Because of this, I played down my ecstatic joy.

That night my dreams were filled with otherworldly visions of unknown spheres. I woke up the next morning excited by the potential that I might experience that day.

Same as the day before, once everyone at the *posada* was ready to go, we were brought over to the Casa. After eating the spiritual soup, we began filing into the meditation rooms.

This time my host from the *posada* accompanied me to help translate my very specific request to John. They told me that John knew what I needed, so it didn't matter if I asked, but I wanted to anyway.

When it was my turn to be in front of him, he began speaking to me in a very quick-witted manner. Even though I didn't speak Portuguese, I was able to understand that I was being lectured to. The interpreter told me that the entity speaking through John said, "You do not need your spiritual eye opened. If anything, you need to not look through it as much as you do. If you start looking at life by softening your gaze through your two eyes more often, you will find the balance you are looking for. Go sit in the third room and keep all of your eyes closed!"

His message hit me like a ton of bricks. My request was to more fully open my spiritual eye so that I could see through it clearly. I had hoped this would bring me balance. Not only did the entity speaking through John know what my request was, but its advice was also the opposite of what I was going to ask for. It implied that I looked through my spiritual eye too much, that's why I was off-balance, but I didn't feel this was the case.

I went and sat in the third room as I was instructed. As I sat down, I made sure to focus all of my awareness in my body. Eagerly I anticipated some kind of intense contact with an entity as the day before, but there was nothing. I sat there meditating for around fifteen minutes, but nothing out of the ordinary happened.

I spent the bulk of my days at the Casa meditating and meeting fascinating people from all over the world. It was on this trip that I first learned about eating an organic raw vegan diet. The group of people who told me about it and ate that way were all happy, vibrant, and glowing. I knew that when I got back to Maine, I was going to learn as much about it as possible.

Every day that John was there, I would file into the current rooms for spirit healings. One day he told the interpreter that he wanted me to stay at the Casa so that I could work. Everyone around told me that this was a tremendous blessing that he offered to very few. Work was his way of keeping someone around so that they could heal and be trained.

At the time there was a man from Portugal that was nicknamed *Little John* because big John had taken him under his wing, so to say. Little John had been there for five months when I arrived. The host of my *posada* told me that when he first arrived in Abadiania, no one thought that he would live. While living in Portugal, he had become a severe drug addict with different strains of hepatitis and possibly other autoimmune diseases. There were open sores all over his body, and he supposedly looked like a skeleton. Thinking that he was going to die, he came to Abadiana as a last-ditch effort. John said that he would heal him, and he did. Every month that he was there, his health improved significantly. By month three, John of God pronounced, "You are healed." Little John decided that he was going to stay at the Casa because John and the entities gave him his life back.

Little John and I talked a lot, and he urged me to stay. I told him that I was considering it. But in the back of my mind, I began feeling like that I wasn't ready to stay down in this part of the world for as long as I might need to, in order to work with and be trained by John. Additionally, I had a strange intuitive feeling about being there that I hadn't been able to put my finger on yet, but something felt 'off' about me being there. Before I came down here, I was sure that this was what I wanted to do with my life, but now that I was here, I wasn't so sure. It was a huge commitment, and the life I had in Maine felt like it was good.

With my mind made up, I filed into the current rooms to appear before John for my last time. When I stood before him, the interpreter explained that I was leaving. He looked at me, then he looked at my abdomen, and he told the interpreter that I had not been healed yet.

"Healed? I didn't think there was anything wrong with me," I said.

The interpreter said John's response was, "In this life I had entered into chambers that few have, and because of this, I had a responsibility, but that I'm not fulfilling it. The longer that I ignore this responsibility, the more unhealthy I will become." Then he had me go sit in the third current room.

After the session was over and everyone was asked to leave, I went back to the knoll behind the Casa and just looked out at the landscape, feeling that I had been kicked in the face. I considered what John said. The thing was, I knew he was 100% right. I had a monumental responsibility that I tried to hide from with hard drugs. I knew the whole time that I couldn't run and hide from what I am, but I tried to anyway, and I still was. *What the hell am I doing? And it was at that moment, for the first time, when I experienced what the strange intuitive feeling I had in my gut was – in addition to the bright light of this whole place, there was also a very dark, seemingly evil and malevolent energy here, and I knew that I had to leave.*

I watched a flock of small green parrots in a tree nearby. Two blue and gold macaws were flying in the distance and squawking loudly. I loved that.

Sure, I was aware that I hadn't taken responsibility for making my soul and its direct connection to the divine my number-one priority. I was also aware that I had made the desires of the ego my primary motive, but there was only so much I could do! Damian was done with all this spiritual stuff, so I no longer had the guidance I once did, plus I didn't want to stay in Brazil for months or years. Still, John's words and the way he stared at my stomach concerned me, as did the overwhelmingly evil presence I sensed come out of nowhere. However, in those moments, I concluded that I felt fine, and decided that I was going to leave anyway. Besides, I could continue my energetic practices on my own in Maine.

For the entire cab ride from Abadiania to Brasilia and throughout the flights home, I felt both conflicted about leaving, while at the same time ready to get the hell out of there. John asked me to stay, and I refused the offer. Why would I have turned this offer down when on my way here I was actually hoping something like this would present itself?

Though I didn't want to admit it, I knew the answer. In addition to the malevolent force I felt there, at that point, my ego was still in resistance to serving the needs of my soul. It justified its own narcissism and selfishness by wanting to stay in its state of Maine comfort zone. By doing this, I was denying something else that I knew very well… that higher awareness is only truly expanded outside of my comfort zone.

CHAPTER TWENTY-TWO

Change

Upon coming home, I made health, energy medicine, nutrition, and fitness my primary objectives. Meditation and Qigong were the icing on the cake. My interest in these practices went to the next level. I became a devout Ashtanga practitioner working at mastering what is called the primary series one and two. Bikram was a style of *hot* yoga that I did on the side to bring more variation to my practice. Interestingly, yoga, once intended to be primarily a spiritual practice first, had become a very *physical* practice for me. Most that I practiced with were really only interested in the physical aspect of it. The energetics of spirituality was more of an afterthought for most of the yoga practitioners that I engaged with.

My brother and I rented a house near Damariscotta, Maine, near the ocean. We had a roommate named Neil, who became a best friend to both of us. We all shared the same interests and made a great brotherhood and team. The three of us all started eating a 100% raw vegan diet, and we really enjoyed our *raw* food lifestyle and all the adventures that it created. I worked at a local health food store stocking the produce aisles. The three of us became inseparable and obsessed with eating this diet.

Neil, my brother, and I began attending raw food events all over North America. We'd be in California one week, Montreal the next, Oregon the week after that and then New York. We were constantly going everywhere, meeting lots of new people and becoming inspired by this vibrant community that was sprouting all over the world. There were so many people we met who we felt we'd known our whole lives.

My brother and I have always had an incredible psychic connection. He would constantly complete sentences that I started, and we often knew what each other was thinking. Our bond as brothers and friends grew tremendously. It was very nourishing for my brother and me to bond like this.

Very oddly, during this time period, my ego started to become massively inflated as my interests in materialism and 'pleasures of the flesh' began to take priority over my energetic awareness.

While staying in Montreal, I met a girl named Denise. We fell in love immediately. She was a beautiful woman with a heady intellect. We used to engage each other in constant philosophical conversations even though she often accused me of being an enigmatic egotist. After about a year of me going to Montreal and Toronto to visit her, and then she coming to Maine to visit me, our relationship ended for one major reason. She wanted me to be what I wasn't ready to become - a father. But before she broke up with me, she witnessed me at my worst.

On one of my extended trips to visit her in Montreal, I began to notice a rash appearing on my left leg. I didn't think much about it until later that day when I noticed another rash popping out on my right leg.

After going to sleep, I woke to find this same rash covering my arms. By the third day, my whole body, except for my face, neck, and hands were covered by it. The day after it was so bad that it looked like

I'd walked through a fire. Three-quarters of my body appeared to be covered by third-degree burns. It was so itchy that it was intolerable. On the fourth day, Denise urged me to see a doctor, because whatever it was, was consuming me.

The first doctor I saw told me he had never seen anything like it. He urged me to see a dermatologist at a major hospital in Montreal. The dermatologist said it was a major systematic infection of some type and told me to take antibiotics immediately. Desperately I did as he instructed, but this only worsened my condition considerably. The rash began to itch so badly that it became practically impossible for me not to scratch it until it bled.

My friends, deeply concerned after seeing this reaction to the antibiotics, found a naturopathic doctor for me to see instead. This guy did a bunch of tests and diagnosed the condition as systemic Candidiasis or Candida albicans, and said it was the worst infection of it he had ever seen or heard of. He put me on a few cycles of rotating herbs to help knock it out, but this treatment did nothing to relieve me of the symptoms. After seeing that his treatment was not working, he suggested I go to an ozone therapy clinic that at the time, was only available at underground clinics in Mexico and Canada. Desperate and in pain, I went to one of these clinics.

They had me lie down in a medical reclining chair and then drained quarts of my blood into big IV bags. Ozone, which is thought to kill pathogens and cancer cells by hyper-oxygenation, is then administered into the drained blood. Once the ozone has been infused into the blood, it was then put back into my body. I did this for ten days in a row with no results.

At this point, I was in misery. I had been to four different practices that did nothing to relieve my suffering. Meanwhile, the rash had gotten worse. Whatever it was, in addition to bleeding, it was oozing yellow pus down my arms and legs. This combination would soak through my clothes. It was terrible. Denise was afraid for me. She made a beautiful meal of raw food delicacies, but I couldn't eat more than a few bites. In fact, any bit of food that I ate caused me excessive stomach pain. I kept thinking about a diagram that the naturopathic doctor showed me of the Candida organism. It looked like a net or a spider web starting in my intestines and spreading out through them and into the organs of my body. I began praying to my higher and inner forces for help.

All of my friends in Montreal urged me to go back to Maine so that I could seek specialized care in the States. I drove myself back to Maine from Canada, which was extremely difficult due to the pain, itching, and exhaustion.

Feeling defeated, I decided to see my parents first. I needed their emotional support. When they saw what I looked like my mother burst into tears. They rushed me to the Brunswick Mid-coast Hospital. The doctor who I saw there said that what I was dealing with was beyond the scope of his care. He referred me to an advanced dermatologist in Waterville. Meanwhile, I could no longer eat solid foods. My diet was a mixture of blended and juiced organic vegetables. My weight dropped considerably. I was skin and bones.

The dermatologist was flummoxed as well, so I went to see a naturopath who did a slew of testing. The thing that kept coming back was Candida. She told me that it had probably turned into leaky gut syndrome. She explained that Candida is a micro-bacterial organism that is present in every human's gastrointestinal tract. There is a balance of *friendly* and *unfriendly* bacteria within everyone. Candida is an unfriendly bacteria that is required for proper digestion but kept in check by a host of other bacterial strains. When these unfriendly forms of bacteria overtake the friendly forms of bacteria, either from poor diet, antibiotics, IV drug use or other causes, the Candida can proliferate to the extent it takes over the small and even the large intestine. When this occurs, it begins eating holes through the GI tract. This is called leaky gut. The Candida organism along with particles of undigested food with then escape through the now permeable GI tract and enter the bloodstream. Once it enters the bloodstream, it will find its way into other organs, making it a systemic infection. When food particles escape through the intestines, an autoimmune response kicks in. White blood cells attack the food because they recognize it as a foreign invader. This attack of food creates a formaldehyde-like substance that tries to escape from the body through the skin. This is where the rash comes from.

This was the best explanation I had heard yet. It made sense. Especially the part about how systemic Candidiasis can result from IV drug use. Hearing all of this caused me to remember John of God looking at my abdomen and telling me that I was not yet healed. I also remembered him telling me that if I didn't fulfill my spiritual responsibilities, my health would further degrade. He saw this thing in me four years before it manifested into this terrible condition. *If I had only stayed*, I thought to myself. I considered going back, but with open sores all over my body, I might be too susceptible to foreign infections. I reflected on where I was in my life. I had become an over-inflated ego who took no responsibility for the incredibly rare spiritual gifts I once embodied. "Look at me now," I thought.

THE FIGHT TO ENLIGHT

My lack of appetite and inability to eat most foods caused my weight to steeply drop off again. I was literally skin and bones with a horrid rash covering my body. I became morbidly depressed, realizing that whatever I was dealing with was so aggressive, nothing but time would heal it. There was also no proof that it would even heal. I was at the beginning of a long tribulation.

Despite all the power I had within me, I continued to look towards other places outside of me for salvation and not within where deep down I knew I had to intuitively look if I was to truly find healing. This option failed me, as it always had before.

CHAPTER TWENTY-THREE

Candida

My parents were afraid of how rapidly my condition was deteriorating. They wanted me nearby, so I stayed with them on the coast and then I rented a place down the road. At this point, it had been four months since I first became ill in Montreal.

All but a few weeks of this time was spent eating blended and juiced vegetables. My body was so frail that I couldn't stand looking at myself in the mirror.

The time that I spent in the rental house down the road from my parents greatly contributed to my depression. My energy levels were so low that getting out of bed to use the bathroom or make blended food was a huge chore. It was clear that Denise was avoiding me. Before I got sick, we both knew our relationship would soon end. Her patience with me had already worn thin before I was stricken with this illness. Once I got sick, she became my caretaker, day and night, and although she generously offered to do it, it caused her great stress. Our relationship could not withstand this, and ended. I encouraged it because just the trip from Canada to Maine was too much for her.

As I sat in this coastal Maine house, deathly ill and all alone, a desolate depression kicked in, worse than it already was. What was happening? Was this disease trying to tell me something? Was I ready to listen to it even if it was?

My parents suggested that I get all of the medical testing I could. I made appointments for endoscopies, colonoscopies, blood tests, skin samples, hormone tests, heavy metal tests, everything there was. The results of the test revealed nothing other than Candida. The big problem with this diagnosis was that most of the medical doctors claimed the condition called Candidiasis was scientifically unjustified by the allopathic community. It was looked upon as bad science.

On the other end of the spectrum, the natural health community claimed that Candida is a very real and serious threat with a slew of conspiracy theories as to why the allopathic community doesn't recognize it. Based on my personal observations, I slanted towards the natural community's beliefs; however the natural treatments didn't bring any lasting relief. Medical doctors tried to convince me it was all in my mind, that stress was causing the symptoms. The natural side told me not to listen to them, but nothing they offered had any lasting effect. The theories on both sides were shot full of holes, and neither of them provided solutions. There seemed to be no common ground. Meanwhile, I was wasting away to nothing with flesh-eating bacteria all over my skin and chronic pain all through my insides. Of course, deep down, I knew that the solution was within myself, but I had lost all touch with my ability to know and experience this type of healing.

To deal with my depression, I tried to keep as active as possible. In addition to seeing the beautiful natural sites of Maine, I also took trips around the country. The mission of every one of these trips was to find doctors and healers from all ends of the spectrum. The pursuit of this goal kept my depression at bay. I continued to sell marijuana to pay for my traveling and health care, and it was becoming very stressful. I was caught in a vicious cycle. If I didn't seek treatments that helped my condition, I would lose hope. If I stopped traveling, I became depressed, and if I didn't sell cannabis, I couldn't afford to travel and seek solutions. There were many times I felt like I was fighting a losing battle. In reality, I was. In the back of my mind, I knew I was suffering because I was not being the responsible spiritualized being I knew I really was. I wasn't ready to be responsible for that because I was afraid of living in this world with that type of power and responsibility, or so I told myself.

I maintained a strict Candida diet, all organic, no gluten, no fruit, no vinegar, and no spices. When I ate this diet, the symptoms were all there, but they were just a little bit more tolerable. The chronic insomnia I felt from the pain in my stomach was intolerable, though.

My life would switch from being ok to being a living nightmare. I still refused to *own* my spiritual integrity though I convinced myself that I didn't know how to do it on my own. My life had become the textbook definition of *unstable and imbalanced.* Once I had gotten to the point of sheer frustration, due to lack of sleep, my adrenaline started to surge. My adrenal glands actually began to constantly hurt.

During one of these anxiety adrenaline-filled nights, I ended up falling asleep from exhaustion. During that night, I had a lucid dream, unlike any other dream that I'd ever had. In it, there was invisible guidance. It showed me that I needed to relax and observe my life from the inside out because the cause of my suffering was spiritual, not physical. In this dream, my awareness was more acute than anything I had ever experienced in my *waking* life. Even though it was a dream, I was aware of my body in a way that I have never known. I could sense individually and in unison, the harmonious functioning of all my blood vessels, organs, bones, marrow, fingers, toes, limbs, all of it. My whole body inside and out worked perfectly. In addition to its physicality, there were luminous energy centers lit up inside and around me. I experienced being a holistic, living human temple. It was a near-perfect manifestation of divine consciousness in human form. This invisible guidance was giving me a glimpse of my potential.

To validate what it was showing me was real, the dream itself wanted to provide physical proof for my waking life, and so it showed me a place. It was a location in the mountains of Maine. It was a place I knew the general location of. Buried under the dirt was a vent containing many *pockets* of amethyst crystals.

The next day I woke up with this dream fresh in my mind. I made the two-hour drive to the area I saw. I went with my friend Gary, who had become my closest companion and mentor in these types of crystal discovery missions and who had also discovered the second biggest amethyst pocket in the US in the early 90's, right here in the state of Maine only three miles from the location that my dream had shown me. With my backpack full of food and water, my potato digger and my pickaxe, I began hiking towards the cliffs I saw in my dreams.

As I got near them, I heard a high-pitched sound, kind of like tinnitus, but much louder, ringing in my ears. The closer I got to where I thought I was going, the louder this ringing got. At first, I was confused by this sound. Why was it so loud? What did it mean? But then I remembered my old friend, Crystal Dean. He was a crystal dowser. He could feel crystal pockets in his bones. I sensed this ringing meant that I was near crystals.

I began getting really light-headed, but I pressed on. Finally, I arrived at the locale of my dream. The ringing in my ears sounded like a siren going off. I felt like I needed to sit down, but instead, I swung my pickaxe into the dirt. The very first swing into the dirt revealed a handful of small milky and clear quartz crystals. All my goosebumps swelled up, and a shiver of tingling energy went up and down my spine. The dream was real. The guidance was real.

I broke down into tears of joy. I felt healing energy inside and all around my body. I was so ecstatic that I felt like I was hyperventilating, and I decided to sit down on a stump after realizing how powerful it was to have a dream that turned into reality.

The view from high up on those cliffs was incredible. All in front of me were New Hampshire's White Mountains under a bright blue sky with puffy clouds. The smell of fresh earth and the site of small crystals in my hand invoked a powerful sensation of gratitude. In those moments, many gifts were bestowed upon me. I thanked the guidance in the dream. I thanked the Earth, and I thanked my awareness for being responsive enough to receive this guidance.

Over the next two years, this location produced thousands of amethyst, smoky and clear quartz crystals, although it was primarily amethyst. Some of the pockets produced deep purple gems. One pocket had crystals that were really big. One was the size of my head! This entire experience gave me renewed hope at a time when I needed it most. Little did I know that I would later form a full-spectrum hemp CBD company called Amethyst Elixir Company with the name inspired by this discovery in addition to the massive amethyst pocket my friend Gary had discovered.

However, my dysfunction at this time was programmed deep into my psychology. Even a powerful life-enriching experience handed down through a dream wasn't enough to save me from myself. I was such a victim that invisible guidance through a dream, awakening my spirit with gifts of translucent *rocks* wasn't enough to keep my enlightened focus! I would need to be stripped of all my ego's possessions and find myself at *rock bottom* between a rock and a hard place before I would pay attention and focus on what my spirit was trying to tell me!

Almost four years after becoming ill, I was able to get to a place where my condition was somewhat manageable, but it could change for the worse at the drop of a hat. Even the slightest deviation of my diet would trigger a return of symptoms that were intolerable. My entire outlook on life had become rooted in instability. Instead of digging deep into the core of my issues, which I could have done anytime, I chose to behave like a victim. Instead of feeding my soul, I fed my dysfunctional ego. This led me further and further from the potential that I knew was alive and well inside me. Though there were some good days, most were not, and even on the good ones, I still only sought to avoid the real issues I faced by giving in to the short-term desires of my ego. My life was spiraling down into a hole where I couldn't see any light at the end of the tunnel.

CHAPTER TWENTY-FOUR

Stars

My constantly shifting state of health made it difficult for me to think rationally at times and it created anticipatory anxiety because I never knew when my next outbreak would be, or how much I'd suffer from it. My friends described my state of health as a pendulum. As soon as it looked like I was getting better, I'd start falling ill again, and as soon as it looked like I'd fall off the deep end, I would rebound. There was no solid foundation for me to know what to expect – a true roller coaster of life experience.

After extensive traveling across the US, I returned back home, and my health crashed. There was nothing that I could eat that wouldn't trigger a systemic allergic reaction. I began to feel completely victimized by the whole ordeal. The cupboards in my house looked like a supplement display at a major health food store from all the health supplements I'd buy. I would try mixing up all kinds of different combinations of herbs and supplements with the hope that something would work, but nothing did.

My life had become a whirlwind of constantly looking for solutions to my health through traveling, word of mouth and trial and error that this mission produced. Underlying it all was the exhaustive pursuit to make money by selling illegal cannabis and the anxiety that always looking over my shoulder created. My insomnia was so chronic that I'd go nights with very little to no sleep. No matter what I did, it seemed like the solutions to all my problems would evade me. Depression was at a high, and my self-esteem was at a low. But I still refused to admit what the real issue was. Instead of going inward and being spiritually responsible, my ego searched outwardly for solutions that it somehow knew it would never find.

I forced myself to into self-reflection often, but only superficially. On the one hand I had great potential juxtaposed against a walking, talking bundle of bad habits and contradictions. Mentally I was all over the place from feeling empowered one minute to becoming the biggest victim on Earth the next. I was a very complex person with a very complicated life that no one around me could understand, least of all myself.

Even I didn't see how my life experience, with all of its mysticism, related to this material world that felt in polar opposition to the energetic reality that my consciousness was consciously steeped in.

Using my illness as an excuse, I began spending exorbitant amounts of money on useless materialistic items to distract myself from having to feel the feelings that I really needed to feel if I was ever to truly going to heal.

At the same time, I began subscribing to all of the 'fear porn' that was surfacing on the Internet during that time period (and it still is). I became so convinced that the world as we knew it was about to end that I started becoming very paranoid and fearful. It felt like at any moment the economy was going to crumble, the dollar was going to crash, Korea would bomb us, a solar flare would hit the earth causing the grid to go down and chaos to erupt, etc. etc. etc… and then there were humans and their crazy industrialized systems that are destroying our world. Though deep down, I knew I loved and believed in our species, yet I didn't like what we were doing.

In my paranoia, delusion, and fear, I decided to buy some land deep in the mountains, far away from humans and build a big house designed with angles that all matched the golden mean ratio. It was more like a cathedral than a house – a temple for me to escape from the world, but really I was trying to escape from myself.

On all levels of my being, I was out of control, thinking that this unbridled illness was going to cause my early demise. I wanted to get my house and farm in the mountains built so that I could escape from the world and hide out to deal with my complicated self, all alone. But almost every single action that I made was based on fear and the insatiable desires of the ego. My pain was out of control to the point where I had become my own worst enemy, and I was certainly projecting fear-based emotions on everyone who tried to get close to me. While I frivolously pursued all of my reckless endeavors, in the back of my mind, I knew this was not going to end well.

A close friend invited me on a trip to Eden Hot Springs, Arizona, a gorgeous desert hot springs resort located in the southeast corner of the state. We had both taken many trips there over the years, and it was almost always a great experience. The whole area is beautiful but can be very intense.

There were different pools of hot springs that were as soothing as could be, especially during cool desert nights underneath a blanket of stars. But there were very mixed energies present there. Just a few years earlier a murder/suicide took place near the property and across the roads from the hot springs were old Apache slaughter grounds where colonists were said to have slain many Native people.

During this retreat, I had a tarot card reading with a woman who was there. My friend watched and listened as this woman pulled my cards. What came up hit me like a ton of bricks. There were two death cards and a rebirth. My friend and I looked at each other with a glare that said, *Holy shit.* After the reading, he apprehensively felt that for me to get a reading like that was a big deal because he knew a lot about my history and my current issues.

He looked me dead in the eye and said, "Bro, I've been worried about you because your whole life seems to have become so toxic that you are almost radioactive."

I agreed with him. There was no way for me to hide it.

As people who are really into tarot readings will say, "The cards don't lie." In this case, I knew that some serious stuff was headed my way. I just had no idea what it was. That night I went to one of the private pools that is known as the *guitar pool* and soaked my body in these healing waters. I was the only one in it. Under the shooting stars above and the dark chill of the deserts night air, I sat in this rejuvenating water, taking it all in. Coyotes were barking in the distance, owls were calling out into the night, and the wind rustled the chaparral bushes that were all around me. I so thoroughly enjoyed every moment of that experience because I knew that it was the calm before the storm, literally.

I awoke the next morning to a bunch of frantic text messages on my phone from a close friend and pot-dealing partner in Maine named Mick. "Bro, call me immediately—call me now—something happened—bad news—gotta talk—call ASAP."

Here we go, I thought.

Mick, who I trusted with my life, told me that thieves had apparently been staking out the garage that we kept our Cannabis at. We were always very careful about how we conducted our business, but there were always blind spots due to unforeseen elements of being involved in a criminal enterprise. Once it was harvested and brought to this location, it was immediately split apart and then brought to a storage unit so that we didn't have all our eggs in one basket, so to speak. But our driver did not get in until late the night before, so to be safe and not risk driving around late at night with many pounds of weed, Mick decided to leave it there and split it up in the morning. When he went inside the garage the next morning, he discovered that someone had stolen all of it. Just like that, all of our hard work and risk was reduced dramatically. That stolen pot represented the bulk of my working liquid assets.

That is the first death card, I thought to myself. When I told my friend at the hot spring what happened, he was speechless.

I flew back to Maine to try and gather what resources I had left. Once I had assessed how serious this theft was, I got really paranoid. *What if it wasn't stolen at all? What if DEA agents who had been watching us and were planning on making an arrest took it?* I had it figured out that if I got caught for what I was doing, I'd do about a year in the prison system. I was of the mindset that if I got caught, it would be worth it because of all the money I had saved, but now I didn't have much money left after the recent theft. The biggest problem was what would happen to my health in a prison environment where not only would I be unable to take care of myself, but I believed the quality of food would surely cause me to become ill instantly. The anxiety was overwhelming as I had endless paranoid thoughts streaming through my brain.

In case the DEA was looking to arrest us, the owners of that pot, I decided that I needed to get out of town. I flew to a big event in LA, where my friend from the hot spring was speaking.

Now I was nothing less than a train wreck. I had lost most of my life savings to either thieves or possibly DEA agents, I was running and completely paranoid thinking about all kinds of different ways that the authorities would apprehend me, I had this crazy digestive illness for six years that no one could figure out how to heal and I was dealing with ultra-chronic anxiety that has resulted from a life that even I could not make sense of, and on top of it all, I was trapped in awful negative thinking and feeling patterns that made it very easy to make poor choices. My hot spring friend was right; I wasn't just toxic, I was straight up radioactive.

After my friend's speaking engagement in Orange County, we went to a Vietnamese Vegetarian restaurant in the Little Saigon district of Los Angeles. This restaurant was well-loved in the Raw Vegan community, partly because the food was so incredible, but mostly because the head chef who ran the restaurant had taken a vow of silence over a decade before and still ran this whole restaurant. It was quite a thing to witness. He was of Asian descent and seemingly inspired by some type of esoteric Buddhist philosophies. He communicated with his staff and customers by writing messages on paper; however, even though he didn't audibly speak, he had a way of communicating that was quite masterful, to say the least!

My friend and I were tired after the long day, and from all the socializing at the event he just spoke at, so we were a little reluctant to visit this restaurant, but we did so anyway since we were on the West coast. We loved the place and didn't know when we'd get another chance to eat there again after returning back to Maine.

As soon as we walked into the restaurant, we found that it was packed, mostly with the people that my friend spoke to in front of at his event, so we decided to head back to the hotel instead because we didn't want to talk to anyone anymore after such a long day. But the Silent Chef wasn't going to allow us to just walk out of there. He called us over to say hi to him.

"Hey brother, we had a long day and are flying back to Maine tomorrow morning. We were hungry, but this place is so busy that we don't feel up to waiting around, but it's great to see you!" I said.

But, there was no way the Silent Chef was going to let us just walk out that door. With a huge joyful smile and a heart filled with love be beckoned us to sit down at the elixir bar where he was, and he indicated (through hand gestures and pointing to tinctures on the shelves of his elixir bar) that he wanted to make something special for us.

"Aw thank you," we said, "but we're going to leave."

He shook his head back and forth, indicating 'no!' In his own way, he lovingly demanded that we sit our butts right down on the bar stools in front of him, and that's what we did.

Over the next 20 minutes, he prepared the weirdest concoction of at least 100 ingredients that I'd ever had anyone prepare for me. It took roughly 20 minutes, but it seemed like forever. We almost got up and left twice because we were so tired and just wanted to get back to our room. My friend and I kept looking at each other, rolling our eyes and being like "really?"

And by the time the Silent Chef had finished, he placed two small plates with a small quarter inch by quarter inch cube of some incomprehensible mixture of ingredients, with what seemed like 'holographic' multi-dimensional sauce drizzled onto them, and a toothpick sitting in the middle of each cube.

My friend and I looked at each other like "we just waited that long, for this!?" But now that whatever it was he made was in front of us, we saw no reason not to try it.

I went first, then my friend. Within seconds tears started welling up from my eyes to the degree that it hurt. Within minutes it felt like smoke was billowing out of my ears. I was starting to hyperventilate. No longer able to deal with this situation, I went running outside, but upon reaching the parking lot, it felt like my entire body was literally on fire from the inside out. I was losing my 'shit' and started screaming at the top of my lungs! Out of sheer desperation, I ran back into the packed restaurant and literally started pounding ice water sitting on the tables of people I didn't know who were just in their eating their dinner. In the background of my tortured awareness, I could hear a mixture of people wondering what the fuck I was doing, laughing at me, and others who were concerned. I was in so much pain from this mystery substance that I would do anything to quench the fire. It was unbearable.

After drinking water that I snatched off two different tables of random customers that I didn't know, I turned to see my friend lying on the floor of the restaurant crying with a group of people standing around him.

"Holy Fuck, what is happening?" I thought. I couldn't process that so I ran for the door. Once outside again, I was having out of body experiences because the power of whatever he gave me was too much for my body to process. I felt like I was probably going to die in the parking lot of the Silent Chef's restaurant.

"Why would he do this to us in front of an entire packed restaurant?" I remember thinking for a brief second.

Then my friend, who had fallen apart inside the restaurant, came running outside with at least 15 people following him. He was expressing a mixture of emotions, anger, frustration, sadness, etc. he began punching windows of cars with his bare fist – really hard. None actually broke, but it had to hurt. He was losing it and couldn't deal with it, like me.

We both eventually came to be sitting down on the ground of the restaurant parking lot hyperventilating with tears, snot and drool soaking our faces, shirts, and shorts. The Silent Chef and members of the restaurant staff kept bringing us ice water, cold foods and anything to help reduce the fire burning that as of now seemed to be permeating our very soul's themselves!

After many failed attempts, ice-cold coconut water finally did the trick. As my friend and I regained some sense of normalcy, we had questions for the Silent Chef.

"What was that? Why would you do this to us?" of course he said nothing. This whole incident was clearly set up to completely crush our egos, and it was certainly a success. To have many of the people who just witnessed my friend give a powerful talk, watch us just completely 'lose our shit' in front of a restaurant full of people was humbling, to say the least. Any resistance I had ever had to feeling 'embarrassed' to anything had been completely erased from my mind!

One of the customers, who was also at the speaking engagement, said:

"You guys did better than the last group he did this to. The ambulance showed up for them"!

"What the fuck," we thought.

The experience was so jarring that we canceled our flight back to Maine and went and spent the day processing what had happened in silence at Deep Creek Hot Springs outside of LA. There weren't a lot of immediate answers. But, it was definitely designed to put our egos in check!

After the ego crush outside of Los Angeles, I took a flight back to Maine. I was paranoid as hell that I would be getting arrested, but after the Silent Chef event, I could feel a part of myself surrendering to whatever was going to happen and just allow it to unfold.

Back in Maine, I was running around trying to tie up any loose ends that I had. Almost all of my Cannabis business was done through one guy, a lobsterman out of Portland. I frantically tried getting a hold of him, but he seemed to have disappeared.

The pressures of all the dysfunctional aspects of my life were weighing on my mind like the pressure one would imagine exists deep the ocean. I had a severe anxiety complex. I was having affairs, was all about making money, taking huge risks, and was wallowing in negative thinking by worrying about it. The house that I was building was almost finished, and now most of my money was gone. My health was suffering tremendously, and I once again became skin and bones. My anxiety was through the roof. I had dug a deep hole, and I was becoming sure that I would not be able to climb out of it. I felt like I was always on the verge of a panic attack, and I was certain a nervous breakdown or some sort of 'bad' ending was quickly approaching.

While mining in September of 2010, I got a text message from the lobsterman who owed me a lot of money. The fact that I had not heard from him in two months should have been a red flag in itself, but I had known him for almost fifteen years, and I had seen much weirder things from him. The text message said, "Sorry, been out of town; I need to return what you gave me." At this point, I didn't care if he had money for me, or a duffle bag full of weed to return. I just needed something to help recoup my financial ruins.

So, after a long and tiresome day, I decided to drive from western Maine to Portland to collect whatever the lobsterman had for me.

It was close to 10pm when I finally arrived at his street. The second red flag came as I was driving towards his place. I had a vision superimposed in my mind's eye. I saw a bunch of DEA agents circle me with their guns drawn. It was a shocking sight to see. I hesitated and thought that I should keep driving, but I thought to myself, *No, it's just my paranoia - everything is fine. I really need this money.*

I knew the routine. Usually, he'd leave a window open, so I could crack the door and pick up money that he owed me hidden in its designated spot. I would often feed his cat if need be. Tonight was no different. I opened the window, cracked the door, and went inside. The cat had no food, so I fed her. Then I went into the kitchen where there was a duffle bag on the ground. I opened it up and saw the third red flag. Amongst the cannabis that I had given him, there were smaller bags of different varieties that I did not give to him. This bothered me. I considered leaving it and instead bringing the duffle bag filled with crumpled up newspaper to my truck, just to make sure that the vision I saw driving over there would not become a reality. But I was beyond exhausted, so I convinced myself that everything was fine. I grabbed the duffle bag, walked down the stairs, threw it into the back of my truck, closed the cover on the back of it, then proceeded to get into the driver's seat.

Before I could even open the car door, DEA agents came rushing towards me with their guns drawn, screaming, telling me to get down on the ground. Seeing guns pointed at me from every direction was all the encouragement that I needed to get down on the ground as they commanded.

They cuffed me, picked me up, and then walked me into the van that they had sitting outside of my *friend's* house. I was hyperventilating. They tried calming me down. Once I calmed down, they began talking to me. "We know this is very surreal, and you are out of your element right now, but we want your grow houses. Tell us where they are, and then we will let you go home. This isn't going to go away, but we will talk about how to resolve it over the next few months, but you need to show us where these places are."

All that I said was, "Sorry, I cannot do that."

This made them become very aggressive. "Oh! You're a stand-up guy, huh? What? Do you believe in the cause so much that you are willing to go to prison for it? Stand-up guys do lots of time in prison. I guess you must want to go because you are facing thirty years! You must really want to go because that's gonna be your new home! Last chance! Show us where and then go home tonight or we are bringing you in right now!"

"OK, bring me in then. I'm not telling you anything," I said.

So that's what they did. They put me in an armored van and booked me in the county jail.

From the time that they arrested me to when I was finally brought into a cell in the county jail, it took almost five hours. I couldn't believe that this was happening. *I have ruined my life,* I thought, as the reality of this whole process began to sink in. On top of a steel bed, and inside of a highly secure and sealed off concrete cage, I collapsed with exhaustion. During the night they put someone else into the cell with me. He had to be an undercover agent because for the next few days, he tried to convince me to snitch on everyone and everything that ever lived.

I knew the agent's threats of thirty years were just a ploy to get me to talk. For what I was doing I figured I'd get about a year in prison which would have been a nightmare especially with my health, but if I ate one or two small meals a day, I thought I could survive, even if just barely.

After three days, my parents, with the help of my lawyer, bailed me out. My parents had to put their house up as bail in order to have me released.

Everyone in my life was extremely supportive and scared for me, but beyond that, most were royally disappointed that I put myself into a terrible situation like this. Many claimed they all saw it coming. They said things like, "You were out of control! You were toxic! You were unhealthy on all levels!" These statements were all true. I had not been myself for years. I had become something else, a walking talking egoic nightmare.

As the next few weeks went by I was dealing with the aftermath of the situation and reporting to a probation officer a few times per week, then things changed. My lawyer called and told me that the crime that I had been charged with was going to get me way more time than a year because of draconian distribution laws and the fact that they had me committing the crime on video and audio. The lobsterman, a friend of fifteen years - the guy I had repeatedly gone out of my way to help and constantly allow his debts to slide, had set me up. Now, doing a year in prison was out of the question. I wanted to go to trial and fight the charge, but if I ended up losing, I was getting at least ten years. If I pled guilty to the charge, then they would give me a plea deal for less than ten years. My lawyer advised me to take the plea deal because I was certainly going to lose in a trial with so much audio and video evidence against me. What was already a disaster had now turned into an unbelievably fucking disastrous nightmare.

"Five to ten years in prison with my health could kill me," I told my lawyer.

"Well, you should have thought about that before you did what you did," he said - a statement I would hear often from that point on by many subjective onlookers.

The next thing that I had discovered was that they froze all of my bank accounts and found my farm/home/temple in the mountains that I had built to live in as a personal monastery. They decided they were going to try and take that as well as anything else that I owned that might have been bought with marijuana. Now I was dealing with full personal financial collapse.

The plea arraignment was set to take place in three months, and during that time, my lawyer discovered mitigating factors in relation to my health that could help with my sentencing. Now my family was really afraid for me. Everyone knew how fragile my health was, and they were afraid of what might happen if I did not receive the care that I needed.

When the day came for me to plead guilty or not guilty, I pled guilty. My lawyer told the judge about my health and asked that I remain outside of jail until sentencing so that I can take care of myself.

The judge said, "I am not letting him stay out of prison because of some psychosomatic illness," and then he had me shackled in the courtroom while my entire family watched it all and started crying out loud.

After four days in the county jail, I began having a severe inflammatory response to the foods they were feeding me. The rash that I had began spreading throughout my body. I started to panic. Once the jail's hospital staff read my health history reports and saw what was happening to me after one week of the wrong food and a lack of available care in the prison setting, they claimed to be shocked. They couldn't believe that a judge would have put me here like this.

They began working with my lawyer to try and get me transferred to a medical prison facility where I had at least a better shot of being taken care of. My lawyer, with the aid of my parents and a few of the doctors who have helped me throughout this process, all started compiling information so that my lawyer could file a motion to get me out on health reasons until my sentencing.

After almost four weeks, I appeared in court on the motion that my lawyer filed. He even made the prosecutor aware of the severity of my situation, and he vouched for me on behalf of the judge. The prosecutor himself said that I shouldn't have to suffer like this for a non-violent drug crime. The judge agreed to let me out. It was a hallelujah moment for my family and me.

During this time, I became more depressed than I had ever been in my life. None of my friends were nearby, but I would not have been responsive had I been in their presence. I had the support of my parents, my brother and our friend, Neil. All of my spiritual energy was long gone. All I was able to do was cry, put my hands together, and pray. I prayed with the little bit of life force that I had left. I prayed for my inner sources of energy, the outer sources, the iridescent guides, angel-like beings who once so gracefully supported me and kept me consciously connected to the source of life itself, and then I cried, and cried and cried. I repeated this process countless times.

My life was so beautiful as a child but then so troubled as a teen and then I awoke to beauty beyond anything I could ever imagine, only to dive head-first into drug addiction and living a mummified existence when I realized what it would take to live as a hyper-aware being perceiving the world primarily through the frequency of energy that I truly am.

After recovering from this state of torpor I became ill, and then started breaking down emotionally from this ongoing and seemingly losing battle with the health struggle I'd dealt with for so many years, and now I was facing a long prison sentence.

Amazingly though, as I sunk into the depths of despair, I sensed a power beneath it all, leading me, carrying me through this nightmare. I could feel the same voice that communicated to me during the profound awakening I experienced in the presence of Damian at the age of 18, the one that said

"You know what this is." It was just that I was in so much pain, physically, mentally, and emotionally, that I didn't fully trust it. My victim mentality was in full force, but I also remembered what it was like to be empowered beyond belief. The battlefield of the soul, mind, and body had been set.

I tried reminding myself that I had already made it through the cosmic court of the soul with a trial of a zillion lifetimes. If I can do that, I can make it through the court of man, no matter how harsh or hopeless it may seem, but I had been weakened by years of egotistical dysfunction, my spirit was broken. At this point, I had no option but to completely surrender to the situation, and that became my new focus – despite how difficult was to do during that period of my life.

With the help of my lawyers and the top healthcare providers I worked with, I accumulated a comprehensive health history report consisting of close to 400 appointments with thirty doctors and health practitioners with three months spent in health clinics over an almost seven-year period. It was a serious report. My lawyer told me that I did a great job, but he was unsure how the court would respond to it – because the system is literally heartless and they look at everything as an attempt to use a "get out of jail free card".

They had me on house arrest for that entire year and a half of pre-trial, so I was very limited in what I could do. Most of my days were spent flip-flopping between trusting a higher power was guiding the process and feeling helpless and hopeless.

Meanwhile, my sentencing hearing was now less than two months away. At this point, my parents started panicking. They felt tremendous guilt for the way my life had turned out. Even though I constantly reassured them that throughout my life I had made my own choices and decisions, they felt that trying to repress my hippie upbringing after they had raised me that way, contributed to this mess that I was now in.

Behind the scenes, we hired another lawyer. It was an attempt to mitigate the severity of my sentencing by displaying that my health issues were more than any prison would know how to deal with, which they were. The care that I needed was so specialized that slight deviations in my regimen could create instant and harsh suffering. It was scary to think what a lack of diet, probiotics, supplements, and the array advanced healing technologies that I used daily would do to me if I was abruptly cut off from using them all. The new lawyer, who was not only my lawyer's closest friend, but he was also very close to the prosecutor and judge in my case. They hoped that if anyone could get through to these people, it would be him. My lawyer agreed to team up with his friend.

When my day in court came, over fifty of my friends and associates were there, including one of my doctors, my family, and two lawyers to represent me. There was a pile of letters from people all over the world, some from big names in the health and wellness industry that appreciated my character. There were many documents from a plethora of health care practitioners asking for a sentence of home confinement for health reasons. If they had no choice to incarcerate me, they asked that I be designated to a medical facility next to one of the most specialized and advanced health care centers in the world – The Mayo Clinic in Minnesota. I then got up and read my allocution to the court. It was originally twelve pages long, but my lawyers had me condense it to a page and a half. I spoke with all of the confidence that I could summon and after the judge looked me in the eye, he nodded his head and took a recess where he would decide my fate.

During the recess, my lawyers and all of the people next to me were confident that we all did the best job that we could have done. Everything in that hearing went as smoothly as it was able to go. For a few minutes, there was a very light-hearted feeling in that courtroom. All the people present on my behalf felt like a miracle was about to happen even though quite a few of them were crying.

Then the recess ended, and the judge came out. He said that after everything he had read about me, he found me to be an interesting person and that he wished we were meeting under different circumstances. However, he was bound by the laws of the state to give me five years in prison, but he would not give me more than that. He designated me to the medical clinic that was suggested. Both lawyers asked that he allow me to self-surrender as opposed to being taken into custody on the spot and then sent through the hellish transport system that would bring me to the prison I would be designated to stay in. He agreed to this as well. Despite the intense pressure, this allowed me to feel a sigh of relief.

In about a month's time, I would receive papers asking me to self-report to the prison on the date that they would give me and with that, the court was adjourned.

I was relieved to not be taken in right there, and I was happy to not get more than five years, but it was still a long time, especially in my delicate health condition.

My close friends and family were all trying to be strong, but they could not help but cry. I had put them through hell, especially, my parents. The lawyers said they would stick with me to make sure I was getting adequate medical attention. My life was about to change dramatically one more time in what had already been a life filled with constant and extreme changes.

CHAPTER TWENTY-FIVE

In the Prison of Mind, Body, and Soul

It was 30 days before I would be surrendering myself to prison. I wondered that if the supposed Mayan prophecy of the world coming to an end in 2012 did not happen, might it still be the end of my world from whatever potential horrors I might be facing within the prison system?

I celebrated New Year's Eve 2012 in Portland, Maine. It was bittersweet to be with my friends knowing that not only was a change coming, but a dramatic one at that. A friend at the time had a few A-list movie star friends. That evening a group of us had dinner with the A-list actress Kirsten Dunst. At one point during dinner, my friend leaned over to me and said,

"Dude, I cannot even believe how crazy your life is. Here you are having dinner with Kirsten Dunst and then shortly you will be headed to prison for five years, what a trip".

"Yup," I thought to myself, this life seems more like a dream than reality.

At that point in my life, everyone was as supportive as they could be, but what do you say to someone who had just had their life crushed by the state for a plant medicine that's on the verge of becoming legal nationwide? Good luck? It will be all right? Most didn't know what to say, but one person did:

"There is no better teacher than life itself." Those words have not only stuck with me since she said it, but they have rung more true every day.

One day, early in the first week of 2012, I went to my mailbox and there it was, a letter of designation from the state telling me to self-report to prison on 1/11, 2012. Knowing a little about numerology, I recognized the number eleven as symbolizing the principles of spiritual awakening and enlightenment. But most of all, those numbers represented having gratitude for the divine, something I wasn't fully feeling at that point! I took a deep breath, and in those moments, I connected to that inner voice that said "you know what this is," and I really wanted to believe it. Then I continued reading further in the letter. *What? What the fuck is this?* It said I was to report to a regular prison, not the medical prison the judge had initially agreed to. *This has got to be a mistake,* I thought. The judge told me I was going to a medical facility, not a regular prison without medical treatment. I'm a small-time non-violent cannabis dealer. There is no way they would be sending me to a facility without medical attention! My body and face became flushed with anxiety. I felt panic.

My lawyer made some calls and discovered that there was no mistake. I was *not* going to the medical facility. I was going to a regular prison without medical treatment.

"How are they going to address my health issues if my symptoms return," I asked my lawyer.

His answer was that they were probably not going to and that most likely I'd be on my own when it came to my health. My head dropped, and my heart sank into my stomach. I now knew that if healing was to occur, it wasn't going to come from any outside help.

It was now January 9, 2012. The very next morning, my brother and Neil would be driving me to the mid-Atlantic region to begin my bid. I was prepared as I was able to face this unknown. I just kept telling myself that this was nothing. I have faced and made it through so many experiences I didn't expect to live through. However brutal this might be I was determined to survive.

Early the next morning, my brother and Neil showed up to get me. Sorrow radiated from their faces. The ride down to the mid-Atlantic region was as depressing as could be. We hardly said a word to each other.

When we finally arrived in the town where I would be incarcerated, we stopped at the local health food store. I was able to have one last healthy meal and fill my stomach with probiotics and cultured yogurt before I was dropped off. Since we still had a couple of hours until I had to surrender to the prison, we decided to go for a walk on some trails that we were told about. It was my last excursion in nature on my own free will for potentially years to come. In a few hours, I would no longer be able to do something as simple and pleasant as walk through the woods. I didn't know what to expect, but I knew it would be radically different than the life I had been accustomed to.

While still parked at the hiking trails, my brother and Neil gave me a huge hug, an inspirational talk, and they let me know they would always be there for me. They said they would be there when it was all over. A better life would be waiting. I broke down in tears, waited a while pulled myself together and then we got in the car so they could drop me off at the prison.

As we made the long drive up the prison driveway, the first thing I saw was a giant sadistic-looking tower, then the rest of the compound comes into view. It is an ominous-looking structure with dark and intricate gothic architecture. The architecture on the inside of the prison is almost beautiful. I say almost because beautiful is a strange word to associate with a penitentiary that has such a notorious reputation as this place did. Gun towers and vicious-looking barbed wire fencing surround the compound. In the middle of the whole place is a phallic tower, shooting straight into the sky. This prison is unlike almost all of the new *state of the art* facilities that have sprung up around the country as a result of the domestic prison industrial complex boom. It is the oldest penitentiary in the country, and it has housed some of the most notorious criminals in U.S. history.

After alerting the front gate that I was here to surrender, they told me to turn right and drive down a hill at the bottom of the prison complex. Once we arrived at the bottom of the hill, I hugged my brother and Neil one last time and watched them drive away, leaving me in the belly of the beast. It hurt so bad to see them go.

I tried to reverse my feelings by remembering that I had always regretted not going on an extended meditation retreat. I wished that I could go to the Himalayas, to a Buddhist monastery or somewhere like that - a place where I could spend a few years meditating, praying and connecting to the divine within. "*Well*, I thought, *I didn't make it to the Himalayas, but I made it to a few years of retreat! What if coming to prison is that monastic wish come true?*" Did I have a choice? No.

But I could definitely choose what my attitude towards this experience would be, as difficult as that was appearing to be.

After my daydream, a correctional officer, (C.O), brought me into a big brick institutionalized-looking building. They processed me, gave me an ID card, fingerprinted me, gave me bedding and the *khaki* uniforms that would become my new wardrobe. Once I was processed, they told me about the compound, its rules, and what was expected of me. After that, they assigned me a bed in a building called *Unit 2*.

Unit 2 is what they refer to as *the ghetto*, and that night, I found out why. They put me upstairs in a cube with two other guys, Chuck and Uncle Joe. Uncle Joe and I would become close friends, but that was a couple of years away. Through sheer exhaustion and depression, I actually fell asleep. I awoke to the stand-up count where all the inmates stand up and are counted by the C.O.'s.

Once they were gone, inmates would guard their windows to alert everyone if they were coming back. Then out of nowhere, Unit 2 turned into a prison party. Inmates broke out their cell phones, drugs, and alcohol, and the party began. The inmates were a strange mix of drug dealers, thugs, young and old, mixed up with corrupt cops and white-collar crime guys. *This is not at all what I expected prison to be like. What is the point of this,* I thought. They are behaving here the way they behaved on the street. Is this supposed to be punishment or rehabilitation? It really isn't either, and I'm in here after losing everything for a plant that is about to become legal (hence my feelings of victimization in those moments).

I found myself entering a deep, deep state of self-reflection regarding my current incarceration…it was so surreal it just didn't seem like it was actually happening. I started by reminiscing about a story that has been playing out over and over in my head since my early teens; for as long as I could remember, I devoutly wanted to know what the point of this life was. It was all that mattered to me. But then I actually got a glimpse of it in Damian's presence when I was 18. I discovered way more about my true nature then I could have ever imagined possible. But I got 'turned on' to a degree that I did not know how to manage in my human self. My psychic awareness was turned up to 11, and I could not be around other humans without feeling their thoughts, feelings, and karmas, I couldn't handle living in that 'open' of a state without wanting to run and hide.

Then, roughly one year after living in such a highly illuminated state, I turned my back on all the gifts bestowed upon me through these intense experiences. Besides my trepidation of this awakening happening so fast, and despite my inability to integrate all of these 'superpowers', I was all set and supported by powerful, loving forces, yet I decided to numb my perception of them with heroin and hard drugs. That was ridiculous because I knew deep down, and on the surface, that something as eternally profound as actually *becoming one with the universe* was not something that even death itself could numb out. Still, I vehemently attempted to do it anyway.

Additionally, I turned my back on my family and friends. I turned my back on any shot I ever had of living a sheltered and simpler life.

But worst of all, after becoming the source and being shown where and how to drink directly from its divine nectar, I turned my back against even that. The supreme source for which countless religions have given countless names to, going back to the very first beings who pondered the meaning of life itself. I turned my back on what most refer to as "God" and chose my ego instead, but it was out of fear of the power that pulsed through my veins.

Because I didn't want to *own* my responsibility in regard to being an instrument of 'divine expression' I had been running ever since. I had been running, hiding behind egoic habits and suffering as a result of making such choices.

Now I was locked inside of a physical prison, facing some deep shadows in this environment, and in my own awareness. This was all because I was afraid of my potential, the world's reaction to my potential, and my responsibility to maintain it. Physically, mentally, emotionally, I was a tired and pathetic human being. I was at rock bottom, but I was still afraid to accept how powerful I had the potential to be, so I prayed. I prayed long, and I prayed hard. *Please, please, please, awaken me from the misery of my wrongdoings. Please awaken me from the nightmare of my conscious slumber. Awaken me, dear Universe, and let me stay awake. Please awaken within me the strength to surrender to your peace and serenity.*

As I lay there detesting myself and this prison that I was now in, I made a resolve that I would meditate and do internal energy work for hours every day. I resolved to fast, eating minimally, as much as I had to, because I knew the food would be a problem with my condition. I told myself that this was my time to become free from the bondage of years, and lifetimes of mental and emotional incarceration. This was my retreat in the Himalayas, my monastery in the mountains. This was my time to own what I always had the potential to be! I resolved that no matter what it took, or how hard it was, I would overcome, and rise above this situation, better and stronger than I had ever been. I knew I needed to just surrender to this whole experience and trust it, but I wasn't ready yet, although I felt I was close.

The vibe of the whole compound was depressing, dim, and dark. The stench of negativity permeated the air just as the noxious odor of the many skunks outside on the compound did as well. Men who were not at all happy about the outcome of their own lives surrounded me. They were miserable, and they wanted to co-commiserate with anyone and everyone who would lend their ear. Many here on the compound were like this. They are known as *haters* because they basically hate everyone and almost everything—themselves at the top of the list. The attitude of most people in there was beyond nihilistic, and it bordered on something more like a spiritual apocalypse.

I had hit rock bottom. It was time to face the shadow of my own awareness, but how? Was I locked in a prison, or was a prison locked in me? Deep down, and even at the surface, I knew the answer and I also now realized that I had been mentally, emotionally, physically and spiritually incarcerated long before I was ever placed inside of the government's prison gates.

CHAPTER TWENTY-SIX

There Are No Victims, Just Volunteers

In the beginning, prison life soon became routine. Each day was the same. I would wake up depressed and filled with self-loathing and would attempt to find some sort of peace through meditation. It was not working at first, though. It took some time before any substantive breakthroughs occurred. My self-depreciation was initially winning.

One day while walking through the compound I noticed an area sanctioned off with a sweat lodge, surrounded by a beautifully landscaped ceremonial grounds. *What? How could this be... a sweat lodge at a prison?* I walked closer to the grounds to see if my eyes were playing tricks on me, but they weren't. There in front of me was the frame of a sweat lodge with a pit for the heated rocks in it and a massive fire pit about twenty feet in front of it. There were buffalo skulls, colored beaded flags and other Native American-inspired regalia around it. There was no one there, but it was clear to me that, whoever used it for ceremonies, used it often. I felt joy come into my heart for the first time in a long time. It made no sense that such beautiful grounds were located in the midst of such a dismal location, but I saw it as a beacon of hope, a light in the dark.

I had attended quite a few sweat lodge ceremonies in my life before prison all over the U.S.; most of them were with my friend from Maine named Ron. Ron knew tribal leaders and elders from all over North and Central America. I have been fortunate to sweat with a few powerful Native American leaders in my work with him. Ron was a mixed tribe Native brother who was also a forty-one-time Sundance chief. Most of the Sundance Ceremonies he attended were in Mexico where he would climb a huge mountain, dance for four days and four nights with no food, no water, and no sleep. At the end of the fourth day, all the dancers who made it through the entire ceremony would pierce their chests with a big ring tied to a tree and then dance around the tree until the ring ripped out, leaving a massive scar. These ceremonies were very serious.

Seeing something as powerful as a sacred sweat lodge in a prison was really surprising. I can't believe it was allowed to be here, especially considering how the Government prevented native peoples from engaging in their traditional practices, even on their own lands as they raided and still continue to abuse them/and most of us.

As I walked off the grounds, I felt really glad that such a place existed in what at face value can only be viewed as a place that is the polar opposite of sacred. I knew that I needed to meet whoever was conducting these ceremonies, but I also sensed that they might not be so open to having me around there.

I found another place of respite in the prison, in the craft room. Aside from the regret of not having gone to the Himalayas on an extended meditation retreat, there was one other thing I always wished I had done, and that was to isolate myself with nothing to do but write and practice songs on the guitar. I was confident that if I were able to do this, I would create some great songs. *Was this that wish coming true?* Only time would tell.

I met two guys that hung out all day playing guitar named Jerry and Bill. They were fantastic players, and the three of us spent many days playing guitar in the craft room. There was not really anyone else who used the room for arts and crafts, so we pretty much had it all to ourselves. It was a decent sized structure, about twenty by forty feet, but it had been abused through the years and years of inmates who clearly had no respect for it. The white floors were dirty and scuffed up badly, the tables and chairs were almost in shambles, and the walls looked like a twenty dollar per night ghetto hotel, darkened yellowish through years of cigarette smoke. But it was low-key, and it had guitars!

Over time we transformed it into a sanctuary where we could get away from the stress and stupidity of the compound. It became a monumental blessing for the few men who made it our own. I named it *the temple at the monastery in the pit of hell*. That room blessed me with countless hours of alone time where in addition to developing my awareness through meditation, energy work and Qi-gong, it allowed me to entirely handwrite this book (over 1000 pages before being edited).

Again, my days were routine. I would wake up and meditate hour after hour in my cell before the CO's would allow me to go to the guitar room. It didn't take long until I became the laughing stock of the compound. People would often walk by my cube, just to catch a glimpse of me meditating or doing qi-gong. This almost always resulted in laughter that would often break my concentration (at first). Most of these inner-city guys didn't even know what meditation was, and even more ornate was my Qi-gong display. When they saw this, I was instantly elevated to the status of super-freak.

My feeling of helplessness, combined with feeling stuck was palpable. Being physically incarcerated has a way of doing this like nothing I had ever experienced in my human body. Nothing about it was comfortable in any shape or form. You are just stuck there, and you know you will be for many years to come. It is crushing to your self-confidence. I had never been this homesick in my life. My only release was music and the transcendent moments of meditation.

In addition to meditation, I was spending hours and hours every day playing the guitar. It was such a profound way to focus my attention. I had always loved to sing; I just wasn't very good at it. But just as the refinement of organic matter through countless years can create the dazzling colors of an opal, just as constant irritation of sand and shell can create the delicate beauty of a pearl, and just as intense pressure can create the rare elegance and prism flashes of a diamond, so too was my singing voice forged through such alchemical extremes in the context of my human lifetime.

One day while my jam partners were playing, I opened my mouth and out came this sound. Like a primordial soul singer, I belted it out like someone whose voice was freed after a million years of being silenced.

I sang with my heart of hearts. I sang with the passion that only a human who had been to hell and heaven and back again would be able to do. Unrestricted, the floodgates of my throat opened wide, and my spirit gushed through my voice with force, precision, and inflection. I sang with the ferocity of a man who had everything taken from him, but his soul, heart, and voice. A voice that despite all its tragic power and grit also knew a deep infinite sense of true joy, that was far more potent and soothing than the devastation of the human condition. In that infinite sense, it allowed itself a few moments where it could be delicate. Jerry and Bill stopped playing and exclaimed at the same time, "Holy shit!" Then for a moment, the room was silent. "Where did you learn to sing like that?" Jerry asked me. "Right here, right now, where I'm standing in this prison!" I exclaimed. They both broke out in laughter.

About a year and a half into my sentence a guy named Don Luzecky walked into the craft room and heard me sing.

"Holy Shit!" He said. "You're good, but you could be great! There are singers, and then there are saaangers, those who can sing with true heart and soul. If you suck in your stomach before every vocal line you sing, and keep it held in, your vocals would soar". From that day forward Don spent almost a year with me, helping me to do just that, and he was correct, my vocals went to a whole new level.

My health was not improving, though. After a couple of months of the prison diet and a lack of all the nourishing supplements I was used to taking on the outside, all of my symptoms returned. My weight plummeted, the rash returned, and worst of all, the insomnia became chronic. With all this, my self-esteem and my confidence in self-healing began diminishing. Fears of all types began to surface as I thought of the worst outcomes I could be facing.

I made an appointment with the medical department and was shocked, but not at all surprised by what they told me. After reviewing my health history reports a little old man who smelled like an ashtray with the qualification of "PA" told me, "It will take an act of Congress to get you approved for even a gluten-free diet. All of your other requirements and restrictions are out of the question. This will never happen while you are doing time here."

"But sir," I pleaded, "What am I supposed to do if this thing progressively gets worse? I may end up looking like a burn victim in no time. If unchecked, there is no telling how ill I may become."

He began barking at me. "Well, you should have thought about that before you broke the law! I turned away from him in disgust.

In those moments walking out of the prison medical clinic, I realized that I was on my own. No one was coming to my rescue. I then did the only thing that I was able to do. I went back to my cube to meditate. I dug deep. I asked the source of the universe for help. *"Please, please, please...Great Spirit, please help me and show me how to heal in this place,"* I prayed over and over again. No answers of any significance appeared to me. Again I resolved that I would spend as many hours in meditation as possible and that I needed to fully commit to convincing myself into realizing that somehow, someway, I would heal this condition while I was at this place. I also concluded that I would spend a lot of time fasting and only eating small amounts of the foods that wouldn't trigger my symptoms too badly. Mackerel, instant rice, olive oil, and canned vegetables became my new diet.

Although I asked the invisible forces of the universe for help, there was one person that could help me that I had not truly spoken to yet - at least not in the right way, and that person was myself. I had the power to heal in my soul, I just needed to make the choice to connect and commit to it, but I was not ready to do so. Not yet...but I felt it coming...

CHAPTER TWENTY-SEVEN

Sweat Lodge

Saturday came a few months into my sentence when I noticed people preparing the Native American sweat lodge grounds for a ceremony. Without hesitation, I walked down there to introduce myself. The moment I stepped one foot onto the grounds, a guy started yelling at me. "Hey! These are sacred grounds! You are only allowed down here by invitation!"

"I apologize! I didn't know it was invite-only. No one told me. But I came down here because I wanted to find out about becoming a member."

He eyeballed me suspiciously. "Have you ever done a sweat before?"

"Yes, quite a few times. One of my close friends is a 41-time Sundance chief. He holds a ceremony at his place every month, and I've been fortunate to meet and sweat with many tribal leaders and elders from all over North and Central America."

After hearing that, his entire disposition changed. "I'm sorry to have come off so strong. It's just that most of the inmates here don't recognize how serious we are about this ceremony and these grounds."

"That's okay; I'm not offended. I'm very serious as well." He gave me a big smile and told me that my heart was in the right place and that he was looking forward to getting to know me. His name was Jayce, and he was Tainos, a Puerto Rican tribe of Natives that once emigrated from North America. We set up an appointment to meet later that day.

Jayce asked me a lot of questions. He explained how new members joined the circle. There was administrative stuff that I had to file with the prison, and then the members of the sweat lodge grounds would meet, talk, and then vote me in through their own democratic process. He warned me that at that time there was only one non-full native member of the current 8, and that getting the natives to accept a non-native member would be difficult. However, after our conversation, he recognized that I was far from the normal non-native. He shook my hand and said that he would talk to me soon. Two weeks later he let me know that all but one member voted me in and that the 'brothers' would like to meet me the following Saturday. I thanked him and agreed to be there on Saturday.

When Saturday came, all the members of the grounds, except for one, greeted me warmly, and his name was Charles Axtell, or Axe. I had seen him on the compound. He was impossible to ignore... tall, and big-boned, with long black hair. He possessed the stereotypical profile of a fierce Native American warrior, such as one would see in old photos. When I walked onto the grounds that day, Axe walked away.

After meeting everyone, they said that I was required to be the fire keeper for the next four sweats they do. This way, they could see how I both conducted myself during ceremony days and how committed I was to being a member. I told them I would be honored to do the fire and so I did for the next four sweats.

In a sweat lodge ceremony, the fire keeper has many responsibilities; the most important include building the sacred fire where the rocks (also called grandfathers) are heated and then bringing them into the Inipi (sweat lodge) for the ceremony. The ceremony we did was known as a traditional Lakota sweat, so along with the fire keeping responsibilities, there are many prayers that I was required to make.

After I completed my fire keeping duties every Saturday for four weeks, I was invited to sweat. To engage in this ceremony while incarcerated was incredible while at the same time, highly emotional. To do a sweat lodge ceremony is to experience all of your senses heightened and responding to the physical elements at their extremes. Once the door of the Inipi is shut, it is pitch black in there no matter how bright it is outside. There was the powerful smell of sage, cedar, sweetgrass and willow burning after being dropped by hand on the grandfathers or by way of the medicine water being splashed upon them. The distinctive taste of the herb bitterroot, used as a purifier when entering the Inipi. The sound of the rocks snapping and cracking, both on their own and then with the medicine water added to them. Then listening to the men sing their intense prayer and passion-driven songs. The combined extremes of Earth, air, water, and fire raise your body temperature so high that it invokes a healthy "mini-fever", burning out viruses and pathogens that lead to the pinnacle of the whole ceremony; for the sweat lodge participant to become aware of the otherworldly sensations where they are hopefully able to get in touch within their own soul.

To do this ceremony at any time in one's life can be life-altering. But to do it in prison where it becomes a way of life for the next few years is to fully face your darkest parts of and have no choice but to be dramatically changed as a result.

The first time I sweat in prison, I was 100% confident that the mysteries and oneness of the universe had put me into this situation in order to work its way through me - thus cleaning out any self-imposed limitations that I had subjected myself to as the result of becoming an egomaniac.

But after the intensity of the first ceremony was over, I considered the gravity of my situation, and that I'd be in prison for years to come. This caused me to completely break down. There were so many thick psychic layers of self that I would have to remove to uncover not only the 'awakened' being I once was, but even more important, to develop the more mature awakened being I had the potential of becoming. I hung my head low, put my face in my hands, and silently allowed tears to flow from my eyes. I had royally fucked my life up good…

I was becoming more and more down on myself. The reality of the human condition hit me like a ton of bricks. The average human today is the inmate their own conditioning as they dwell on the global compound of a prison planet. Most are incarcerated by an intellect that is at junior high school level. They are slaves to junior high-level emotions. They are insatiable consumers of all 'brands of form' aka egoic masturbation. Their narcissistic values are focused on instant gratification first and are in direct opposition to their value of developing virtue. But the root of the problem is that people have no idea who they are because they have no idea what they are. It's all backwards, and I have contributed to the above conundrum as much as anyone else. What have I been doing with my life? I've almost always known better, but I haven't done better. And that's why I'm here - to do better.

At that point in my life, it became crystal clear that I had been in a prison of mind, body, emotions, and soul long before the government ever physically incarnated me. I had hardwired a software program that played a story of emotional victimization on autopilot.

It very peculiarly started to make sense that if I was ever truly going to be free of all that has ever held me back – the isolation of being physically incarcerated was a perfect place to do just that...

I resolved to take my energy-based human development to the next level. I decided that I was going to *reverse the world*. Instead of becoming a by-product of society by viewing the world from the outside in, I would live from the core of my being, creating spiritually aware fruits from the inside out.

What would a modern mystic in a monastery do? No more masturbation, no more desecration of sex by looking at images that decreased the sanctity of sex. Heck, there's no need to even think any thoughts about sex because I'm not having it now or any time soon, and even when and if I ever decide to have it again, I only want to do it with the utmost sanctity and integrity! No more mental masturbation. No diarrhea of the mouth. I don't need to talk or gossip about anyone or anything regardless if it's justified or not because that's a waste of energy that I could be using to improve myself. But most important of all, I vowed to end my addiction to obsessive thoughts, anxieties, and fears and to live with confidence by focusing on the higher-frequency aspects of my consciousness. Besides, what else do I have left? I'm in prison. I've been stripped of everything I 'owned', that I didn't really need in the first place, and I am left with one thing, the only thing that I actually need, my will to improve my life and this world, by becoming hyper-aware of whatever limiting personality traits have blocked the naturally occurring flow of divine consciousness that seeks to express itself through me. That's all that I have left! That's the only thing left that's rational. That's all that matters. Period.

I've always had really strong sexual energy, and knowing that I was in prison, and not going to be having sex anytime soon (I have gay friends, both men and women who I love and respect, but am not gay myself), I resolved to practice abstinence from masturbation and even thoughts of sex while I was incarcerated. But this did nothing for the 'feeling' of sexual energy that accumulated naturally in my body. Interestingly, I intuitively began engaging in a practice where every time I felt it, I would breathe the 'feeling' of this energy up into my body.

When I first started doing this, I could only move the feeling of the sexual energy into my lower stomach, and then it would dissipate. But over time, and with a lot of consistent practice, I began being able to move this energy higher and higher into my body while concentrating it in different organs, plexus centers and glands, forming new neural circuitry (such as I learned with Damian). Doing this was incredibly healing. The effects are beyond the scope of words to explain.

The first time I was able to bring this energy into my heart, it literally caused a reaction where my capacity to 'feel'- opened up dramatically. And then one day after a year and a half of practicing this, I brought that energy into my brain, and something profound happened. It felt like time stopped, and I could observe the inside of my brain almost as though I had a microscope, and then my self-healing abilities really began to accelerate.

But before that, there was a day when I waited in line for a meal that I could eat very little of, around people whose normal conversation skills consisted of screaming and yelling with ghetto swagger, I noticed Axe, the Native American guy who walked away from the sacred grounds when I walked onto them for my first sweat in prison. After my resolve to take my spiritual and human development to the next level, I was compelled to communicate with him. I wanted him to know how serious I was about changing myself. To me, whatever it is about him that evoked fear in others was the indicator that he possessed something powerful, something real. And like Damian before him, I assumed that Axe's hardened out shell was a barrier to protect something that not only would most *not* understand but also something they wouldn't have empathy for even if they did, or maybe they would? I was determined to form an alliance with this man.

After the chow hall slop was piled onto my plate, I walked over to his table and sat directly across from him. He paid me no mind. Every few bites, I looked up at him, but I could see he refused to acknowledge my presence. I decided to break the silence.

"Dinner is pretty good tonight, huh?"

Finally, he looked at me with a glance that said,

"Who the hell do you think you are to say anything to me?"

But still, he said nothing.

With the conclusion that this guy didn't want to budge, I began to gush.

"Listen, I know you don't know me from Adam, but I didn't come here to play Indian or anything else. I came here to get to the heart of what matters in my life and in this world. I've got massive love in my heart no matter how fucked up this world is, and I've joined your circle because I want to heal every part of my life. I know that you're for real, and I believe you know that I'm telling you the truth."

He looked directly at me and after a long pause, spoke with a chuckle and an ear-to-ear smile.

"Chow is pretty good tonight!"

I responded with a laugh, and for the next 15 minutes, we shared awkward small talk. Although not a word about the sweat lodge was uttered, I could feel that he appreciated me approaching him so bluntly.

When it was time for all the sweat lodge members to gather on Friday night to build the sacred fire for Saturday's sweat, Axe showed up. He equally participated in gathering the grandfathers and building the mantle, but he said very little as he viewed every move I made like a hawk watching a rabbit. The next morning he came and did the sweat with us. We usually did four "doors" that lasted around 20 minutes each, and sometimes we did five. Between each door, new grandfathers would be brought in, commencing the start of new prayers. On the first door, we called on the spirits of the directions to join us. The second door we prayed for women, children, and the elderly. During the second door, Axe began to sing in his native language while drumming. It was so powerful. The heat was so extreme that it was unbearable that we had no choice to withstand it until the prayers and songs were over, unless we feebly admitted defeat and called for the door to the sweat lodge to be opened, something that few would ever do.

And just when it seemed that Axe's song was about to end, he would then launch right into another verse, more intense than the last. I could hear the other guys groaning because they were pushed to their limits. It was so hot that it felt like my skin was going to peel off- literally, and then I felt like I was going to faint. All that I could do was get on my elbows and knees with a towel over my head, my nose and mouth to the ground, desperately trying to inhale even a wisp of cool air. Finally, Axe finished and in unison everyone called for the door. When the door was opened, the daylight revealed 7 men in a circle drenched in herbal steam and sweat, gasping for air. Axe then spoke with his thick Native accent.

"For the most part, nothing in our day to day life is going to be as intense as what we do here in the lodge. But that's why we sweat. The heat like that makes you confront your greatest fear...the fear of your own death. When we confront this fear every week, month after month, year after year, you eventually realize that there is nothing in our life that you cannot face with confidence."

As he was telling us this, we were all still breathing heavy, stealing oxygen from the atmosphere, hearts beating like freight trains burnings coal. Then the fire keeper passed around ice water and medicine tea. The sage, cedar, and apple infusion tasted better than anything I had ever tasted. I dumped it on my face and chest, then onto the still glowing grandfathers. The scent of candied apples perfumed the air. Axe then called for more grandfathers for the next door. It's a general prayer round where each of the members is allowed to pray for themselves, only after praying for others.

Again, as in round two, the face-melting heat pushed us to the edges of our self-limits. The beautiful yet haunting song he sang seemed to never end, but it eventually did to my relief. Like I said earlier, to do this anywhere is life-altering; to do it in prison is to experience an internal personal pole shift.

At the end of round three, once the door is raised, it's time for the pipe ceremony. The pipe ceremony is the focal point of the entire sweat lodge ceremony. The soapstone bowl of the pipe and the wooden stem fit together to represent the masculine and feminine aspects of the creator. The burning of tobacco and sage through the sacred pipe represent the harmonization of the Creator's physical and non-physical aspects. It's father sky and mother Earth, meeting each other halfway during the pipe ceremony. It is said that prayers by-pass the spirits of the directions and go straight to the creator.

During the pipe ceremony, I became Axe's focal point. He started out with,

"When you spoke to me a few days ago, I was able to listen very closely because you were speaking my language. The language of the heart; I am a full-blooded Nez Pearce, people of the heart. I am a direct descendant of Chief Joseph. I've never had a non-native, much less a white man speak to me in such a way. I recognized that you have a native soul, an indigenous soul."

I was a little troubled to find something of substance to say, but I responded.

"Thank you."

I meant both of those words.

His body was covered with deep scars, including a massive gash on his leg that was punched all the way through by a makeshift shank in a penitentiary fight. He continued. "After talking with you, I called my grandfather because I didn't want to sweat with any more white men. I've been sweating with my grandfather since I was born, so I wanted to see what he would say. What he said was,

"Grandson, it doesn't matter what color a man's skin is, it only matters what's in his heart." I knew he was right, so I decided to sweat with you."

CHAPTER TWENTY-EIGHT

Reverse The World

With my decision to "reverse the world" set in place, I focused on all matters inward. Whenever negative thoughts or thoughts that distracted me from this inner focus surfaced, I replaced them with non-thoughts, the result of focusing on the subtle nature of my awareness itself. At times I would gently ask myself the question *"who and what is seeing through my eyes"?* The longer I would do this, the more the field of pure potentiality that Damian spoke of would emerge through my perception of this world. There were months that went by where my awareness was constantly teetering between these two worlds with one foot in each, not fully committed to either yet.

In addition to hours of daily meditation and energy work, I made planning for and attending the sweat lodge ceremony a major focus. I found un-abiding comfort and intuitive guidance by just going outside and sitting on the earth. No one other than the sweat lodge members came to the sacred grounds. I was able to escape from the festering concrete jungle inmate population by spending as much time down there as possible.

Since I was able to use most of my time to develop awareness of the energetic aspects of my consciousness, at times, I would forget where

I was, that is until I walked into the 'chow hall' or the units. That was always a smack in the face that said, "Don't forget - you're not a monk in the Himalayas, you're an inmate in prison." It was the constant clash between ego and soul, but I realized there was a powerful lesson of detachment that consistently presented itself to me.

Amidst all this inner focus, I still struggled with my gastrointestinal condition, the rash, and only having access to low-quality food. However, this all changed during a sweat a couple of months into my friendship with Axe. With every sweat, we all focused on our hearts while sweating and praying with every bit of energy we had. All the members prayed for each other in every ceremony. They all witnessed how much I suffered as a result of this condition.

During one particular sweat, I experienced a breakthrough. Like when I was a child, the profound meditative state that I regularly engaged in, lit up within, and surrounded me. I felt the deep eternal peace that gave birth to my soul. As this happened, I literally felt my condition "leave" my body. I was so grateful and deeply humbled by this, and since that one sweat, the rash never returned during the rest of my incarceration.

It was then that everything changed for me. It was not that I had to work or train hard to become hyper-aware of the energetic substance of my own awareness. It was always there. The difference now was just that I trusted life itself' enough exist in this state without wanting to denounce it, and more importantly, instead of focusing on my past or current problems, I focused my awareness on this energy more then anything else.

I felt a massive shift in my consciousness. On an animalistic level, it was like a young animal learning to hunt. The more it focuses on seeking out the food that nourishes its life-force, the better it gets at catching that food and integrating it into its being. It is flexing its muscles, and its muscles are being driven by an instinct that becomes keener with each hunt.

Human spiritual awareness works in a similar manner. The more you focus your awareness on the nature of your awareness itself, the more you come to realize that what many call "spirituality" isn't at all this mysterious hidden force available only to those who renounce the ways of the world and live at monasteries in the mountains. It becomes a reality more real than the reality that your mind has been conditioned to accept as real.

Jokingly I would state that the next most miraculous thing there is - next to the miracle of life itself, is how few have any recognition of how miraculous life truly is!

I allowed my awareness to naturally be present in the here and now, but when I was in that state, time and space didn't exist, so what I was truly doing was becoming hyper-aware of the very nature of my consciousness itself.

Instead of constantly worrying about the imagined future or the remembered past, both of which would take me out of this expansive awareness I was consistently in, I would focus on the autonomic sensations within my body and mind; the feeling of my heartbeat, the rising and falling of my lungs as they breathed and my pulse as it echoed in any area of my body that I chose to focus on.

The more aware of these sensations I became, the closer I got to the "source" of what it is within me that actually perceives these sensations. When one is able to perceive the source of their own perception, that person becomes aware of what it is that's actually powering this source to project itself through their human senses.

At 'awareness points' like these, universes 'open their doors to you.' What actually happens when this occurs is that the limited animalistic aspects of your ego become illuminated with a 'higher' frequency of potential that has essentially been dormant in your awareness itself, but it was always there... this illumination represents the sacrifice of the limited animalistic aspects of the ego. These animalistic traits aren't actually sacrificed or killed per se; they are augmented and expand into a more holistic expression of what they have the potential to be. The more committed I became to engaging in this process, the more being in this state became second nature – like the development of a positive habit, and then it eventually became 'first-nature.'

It felt like the scales of my awareness tipped from being primarily aware of my human mind and it's fear-based obsessive thoughts, to becoming primarily aware of the "energy" that powered my body and more importantly, the source of my consciousness. This shift marked the beginning of a series of such shifts where the bulk of my awareness became focused on this energy that powered "me," as opposed to just being aware of my thoughts and my human body. The more that I focused on, not my consciousness itself, but the source that was powering my consciousness, the more my normal awareness itself expanded. This expansion of consciousness resulted in what at first seemed like two different experiences; one was being aware of incredible non-physical energetic realms while the other being hyperawareness of this energy source as it worked its own agenda in my body. But the reality was that these were not two separate experiences. What I was coming to terms with was the balance point between the two.

As my energetic development was now returning to the powerful and sustainable levels that I always intended it to, many of my own gifts began reemerging. Anytime that another or I would get hurt through exercising or whatever, my ability to dissolve the energetic blockages that were causing the pain was often instantaneous. While in prison, I was able to help a lot of people in this way.

These periods of inner self-recognition/advancement marked the beginning stages of a clear point of spiritual/physical balance that I had sought since getting clean of heroin in my early twenties. It took being locked in prison, with everything that I didn't need taken from me to get back to that place. In this situation, I was left with the only thing that I did need: my willpower to take my energetic awareness to the next level. Now that I was locked into this commitment, the freer I became – an indescribable freedom.

Here I was physically incarcerated, and feeling the way that I had always wanted to feel. Healing was occurring naturally…

Interestingly one day on the compound a couple inner-city guys who really liked me came running up to get my attention "Yo, Seth, my Nigga, you got to come over here! A bird flew into a window cracked his neck and died, you got to do something about this!"

I walked over to where a beautiful little green and yellow bird sat in the grass. I could see that her neck wasn't cracked and she was just in shock from the impact of hitting the window. As I bent over to pick her up I heard one of my friends say "Oh no he isn't!" As I cupped the bird in my hands and began making a soothing, light tone with my voice she perked up and then flew away. My friends lost it and started proclaiming at the top of their lungs "Holy shit! Did you see that? That Nigga Seth healed that bird and brought it back from the dead! He's like Jesus!"

Of course I couldn't help but smile ear to ear as I told them the bird actually wasn't dead, but they didn't want to hear that. They wanted to believe that I brought it back to life because I could see in that moment that it brought hope back into their own lives.

From that day forward I became known as "the healer." Many of the inmates began approaching me, asking for help and advice with all that plagued them. I gladly did all I could as it brought them, and me great joy and hope that a better world does exist. It doesn't matter who we think we are or where we come from. Almost everyone wants to feel love, even in its most basic form – just another human being showing them a little appreciation. And if someone appreciates that, why wouldn't they also want a better, more compassionate world. The inmates in prison are no different except that they have more of an opportunity to seek within and change themselves than those who are living in the 'regular world'. They just needed to be taught how.

Universal love was in the air, even in prison.

CHAPTER TWENTY-NINE

Free While Chained

I was born hyper-aware of the energy field that animates my human body. This hypersensitive awareness provided me the opportunity to develop a conscius amplification of this energy within my organs and around my entire being.

When I allowed my awareness to remain in that field, instead of focusing on the external world around me, then my consciousness itself would actually expand as I embodied a deeper understanding of my own true nature. This gave me the confidence to push myself through any challenges or triggers that were in my way. It was because of this feeling that I trusted the greater essence of what life was teaching me, and so I sought out the unknown instead of staying in the comfort zone of familiarity.

However, it is interesting to note that even though I had been hyper-aware of elevated states of being throughout many junctures of my life, it wasn't until I became a mature adult that I decided to make the perception of my energy field the number one priority of my life. Until then I consciously and unconsciously became distracted, and then disempowered, by the world around me, and this caused me to suffer.

However, every time I was able to move beyond the distractions of the world and trust in the innate power of my energy field, I eventually discovered that life is always the best teacher, no matter what it is was teaching me, and no matter if I thought I was actually learning the lessons presented to me or not. I experienced first-hand that the universe is a perfect accounting system in that it will ultimately balance itself from its own "zero point"– the potent place of creative power that gives birth to all things.

But the collective human dilemma is that most of us have forgotten that this energy exists in our perception of reality and so we feel disconnected from it, and from something greater. This causes our bodies and minds to stay in an almost constant state of stress, so we seek external distractions -people, places and things to satiate the lack of wholeness we feel inside. And even if we find something that momentarily fills this void we almost always discover that it is temporary and unfulfilling. People have been collectively feeling this disconnection for more generations than anyone knows, and so they perpetuate this limited reality through their thoughts, feelings, behaviors and actions. This creates more disconnection in and all around us, until eventually a crisis occurs - because something greater is always trying to get our attention. But our senses and our will power to change into the best version of ourselves, has become so blunted by the density of this reality. We usually don't heed or know how to navigate these wake-up calls when they do happen, but if we can surrender to it, something greater leads us through it. It works every time. This is the world we all live in, the world of form, of seeking external experiences to fill the void we feel inside. If only we knew we could generate the feelings we really wanted to feel from inside of ourselves, we would heal rapidly.

As a pre-teen this world began conditioning me to believe that I needed to adjust to what it expected of me. But I knew in my soul that society and the world were not in alignment with the greater reality. They only made up a small, almost illusory subsection of it. But people do not know of any other way to live, other than how other people teach them...and how could they? Most of us just do what we are told, even without questioning it objectively. We are but participants in a manufactured world of others making. As a teenager I intuitively sensed this, and felt helpless to do anything about it, so I began to suffer daily. I became distressed and would not understand why I felt so disempowered. I needed to know why I suffered. I could not accept that this version of the world was real.

Finally, I attracted someone into my life (Damian) that was acutely aware of the deeper dimensions of human perception. Through his perspective I observed many truths and expressions of reality that before seeing them, would have been unfathomable to me. But because of his example, and more importantly my own willingness and commitment to knowing the deeper reaon why I existed, and not settling for anything less, I had a full-blown awakening when I was 18 years old. Everything I thought I knew or believed from a human perspective just melted away, and the reality of what was actually going on completely engulfed my awareness.

When that happened, my perception inwardly and outwardly connected to things that myself, and most others don't usually perceive in their 'normal' waking states. I began to embody the recognition that my own true 'self,' and that of everyone around me, was nothing less than indescribable forms of energy that were animating human bodies, and that this energy always was and is connected to every single thing that there is and ever could be.

At the age of eighteen, I experienced that 'great spiritual awareness' is just one tiny piece of an infinite puzzle, and that it would be up to me to conduct myself virtuously, innocently and consistently if I wanted to develop this expansive awareness to higher and higher levels, thus allowing me as a person, and my soul, to evolve. I also realized that it would be exclusively up to me to really engage my own free will, and constantly choose to make the awareness of my inner world more of a priority then anything externally. Otherwise, the conditioning and density of the external world would be to much of a distraction when developing these crucial aspects of my own consciousness.

However, the distractions of the world are constant, and the conditioning of this dilemma impresses itself deep into our psyches without most of us even realizing what is happening. The habits of identifying with the world, as it appears to be, are hard habits to break. So while I knew there was a much greater force moving through me, the part of me that was able to nurture it energetically was constantly battling with my human self, or more accurately – the parts of my ego that resisted the naturally expansive nature of my consciousness.

I was living in the woods like a monk. But at the same time I wanted to be young, I wanted to get high, and I wanted to be human, not just an energy form. The responsibility I had taken on was immense. I thought I was ready to be 'holy,' but as soon as I found out what being holy actually meant, I didn't feel I was ready for such responsibility at that point in my young life.

Damian was going through his own struggles, but his battle was tempered by the fact that he claimed to have memories of past lives where he had gone through this struggle before, while I did not have that. The past lives I experienced at 18 happened so fast that I didn't know what hit me, and even though all that 'information' was still encoded within me, for much of my life I didn't feel the urge to continue reliving the past, or to create a future from such a powerful place that required such tremendous personal responsibility and accountability to "spirit".

However, I realized that I had opened Pandora's box, and once you open up the gates to that kind of awareness, it does not go away. I was running from something that I knew I would inevitably have to face. So, in my attempt to not face it, I began dealing lots of cannabis, making lots of money, living what I thought was a luxurious lifestyle (according to society), and all of this took precedence over what I really wanted, far above any of it – soul freedom here in this body. I consistently felt that 'ultimate desire' wanting to express itself through me, and yet I would push it down as much as I could, but it was always there, and I knew early on that it always would be. How could it not?

We as individuals become very good at being ourselves according to all of our habitual routines, but there is always that undercurrent of something greater attempting to surface in our awareness, and I always knew that my habituated egoic self would eventually have to face this sobering, truthful awareness that I was running from.

I knew that it would come back and reveal itself to me in unmistakable ways in order to get my attention, and it did. I became an addict, got sick, and then I was arrested, indicted, lost everything, and then sentenced to prison. But even through that whole process, as brutal as it was, I did not 'stay awake'. Instead of focusing on what was real, I spent a ton of money on lawyers, doctors, and specialists, but still, no one could cure me or help me do what I knew I needed to do for myself.

And not even very deep down, I knew the reality was that no one was coming to my rescue. Only I could cure myself, but I struggled with taking that responsibility on because I was afraid of 'my power' and what I thought it meant to live in that state.

Of course, if I were living at the spiritually high-frequency that I was (when I was 18), I more than likely wouldn't have become sick in the first place, but I chose to descend, and numb myself with drugs and material distractions.

The support that we have within ourselves is immense, but we need to constantly nurture it to stay strong. Getting sick was a wake-up call, but I did not want to heed it. I wanted to be a victim. I allowed my sickness to keep me down.

After a couple decades of high-intensity living I was ready to give in and settle for a life that I used to mock and rebel against because I started craving simplicity. However, I still didn't want to take responsibility for focusing on the energy that animated me – the energy that I knew would heal me. I kept going further and further into dysfunction, dealing a plant that at the time was on the verge of becoming legal, buying expensive stuff and wallowing in my own pity. Then the nightmares that followed were truly a massive ego crush. To once have had so much internal power, and then feel like I had none was a sobering realization of dualism.

Yet even after all that I didn't want to recognize what was happening, I kept that victim mentality the whole time that I was being indicted and for my first year in prison, until this internal energy literally welled up within me and started to override my past dysfunctional mindset.

This coincided with the time that I consciously decided I was finally ready to be what I always knew I was, am and will be. I was so firm in my decision to shine that I wasn't going to allow anything to stop me from cultivating the potential residing within me, and prison was the perfect place to do it. There were no distractions worth giving my attention to. I had everything I needed to work with - my soul, and the awareness of my ego that vacillated between resisting it and surrendering to it.

At that point in my life the options were clear to me. I could choose to focus on the parts of me that felt like a victim and feel bad for myself, or I could focus on what I had known I am since the day I came into the world.

It was that simple, so I consistently began to focus my awareness on my heartbeat, my lungs breathing and directing my attention to the place from 'where thoughts arise' before they became thoughts. That place began in the coherence of my heart. I could feel my pulse anywhere in my body, even deep in my organs and when I focused on that, the energy was amplified, and thus the healing potential was increased. By making these choices and committing to them moment after moment, in no time, everything changed.

The runaway train of incessant thoughts and thinking was gone, and what was real was left in its place. The more I focused on this coherent field of energy, the more aware of it I became and the more activated its potential became in me. Then I began to develop it further, and evolve with it.

Instead of dwelling in my thoughts, I focused on the feeling of experiencing the energy that exists before any thoughts arise. The scales of my awareness tipped from being primarily aware of my human mind and it's fear-based obsessive thoughts, to becoming primarily aware of the "energy" that powered my body and more importantly, my consciousness itself. Then, the more that I focused on, not my consciousness itself, but the source that was powering my consciousness, the more my normal consciousness itself expanded. This expansion of consciousness resulted in what at first seemed like two different experiences, one being incredibly aware of non-physical energetic realms while the other being hyperawareness of this energy source in and around my physical body. But the reality was that these were not two separate experiences. What I was coming to terms with was the balance point between them.

After a while, it no longer became a choice; it became an automatic function like a habit. It was almost like having x-ray vision in that I could see through the surface of what everything around me appeared to be. What was below the surface was a living energy source that connected everything near and far, big and small. The previously narrow lens of my egoic filter had been substantially widened. It was now letting in the light of "divine electricity," thereby illuminating my perception of the inner and outer worlds. True balance was now becoming sustainable. This is what I had always truly wanted.

The monotony and stupidity of what the prison experience appeared to be through all of its outward forms and expressions beckoned me to go deeper into the formlessness of my inner reality. It was a place where limitless peace was alive and well, and always ready to embrace me with its expansive comfort. I was finally coming full circle.

Those early and dramatic years had set my life reeling, and didn't stop until I was literally incarcerated. It took having to be put into an actual prison for me to wake up and realize I was ready to free myself from the prison of my own mind.

THE FIGHT TO ENLIGHT

Once I began to free myself, the meditations I would do went to another level. My consciousness reached way out into celestial wonders, far beyond the depths of universal awareness. At the same time, it was rooted firmly in the foundation of the Earth. My anxiety was gone. My body was robust and vital. It was filled with life force. A living geometric field that felt universally orgasmic in nature was reverberating from the core of my bone marrow through all of my organs and tissues and out from the pores of my skin. My muscles were big, and my body fat had all but completely disappeared and more incredibly, I was glowing. People kept asking how I got so healthy. They said that I looked like I had jumped from the pages of a magazine. I was in the best shape of my life. It was the start of true balance.

As this inner alchemical transformation progressed, I realized that the gastrointestinal diagnosis of Candida that almost claimed my life was not caused by past drug use or the foods I ate. It was a symptom of constant anxiety, due to life trying to get my attention, and me focusing on everything but it. And the insomnia I had didn't really result from the discomfort of my stomach. It was caused by a soul that was uncomfortable always being ignored and suppressed when all it really wanted was to remain awake within my ego. It was amazing to not only be healed of this condition that afflicted me for almost a decade but to have done it as the result of fulfilling the spiritual destiny that I had been running from for the past two decades.

A huge benefit that emerged in my life, as the result of regaining my health and coming more full circle spiritually was that now I could laugh again. Even in prison, I could consistently see humor in things that I would have normally seen fear, drama, and horror in.

However, there were still some personality obstructions from previous conditioning in my way. They weren't severe, but they definitely caused interference. Though I had crossed over to the point where the majority of my awareness was focused on the energetic aspects of my mind, body, and emotions, these obstructions would often break this awareness via distractions by negative people. I knew that for my transformation to be more complete, I would need to maintain a continuous stream of focus on my energy field, and through a commitment to rational self-observation, or 'observing the observer.'

Although I had finally reached a place in my own evolution where all of my experiences of expanded consciousness were finally integrating in a sustainable way - through unbridled chaos, it took me two decades to arrive here.

The most difficult thing for those who want to free themselves of suffering is to find the uncompromising will power to make focusing on their energy field their number one priority. And if someone can find it, and consistently makes this focus into a habit, then it gets easier over time. This is because the practice of doing so installs the neural circuitry imprinted by the intention of self-empowerment in their brain and body. The feeling it generates eventually leads to the dissipation of suffering. Suffering is not our natural state; it is a memory of the past. It creates stress hormones in the body and puts our awareness into a constrictive, fear-based state. Our natural state is expansive. Once this expansive state is established, it becomes default and over time we find that we can learn, evolve and heal with much greater ease.

In Poetic Summary

Born awake, I feel asleep, but then I awoke again. It wasn't biological sleep; it was spiritual. This happened more than once. In my life, there were long periods of deep slumber interrupted by many brief awakenings, then came one that was profound. Every time I awoke and saw the state of the world, I was intoxicated by its collective drowsiness, and I fell back asleep.

But eventually, something in me was no longer tired. Even though I wanted to sleep, this something refused to. And so it began, an internal war between the person I thought I was - my ego - and my soul, the energy that animates my brain and body. It wasn't really a war, because my soul didn't want or need to fight. It just wanted to remain awake. And although my ego resisted the sleeplessness of my soul, it eventually surrendered to it and formed an alliance. This marked the ending of my personal battle.

But now I have enlisted for a much bigger one: the collective battle to awaken the masses. It's not a war between good and evil. The dispute is in the ego's resistance to the soul. And although it is not necessarily a war; it's more of a restoration of perceptive balance, and it only develops when a person surrenders their ego to the wisdom of their life-giving soul. And through that surrender, the entire world benefits.

You see, when one human being fully awakens to the revelation that 'who' they are is only an extension of 'what' they are, change can pursue at a quantum level. 'What' we are is the energy that makes our heart beat, causes our lungs to breathe, and provides the consciousness from where thoughts form. It is in the realization of and focused identification with this energy that true awakening takes place.

With this comes a personal healing, whereby an individual begins to think luminous and - for the first time - truly original thoughts. They begin to feel immeasurable life force pulsing through their body that heals their aches and pains. The combination of these two elements leads to the recognition that sustained super-consciousness is not only within reach, but that it is the normal and natural expression of human consciousness.

It is from this point of balance that an individual is able to cut through the dense fog of collective slumber and contribute practical solutions to our human species that has become so out of touch with reality that we are destroying ourselves and every other species whom we share the planet with.

As I write this book, I'm finishing the last couple months of three years incarcerated in an actual prison. It was a meditation retreat that I obviously didn't consciously choose. But although it was a forced sabbatical, it was a much-needed one.

When I look back on it, I wasn't arrested - I was rescued. I was rescued from the part of myself that couldn't tell the difference between illusion and reality. I was rescued from my ego, from the story of the person I believed myself to be. That's where I'd really been doing 'hard time.'

For far too long, I'd been repeating a self-limiting story in my own mind. To break free of that prison, I was extracted from life as I knew it, stripped of my life savings, and dropped into an actual prison. But none of it made any sense until I discovered something in that dungeon that I had always known, but refused to own: that there was nothing worth owning in this world except for that which I already owned within, or more accurately, that, that I was owned by – my soul, the miraculous energy field that animates my brain and body. While everything around us changes, our resistance to it causes us to suffer. The soul remains unchanging in this equation, making it the only solid holy ground that we can count on being there for us when we need it.

Of course, there was no intrinsic blessing in being jailed; it's what I did with my time that made it so valuable. But in all reality, it was an easy choice to make. What else was I going to do with 1,096 days and nights?

It was an easy choice to make at the outset, but the commitment to continue making that choice was the hardest habit I've ever had to build – but only at first.

I had to face every single choice that had led me to where I was and what I'd become - an inmate in a prison. Selling weed wasn't really what landed me in my current situation; as it is with almost everything, this story was a lot deeper than that.

It was time for me to finally face and dissolve all the thick layers of illusion that had accumulated from years of misidentification with what almost everyone assumes is "reality." And like most everyone else, most of that perspective wasn't formed of my own accord. Directly or indirectly, I observed others and learned what to think and how to act from their influence. This left me begging to know: "What is MY perspective of reality, free from their influence? Not the perspective that forms as the result of other people's perspectives mashed into my own, but what would my perspective of reality be if I was able to perceive life free of others' influence on me?"

There was only one way for me to find out: by cleansing my perceptive faculties with hours upon hours of daily mental disinfectant reconditioning; meditation in the present moment. I knew from the outset that it wouldn't be easy. But I also knew that the rewards waiting as a result of committing to this work are valuable beyond measure. I'm incarcerated, yet I'm freer than I was before I was arrested. The wisdom of *what* I am has finally enveloped the knowledge of *who* I am.

What does that mean?

It means that I've finally arrived at the point in my human existence where the wisdom of my soul guides and informs my ego, rather than the other way around. To put it simply, I've reawakened to the innate awareness of what it is to be a spiritual being having a human experience. It is my hope that after reading this often brutal but ultimately uplifting story of my life, it will have brought you closer to your own awakening, of truly knowing yourself as soul.

CHAPTER THIRTY

How does my story help you?

On a daily basis, people ask me many different questions about how they can change their lives. The questions span from 'how do I overcome addiction and other compulsive habits', to 'how do I overcome limiting beliefs that hold me back', to 'how do I find peace within myself' to 'how do I unlock my potential so I can thrive,' and everything in-between. And although these questions might have many different answers based upon the individual, the reality is that even though people ask questions that pertain to specific situations in their lives, there actually is a very simplistic answer and technique that I have found to work universally across all areas of my life. And that answer is "when you as an individual decide to make a habit out of developing an internal state of being called "heart-brain/whole-body coherence," the answers you seek will naturally appear as self-evident truths in your conscious awareness.

What is heart-brain coherence, you might ask? It is simply this:

When the awareness of our heart's energy field supersedes that of our thinking process, the bioelectric nature of our thoughts then become influenced by the powerful bio-magnetic field of our heart. This leads to the synchronization of our heart and brain. It's what is referred to as heart-brain coherence, and it allows these two organs to function as though they are one "super organ."

Once this state of coherence is anchored into our moment-to-moment awareness, we become extraordinarily intuitive, while at the same time mentally rational. The feeling of heart-brain coherence produces a sense of wellbeing so profound that with consistent practice, it overrides negative thoughts, while at the same time becoming a powerful deflector, blocking the negative projections of others. The more that someone chooses to develop this coherent state, the more they realize the endless possibilities that it holds for their physical wellbeing and the universal expansion of their consciousness.

As babies and young children, we usually exist in a naturally occurring coherent state. But as we grow older, most of us become subjected to the influence of western scientific thought. This way of thinking has become the primary model through which most perceive the world. It places the rationale of the logical mind as the predominant thought process without recognizing the heart's influence on the brain. But this way of thinking has led to a dramatic imbalance in human perception. When we are out of alignment with our own inner nature, we don't know how to harmoniously interact with the natural world around us. The effect this has had on our relationship with Mother Nature is apparent to all who are paying attention.

The heart is always giving intuitive guidance to the brain that ultimately promotes the most harmonious and beneficial outcomes for one's self and the world, especially as it pertains to the wellness of our own bodies. Because we as a society have learned to value logical reasoning over intuitive guidance, we have become almost oblivious to this source of wisdom that is emanating outwardly from our hearts.

Logical reasoning inhibits our ability to perceive the multidimensional aspects of our reality that are always operating in the background of our subconscious awareness. These aspects of our consciousness make up the foundation of our human experience. When we are unaware of them, we perceive reality through the tunnel vision of social conditioning that we have unknowingly accepted as our own since we were children. This has resulted in the adoption of preconceived notions and limited belief systems that use the logic of the mind to navigate through reality without the intuition of the heart and even our gut (whole-body coherence is the next level of heart-brain coherence). However, the heart is not subjected to such mental limitations. It freely sends and receives information, signals, and frequencies without the restrictions of mental constructs.

It is through this expansiveness that the heart is able to operate in alignment with the multidimensional and metaphysical components of existence that all but eludes our conditioned minds, and we are the last to know it.

By integrating heart-brain coherence into our moment-to-moment experiences, we then activate what can be referred to as 'whole-body' coherence. This is where the harmonization of heart and mind begin to have a ripple effect through the other organs of our bodies, causing our whole being to harmonize with itself. It is in this state that our vibrancy and health begins returning back to us.

Once we have truly begun to anchor in a state of whole-body coherence accompanied by its vibrant life force, something phenomenal begins to occur that can be referred to as 'whole-soul coherence.' This is where we consciously become hyper-aware of the energy field that's animating our entire human body - both as it resides within each organ inside of us, and then how we become aware of its coalescing into the holistic animating force that's surrounding our body and beyond.

To even begin to recognize one's true self, as this energy form animating our human body is to realize the true definition of freedom. The more we learn how to consistently shift our awareness into this state, the less and less we are negatively affected by anything in the world around us. It is in this state that we begin to bridge our conscious, subconscious, and unconscious awareness as we embody a true sense of self that is unlimited. This sense of self is the unchanging nature of our pure consciousness.

The great thing about the concept of heart-brain coherence is that scientists now back it. Until recently, scientists believed that the brain was the chief organ that sent commands to all the other organs of the body, but now we know that the heart and brain do this together almost as they are one organ. The brain and heart communicate through a number of vast physiological pathways that spread throughout the body. Together they continuously exchange information, signals, and frequencies that influence how well the body functions.

Dr. J. Andrew Armour first introduced the term heart-brain in 1991. He demonstrated that the heart could be viewed as a "little brain" because of its complex nervous system. The Heart Math Institute published, "It is an intricate network of several types of neurons, neurotransmitters, proteins and support cells, like those found in the brain proper. Research has shown that the heart communicates to the brain in four major ways: neurologically (through the transmission of nerve impulses), biochemically (via hormones and neurotransmitters), biophysically (through pressure waves) and energetically (through electromagnetic field interactions)." Its elaborate circuitry enables it to act independently of the cranial brain – to learn, remember, and even feel and sense.

Here is a technique to begin practicing heart-brain coherence from the HeartMath Institute called "The Quick Coherence Technique":

- Heart Focus: Shift your attention to the area of the heart and breathe slowly and deeply.
- Heart Breathing: Keep your focus in the heart by gently breathing – five seconds in and five seconds out – through your heart. Do this two or three times.
- Heart Feeling: Activate and sustain a genuine feeling of appreciation or care for someone or something in your life. Focus on the good heart feeling as you continue to breathe through the area of your heart.

Practicing heart-brain coherence has been the single most powerful technique to transform my reality from both an ordinary day-to-day existence point of view, to the development of the highest states of expanded consciousness. It needs to be practiced until it becomes a habit. It is undoubtedly a practice that if made foundational allows an individual to sense reality primarily through a heart-centric state of perception with mental perception as a secondary support system, as opposed to the other way around. When these two organs function and communicate as though they were one "super-organ," a state of internal balance occurs that endows the individual with virtuous feelings, thoughts, behaviors and resultant actions that greatly assist the evolutionary journey of their soul.

On a physical level, it also brings immediate relief to me when I experience any kind of health challenges or blockages. Additionally, I've found that the more that I practiced this state, the less affected I am by the negativity of this world, no matter what it is because energetically I'm affecting the world more than it is affecting me.

It could be suggested that human beings possess a near dormant, sensory-based evolutionary trait that if harnessed and used, to even a partial extent, could dramatically enlighten the course of our world for the better. The individual, through their conscious commitment, is the only one that can take responsibility for developing this trait if we are to first survive and then begin to thrive as a species. In my own experience, I have found that heart-brain coherence is the gateway to activate this internal evolutionary trait that leads an individual to the awareness of their infinite self, and the potential found therein.

The reality is, this world is not at all what we think it is -nor is it anything that anyone has ever told us about. It also isn't any story that we have ever read, including the story of my life that you just read. The only way that we can truly begin to understand what reality is, and more importantly – who we are, is by first coming to terms with WHAT we are.

And the way for this to happen is to free our minds of any and everything that anyone has ever told us about what reality is- including the words on these pages and experience it for ourselves directly from the heart-centric core of our being.

Once this begins happening, we will, possibly for the first time in our lives, have the ability to deeply and clearly, feel, sense and think for ourselves about who we are and what this world is.

For the soul seekers - that have a deep urge to know the esoteric and often clandestine nature of reality itself - life can be an obscure journey. When we intend to move way beyond the conditioning of our minds, and its perceptive scars, imprinted by a patriarchal and pragmatic society, we often meet a lot of internal resistance to and from others. And often, the deeper we go into the essential nature of our own existence itself, the more we unearth our own hidden egoic triggers. And usually, we become aware of them because they go off like fire alarms as we try to squirm our way out of letting all resistance to "truth" go when facing the ultimate nature of what we really are. It can be very intense if we have not grounded in the deepest sense of peace, and even if we have, it is still usually intense.

When we embark on this path of self-realization our perception of self, others and reality itself will often stretch, bend and twist in ways that can leave us confused, deterred and the rare occasion, even more determined to discover the true nature of one's existence. The further our awareness goes into these realms, the less language and all human understanding are able to follow. This is why some of the deepest spiritual teachings take the form of parables, metaphors, poetry, philosophy, and art, with the difference being that many of the individuals who have directly experienced these states infuse their own awareness and experience of these realms into their written and spoken words with the hope that the reader or listener is activated enough to recognize these profound states within themselves.

This is why I've written the following. It may not give you the linear, step-by-step path to spiritual liberation, but it will point the direction and give you a conceptual idea of what to expect. Considering the following in a state of heart-brain coherence will allow you to more fully tune in to what is being communicated in this writing. Please read it with an open heart, an open mind, and softened senses that are also hyper-aware at the same time. Enjoy!

"Awareness Becoming Aware of Itself"

There is a unified field of conscious energy emanating from the core of our being, and it is connected to all things great and small. The more that we focus our awareness on this field, the more our awareness of its potential within is amplified.

And as our perception of its potential expands inwardly, we soon feel this frequency vibrating throughout every cell of our physical being. They vibrate individually and yet at the same time in synchrony with each other creating alignment within and around the whole our body. This leads to the harmony of our authentic self.

The more acutely aware of this feeling we become, the more this "force" begins to communicate through seemingly countless almost geometric "energy" centers and points of "light" that can be likened to the understanding of what a chakra is. They are like energetic acupressure and acupuncture points naturally existing in and also around the living temple of our human body.

Like countless distant stars in a perfectly clear night sky, our inner view of self becomes like looking out into the Milky Way galaxy while being sensually blanketed by the bright glow of aurora borealis.

And just as significant celestial alignments have the ability to occur in outer space, so too do they here, in this inner space. But the more clear and honest that we get with ourselves, the more we realize the possibility for much greater significance "in here" as opposed to "out there."

The reason for this is that our inner view reveals the potential for a seemingly "perfect" alignment in which this unified field of conscious energy can become more aware of itself through us.

Then when we're able to reach even deeper into this natural meditation of hyper self-awareness, this conscious energy will then give birth to an ineffable living geometric field that can be said with certainty is absolutely self-aware through our own awareness.

Aside from all the obvious words that have used to describe this state such as God, Allah, Brahma, or Christ Consciousness, it can more practically be thought of as "Divine Electricity."

It's a good explanation because it is the energetic precursor that sends signals to catalyze every function in our human bodies.

Through our brain and nervous system, it alchemically sends the electrical impulses that cause our lungs to breathe, our heart to beat and thoughts to arise in our minds. It is what allows us to be self-aware as an evolving human being. It is our pure consciousness, free of any thoughts created by the egoic and separatist mind.

When we focus our attention inside of ourselves, on the place from which thoughts arise, we find this miraculous bio-electrical substance coiled up and waiting for our ego to perceive it. It is the soul. And upon our ego's acknowledgment that it is indeed the soul, it reveals that it never was separate from the person we believed ourselves to be.

All that happened was that we unknowingly allowed the world to condition our mind to the degree that we weren't perceptively aware enough to know this part of our self. This left us lost and incomplete, a ship to wreck in an endless sea of energy.

But all that has changed now because we are able to find what we've always been looking for. Or is it the other way around? Maybe it is finding itself through us?

In any case, it truly is Divine Electricity, the miracle of life in action. All that we need do is surrender our egoic awareness to it, and it does the rest.

When we focus the dysfunctional aspects of our human perception on this Divine Electricity, it imbues itself into them. Doing this heals our whole being, and it brings about a balance that causes us to function in a way that's supported by forces so much bigger than we are able to perceive with our human senses.

We become deeply humbled to have learned that our soul is able to perceive this spiritual magnanimity because it actually "IS" that spiritual greatness! It just takes intentional union on the part of our focused ego to realize it.

Before long we begin to understand that this state is potentially a paradigm of perfection because it produces a feeling that can only be described as "the best orgasm ever felt multiplied by infinity" and it exists in every part of the body, not just between our legs. But even that says very little of the sensation this feeling produces because it's hardly sexual in the way that most people would consider sex to be.

It is filled with a love so great that words on their best day could not even come close to describing. But it's also not love in the way that most people would consider or think love to be. It's like the feeling one would get knowing that everyone and everything that they've ever loved and cared about is right by their side and will always be. It's the greatest and most unimaginable love that we've always imagined wanting to feel multiplied by infinity if we can imagine that!

That intensely blissful super-sensual-beyond-sexual feeling is the creative impulse of life itself. And of course, that's how it feels! How could life beget life without such a feeling of rapturous ecstasy? It has to feel like that, and of course, that's only the beginning of how miraculous it can be.

On a more practical day-to-day level, our focus on this energy causes bio and neurogenesis to occur within the living tissue and cells of our human anatomy. With our expanded awareness, this force amplifies itself causing our physicality to regenerate, heal, and become stronger. This IS the most potent medicine to be found anywhere in the universe. There isn't a pill, potion or lotion, or a fountain of youth yet discovered that can come anywhere close to matching its potency!

We can find full confidence in our heart of hearts and soul of souls that this state of awareness represents the next stages of humanity's evolution towards supreme levels of super-consciousness. This IS the razor-sharp cutting-edge potential of human consciousness as it is evolving in real-time, in the here an now, and yet it is completely beyond any concept of time because there are no moments, there is only consciousness perceiving itself through our awareness.

But, despite the enormity of deep peace and blissful satisfaction that being in this state provides, it isn't something that's a luxury. At this point in the human species evolution, it feels like it's probably a necessity to self-actualize if we are to survive the destruction that we've unleashed on this planet and more sobering - to our personal and collective soul.

While the mob mass of human awareness and societal progress seem to be in a contracted and disharmonious state - out of alignment with nature, the universe is not. Even in its chaos, it is expanding according to its own essential nature.

So why then should our consciousness not be expanding along with it? After all, that expansion makes up the bulk of what exists in the entire known universe.

But becoming enlightened is one step; staying enlightened takes countless steps. It's like a choice; only it's a choice that one has to make over and over again almost endlessly until the wisdom of their limitless soul supersedes the knowledge of their limited ego. When one succeeds in choosing the wisdom of the soul, the ego dissolves its boundaries into the limitless of it, until there is no more perception of separation.

But even then we have to remain vigilant and incessantly choose, "Should I identify with the way things appear to be in the world around me? Or am I choosing to have faith and identify with the way things really are inside of me?" This is a constant process, but it is one that is very predictable no matter what choice we might make.

Once it was our ego, the limited and often confused human personality we so often believed ourselves to be along with the personal narrative we usually told ourselves, the story that blocked the awareness of our eternally wise soul - until common sense finally kicks in.

Then the tables turn, and we learn how to reverse the world, our world-the stuck, suffering, confused, hairless ape world of our ego.

Where once a brutal prison guard known as "the ego" incarcerated the innocent inmate that was our seemingly the perception of our nonexistent soul- now it's the other way around. The innate intelligence and infinite wisdom of our soul guides our very ego, and our whole being loves it!

It's quite poetic that I'm writing these words from inside of an actual prison. It's ironic that it took being physically incarcerated in order for The Ego to finally surrender to its infinite soul. It fought a relentless fight for so many years, and only when it was wearied and beaten to the ground with barely a breath left to breathe did it recognize the value of this surrender. It realized that all of its pain was self-inflicted and self-chosen, and in prison, it just simply chose to stop identifying with that dysfunctional part of itself.

In its place, it chose to identify with what it knew always was- and will be there...the "invisible" energy that animates the human heart and the entire world it lives in. And beautifully, in that choosing, what was once invisible...became visible, vibrantly visible!

What's crazy is that I fully knew myself as "soul" as a young child, and I knew myself well! How could I have been born with this only to fall so far? Oh yeah, that's right, the conditioning of the world...

But it's in going through these processes that we learn the value of what we've always known. That's how it was for me anyway.

And while the story of my journey seems to have come full circle, it's actually more like a spiral in that even though it's circular; it's not really coming back to where it began. It appears that way from the outside, but the closer one looks, the more they realize that like a spiral, it's expanding upward and sometimes outward with each revolution, evolving if you will.

One of the greatest rewards of this spiraling path is "dramatically enhanced perception." The more that our perceptive abilities are strengthened, the more the unseen "spiritual" worlds that we intuitively know exist become seen and known. Perception is like a muscle that we can learn how to flex through our keen awareness of life experience.

I've often said that the second most miraculous thing there is next to the miracle of life itself, is the fact that there are so many people alive who so infrequently contemplate how miraculous life truly is! We came into this world with the hardwiring to fully realize this miracle that's called "life." But it's up to us as individuals and us alone to do the constant work of coming to terms with that realization.

It is my hope that human beings learn how to strengthen their muscles of perception. I hope this with all of my heart and soul because we all deserve to know the truth of reality; that we are not just hairless apes seeking out spiritual truths. More precisely, we are spiritual beings having a human experience- and that spiritual being no longer wants to be locked up in the prison of our minds. It wants us to set ourselves free! And we are entirely capable of doing this!

But it comes down to a choice that the individual is required to make: do I want to live the life of a hairless ape (not a real ape, real apes are in tune with reality)- concerned only with my own survival? Or, am I a being of divine self-realization-concerned with the superconscious evolutionary growth of our entire species?

I know what choice I've made and will continue to make! What about you?

In Conclusion (what I'm doing now and where to find me)

It is now Summer of 2020. It has been 5 years since I've been released from prison, and I am finally ready to publish this book. I decided to wait because I knew that the time to release it needed to feel right. It is a deeply personal decision to make my life experiences an "open book," and I had to really learn how to be emotionally detached from the severity of what I share in these pages.

Another reason I waited is that I recognized that I have a big responsibility to compassionately communicate with those who either resonate with or relate to what I have shared. For me to truly help people overcome the challenges that they might face, I knew I had to truly be ready to put myself out there and use my story as a force for inspiring healthy change in our world. I'm now clear about how to proceed in sustainably achieving that.

During the time of Covid when people are collectively experiencing serious hardship, I feel my book couldn't be any more relevant for those who are suffering or looking for a healthier way of being.

Since my release from prison, I have reunited and healed the relationship with my family who has always wanted to be a part of my life despite my resistance to them, and their inability to understand the complexities that make me who I am. My brother and I continue to own and operate Living Nutz "the best tasting, most healthy snack food on the planet" and we have managed to keep our first hemp body care company The Maine Intellihemp Company alive and well since 1998.

You can find them at:
LivingNutz.com
Facebook.com/LivingNutz
Instagram.com/LivingNutz

The Maine Intellihemp Company
Intellihemp.com

After my release from prison, I was inspired to create a new company that reflected the deep healing and inner work I had experienced while incarcerated.
Likening my healing process to a natural spring bubbling to the surface of the Earth, I wrote the following before I was released from prison:

"Like natural spring water bubbling to the surface of the Earth deep in the woods, so too is our consciousness like this - originating from deep inside of our being and bubbling to the surface of our awareness so that we can remember and embody the purity that we truly are. This remembrance enables us to go out into the world and help sanctify it for the health of all."

It's not at all surprising that I reconnected with an old friend who has preserved one of the last great natural sources of spring water in North America (a source of water that compares to none on earth as far as quality and the sustainability as a small bottling operation) and we went into business together. He allowed me to bring his vision to life and infuse it with my own vision. We made a significant impact regionally in New England, and in 2018 we received global recognition when literally every major and minor mainstream media outlet in the world began attacking us (and another company publicly) for offering untreated spring water to the public, just as our company has been doing for almost 140 years without a single health complaint or even a negative complaint about taste on state record. The media called it "The Raw Water Trend," and they claimed it was the biggest health trend of 2018.

As a result of these attacks, my business partner and I defended our company's position, and we were able to change much of the collective perspective regarding many of the major media outlets that attacked us. Those that looked deeper into what we were actually doing came to respect our operation and us. They were just doing their jobs and covering the mass-hysteria that spread virally through the world about The Raw Water Trend. We appeared on the CBS morning show, The Doctors Show, the Guardian, even Comedy Central, and scores and scores of others Internationally, Nationally, Regionally and Locally. It was every small business owner's greatest dream and biggest fear coming true at the same time. As the media attacks began to slow down, we ended up winning two top-place awards at The International Fine Water's Tasting competition in Ecuador out of hundreds of different waters from all over the world. It was an exciting achievement, but more importantly, because of the Raw Water Trend, we were able to voice the perspective that human beings are disconnected from both the natural world around them and more importantly their own inner-nature.

Looking at what our species is doing to our planet, each other, and ourselves many couldn't help but agree.

You can find Tourmaline Spring and our new CBD Water, a product far superior to any of it's competitors out there at:

TourmalineSpring.com
Facebook.com/TourmalineSpring
Instagram.com/TourmalineSpring

I'm quite happy to say that I've launched a podcast called "The Integrative Science of Water & Consciousness Podcast" with my close friend from New Zealand named Veda Austin, who has become known as "The Water Whisperer". Veda has just released her own book on water crystallography that is nothing short of awe-inspiring. When you can visibly see the effect that consciousness has on water, it causes one to seriously question the nature of reality! The podcasts are available on the Tourmaline Spring website and in our Facebook group: The Water Consciousness Movement at:
Facebook.com/groups/thewaterconsciousnessmovement/

Regarding Hemp and Cannabis, the times have certainly changed dramatically since I was incarcerated. From growing up in a 'cannabis-friendly' household, to witnessing how socially taboo the topic of legal cannabis was in mainstream society, to starting our first hemp company in 1998 in order to create greater awareness around the importance of this plant, to watching recreational marijuana become legal in 10 states, medical marijuana become legal in 33 states, industrial hemp become legal in all 50 states, and then to watch the unprecedented onslaught of money-hungry entrepreneurs many of whom are bastardizing the integrity of an industry that has the potential to change the world – I knew that my team and I needed to take action.

Amethyst Elixir Company was influenced by the naturally pure spring water and branding of Tourmaline Spring. Right now the line consists of a water-soluble, whole hemp extract that is suspended in our spring water. Unlike tinctures that are oil-based, our water-soluble that is suspended in water is rapidly absorbed in our bodies, making it much more bioavailable and effective for those suffering from a host of modern health conditions.

My family and I started selling hemp shoes in 1991, we started our first hemp body care product line in 1998 and my brother and I have been advocates of all things legal cannabis since our childhood because we have always known that legal hemp has the potential to disrupt all sectors of industry that are toxic, thereby hurting the health of people and the planet. However, while I fully stand behind the use of plant medicines for healing, I certainly do not advocate addictive consumption of any substance, behavior, or even belief system. Addiction means different things to different people, but the ravages of addiction are something that I wouldn't wish on anyone.

You can find Amethyst Elixir Company products on the Tourmaline Spring website at:

TourmalineSpring.com
Facebook.com/TourmalineSpring
Instagram.com/TourmalineSpring

Since my release from prison, I have continued to play music, forming a band called "In the Wind" with some local contacts that have built up steam since we started. We now have over 60 songs, are in the process of recording two albums, and we have played many local gigs in addition to being invited to play at a massive talent show. Every time we play out, we deliver powerful and inspiring performances leading to our inboxes filling up with the requests to play more shows. Once these two records are done being recorded, we will actively be out there playing live!

We can be found at:

Website: www.InTheWind.band
Facebook.com/inthewindband
Instagram @inthewindband

Another project that I'm very excited about is a non-profit I started called "I'm Awake, Now What?" The concept behind it is to create fun live events that inspire healthy change in our world by bringing conscious people together through festive parties that encourage compassionate communication and networking. It's for all those who are "aware "and don't want to go to bars in order to mingle with others, but who also want to improve the state of our world and need a starting point. My plan is to make these events a starting point for those who are ready to seriously effectuate positive world change. My team and I are actively putting these events together as I write this and will be launching them soon.

This project can be found at:

ImAwakeNowWhat.com
Facebook.com/ImAwakeNowWhat

And a FB discussion group Facebook.com/groups/Imawakenowwhat/

And of course, for anyone who wants to read my experiences on everything I've expressed in this book and way more, my personal Facebook page has become a blog of sorts and where I'm most active on social media. It can be found here:

https://www.facebook.com/SethLeafPruzansky

To contact me go to by business website at:

TourmalineSpring.com or email me at:

info@tourmalinespring.com

Thank you for reading my book and I hope more than anything that it inspires you to take responsibility for changing your life according to a vision that serves your best potential growth in this life!

Made in the USA
Middletown, DE
30 January 2025